Social Identities

Social Identities: Multidisciplinary approaches addresses a topic at the heart of social and political theory. It argues that we have a collection of social selves and that our identities are influenced by such things as class, gender, sexuality, race, nationality, religion and the media. The book includes contributions from leading scholars in the field and provides an undergraduate audience with an accessible and insightful introduction to a fascinating subject. *Social Identities: Multidisciplinary approaches* is particularly useful for students studying courses on social identity, sociology, social and political theory and contemporary culture.

Gary Taylor is Senior Lecturer in Social Policy at Sheffield Hallam University. He has written books on social and political theory, the media and social policy.

Steve Spencer is Lecturer in Sociology at Sheffield Hallam University and has previously taught Communication and Media Studies in Australia.

Social Identities

Multidisciplinary approaches

Edited by

Gary Taylor and Steve Spencer

Routledge
Taylor & Francis Group

LONDON AND NEW YORK

First published 2004
by Routledge
2 Park Square, Milton Park, Abingdon, Oxon, OX14 4RN

Simultaneously published in the USA and Canada
by Routledge
29 West 35th Street, New York, NY 10001

Routledge is an imprint of the Taylor & Francis Group

© 2004 Editorial material and selection, Gary Taylor and Steve Spencer;
individual chapters, the contributors

Typeset in Times by
Newgen Imaging Systems (P) Ltd, Chennai, India
Printed and bound in Great Britain by
Cromwell Press, Trowbridge, Wiltshire

British Library Cataloguing in Publication Data
A catalogue record for this book is available from the British Library

Library of Congress Cataloging in Publication Data
A catalog record for this book has been requested

ISBN 0–415–35007–7 (hbk)
ISBN 0–415–35008–5 (pbk)

Contents

List of Contributors

Dr Timothy Baycroft is a Lecturer in Modern French History at the University of Sheffield. He is the author of *Culture, Identity and Nationalism: French Flanders in the Nineteenth and Twentieth Centuries* (Boydell & Brewer, 2004) and *Nationalism in Europe 1789–1945* (CUP, 1998). He is currently co-editing a book on nineteenth-century European nationalism, completing the volume on France in the 'Inventing the Nation' series (Arnold), and engaged in research on identity and borders in Europe.

Dr Jenny Blain is a Senior Lecturer in the School of Social Science and Law at Sheffield Hallam University, teaching ethnographic research and leading the ESRC-recognised MA in Social Science Research Methods. Her book, *Nine Worlds of Seid-Magic: Ecstasy and Neoshamanism in North European Paganism* (Routledge, 2002), is an ethnographic study of North European shamanic practice today, and she has articles in *Journal of Contemporary Religion, Folklore*, and (forthcoming) *Journal of Material Culture*. Her research interests include constructions of identity within Western paganisms, gender and sexuality, sacred sites, spirituality and marginalised groups: she co-directs the Sacred Sites, Contested Rights/Rites project on paganism and ancient sites in the UK, working within theoretical research frameworks influenced by recent moves toward auto-ethnography and increased reflexivity in anthropology.

Dr Serena Bufton is a Senior Lecturer in Sociology at Sheffield Hallam University. Her publications include 'The Lifeworld of the University Student: Habitus and Social Class' *Journal of Phenomenological Psychology*, 34 (2): 207–234, 2003, and 'Learning to Play the Game: Mature, working-class students' experiences of higher education' *Centre for Sociology, Anthropology and Politics Monograph No. 2*, University of Birmingham, forthcoming. She is currently working on a number of projects related to the student experience in higher education, with a particular emphasis on issues related to skills development.

Dr Lorraine Green is Lecturer in Social Work and Social Science in the Department of Applied Social Sciences at University of Manchester. She has written widely on sexuality and sexual abuse of children and on issues around the punishment of children. Her publications include chapters in P. Cox, S. Kershaw and J. Trotter (eds), *Child Sexual Assault and Feminisms* (Palgrave, 2000) and J. Hearn and W. Parkin, *Gender, Sexuality and Violence in Organisations* (Sage, 2001). She is currently conducting theoretical research on child sexual abuse, anorexia and obesity.

Dr Julia Hirst is Senior Lecturer in Sociology at Sheffield Hallam University. Her previous publications include 'Researching young people's sexuality and learning about sex: experience, need, and sex and relationship education', *Culture, Health & Sexuality*, 6 (2): 115–129, *Evaluation of Sheffield Sure Start Plus* (2003) and 'Voices of Experience: Muslim and African Caribbean Teenagers' *Insights on Pregnancy and Parenting* (2003). She is currently working on an evaluation of initiatives to support people at risk of social exclusion.

Dr Victor Horboken is Senior Lecturer in Media Studies Faculty of Arts, Media and Design Staffordshire University. He came to media studies after ten years experience of print journalism in Eastern Europe. His research interests include ethnic minority media, diasporas, interethnic communication and ethnic ideologies, nationalism and identity-building in Central and Eastern Europe. He is currently researching UK Ukrainian community media and ideology of secession, religion and political identity of Eastern European transnational communities.

Dr Barry King is Associate Professor and Head of the School of Communications Studies at Auckland University of Technology. His most recent publications are 'Über die Arbeit des Erinnerns: Die Suche nach dem perfekten Moment' in H. Wolf et al. *Diskurse der Fotografie* (Suhrkamp, 2003) and 'Embodying an Elastic self' in Martin Barker and Thomas Austin (eds) *Contemporary Hollywood Stardom* (Arnold, 2003). He is currently co-editing, with Sean Cubitt, Thierry Jutel and Harriet Margolies, *Studying the Event Film: The Lord of the Rings* (Manchester University Press).

Dr Kevin Myers teaches social history and education in The School of Education at the University of Birmingham. He is a member of the DOMUS research group that is based in Birmingham and co-editor (with Stephanie Spencer) of the *History of Education Researcher*. His doctoral thesis examined the settlement and education of refugee children in Britain between 1937–1945 and he has published widely in this area. He was awarded the inaugural ISCHE prize in 1998. His more recent research is focused in two areas. The first explores histories of outcast children in the 19th and 20th centuries, with a particular interest in the emergence of mental health services and policies for young people. The second examines the philosophy and presentation of community histories in urban regeneration policies.

Dr David Parker is a Lecturer in the School of Sociology and Social Policy, University of Nottingham. Previous publications include: *Rethinking Mixed Race*, co-edited with Miri Song (Pluto Press, 2001) and 'Diaspora, Dissidence and the Dangers of Cosmopolitanism', in *Asian Studies Review*, June 2003. Currently he is working on issues relating to urban social change, and the role of the Internet in the expression of ethnic identities in Britain.

Dr Michael Pickering is Reader in Culture and Communications in the Department of Social Sciences at Loughborough University. He has published in the areas of cultural studies and social history as well as media analysis and theory. His books include *Everyday Culture* (1987); *History, Experience and Cultural Studies* (1997); *Researching Communications* (1999); *Stereotyping: The Politics of Representation* (2001); and *Creativity, Communication and Cultural Value* (the latter with Keith Negus). He is currently working on a co-edited volume with Sharon Lockyer on the ethics of humour, and is involved in an AHRB-funded research project on the relationship between work and popular music.

Professor Anthony Rosie is Learning, Teaching and Assessment Co-ordinator for the School of Social Science and Law at Sheffield Hallam University. His previous publications include journal articles on teaching social theory, using models of dialogue in online learning. He holds a national teaching fellowship (2001) and with two other NTF colleagues is researching the experience of award holders in learning and teaching in national schemes.

Steve Spencer is a Lecturer at Sheffield Hallam University. He has lived and worked in Australia and has a background in Media and Cultural Studies. He has researched ethnic identity in Guyana, and currently issues of Aboriginal identity, consumerism and the management of the media during the Iraq war of 2003. He has two books in preparation: A Dream Deferred: Ethnic Conflict in Guyana and Race and Ethnicity: Culture, Identity and Society

Dr Gary Taylor is Senior Lecturer in Social Policy at Sheffield Hallam University. His recent publications include *Democracy and Participation* (co-edited with Malcolm Todd, Merlin, 2004) and *Ideology and Welfare* (Palgrave, forthcoming). He is currently researching for projects on educational theory and on the social context of health.

Dr David Waddington is Reader in Cultural Studies at Sheffield Hallam University. His previous publications include the Routledge titles: *Contemporary Issues in Public Disorder: A Comparative and Historical Approach*, and (with Chas Critcher, Bell Dicks and David Parry) *Out of the Ashes? The Social Impact of Industrial Contraction and Regeneration on Britain's Mining Communities*. He is currently interested in the policing of the anti-globalisation movement in Europe and North America.

1. Introduction

Gary Taylor and Steve Spencer

The question of 'identity' is being vigorously debated in social theory. In essence, the argument is that the old identities which stabilized the social world for so long are in decline, giving rise to new identities and fragmenting the modern individual as a unified subject. This so-called 'crisis of identity' is seen as part of a wider process of change which is dislocating the central structures and processes of modern societies and undermining the frameworks which gave individuals stable anchorage in the social world. (Hall, 1992: 274)

Identity has a unique and contentious place in social and political theory. On the one hand it is a concept which embodies our sense of uniqueness as individual beings and as members of groups sharing values and beliefs. On the other it is an intensely political field in which the expansion of critical theory has allowed the emergence of competing voices demanding space for recognition of fragile and previously often fugitive and unspoken subjectivities. As the above quote suggests, challenges to the grand narratives of modernity have begun to detach identity from the moorings of a stable social consensus, drifting to new, ambiguous, and hybrid forms. Bauman quite rightly suggests that 'identity' is an uneasy concept, that we examine when confronted with uncertainty and that one '…thinks of identity when one is unsure where one belongs' (Bauman, in Hall & Du Gay, 1996: 18). Recent interventions question the attempts of dominant groups in society to impose single definitions on such domains as sexuality, race, ethnicity, age, disability, and class. It could indeed be argued that to study identity is to recognise the troubled nature of the individual.

Understanding identity

In order to understand the nature of identity, a number of questions must be raised. Is there a single unitary self, or a collection of social selves? We each possess a number of social identities: father/mother, brother/sister, son/daughter, employee/employer, friend/lover, British citizen/Australian citizen, football team supporter and so on. Yet is there not simultaneously a self who oversees the faces we present and choreographs these different roles

1

to portray a pattern of predictable reactions consistent with some core personality?

Craib argues that this is not necessarily an either/or question and that it is possible for us to be both the single unified self and plural selves simultaneously (Craib, 1998). Indeed the work of George Herbert Mead implicitly accepts this dichotomous nature. The division between the 'I' and the 'me' recognises that people are 'reflective, symbol-using beings' and that:

> We cannot realise ourselves except in so far as we can recognise the other in his relationship to us. It is as he takes the attitude of the other that the individual is able to realise himself as a self.
> (Mead, 1934: 194)

There is a constant dialogue between the 'I' and the 'me', a negotiation between the internal and the external worlds of the self, what Jenkins in his discussion of Goffman and others calls the 'internal/external dialectic' (Jenkins, 1996: 22). In any social situation we project an image, an identity to those around us and may face approval or disapproval, acceptance or rejection. We decide how these reactions should be assessed; we may choose to modify our future presentations to that group, ignore their response, or feel a positive affirmation of our identity. So we constantly monitor our self-presentations, and as a result individual and collective identity is open to continuous reassessment.

Ethnic identity is a case in point. Terms such as 'black', 'brown' or 'white' are political and social boundary markers rather than iconic signs representing actual categories, and function in an interlocking fashion to raise or lower boundaries, exclude or unite. In *Brown Britain* Pauline Black (a woman of mixed-race) commented on her self-designation as 'black':

> I will still continue to define myself as black, until white people turn around to me and say, "Hey I'm mixed race as well." You know – the Vikings came over one time, the French came over one time – and actually recognise that everybody on this planet is really a mixture. (*Brown Britain*: 2001)

This is a vivid example of the manner in which human identity is socially, historically and culturally constructed. While there is individual choice and freedom of movement, in practice this is circumscribed by shared conventions, codes, values, by what Pierre Bourdieu (1992: 66) calls 'the feel for the game' a second nature instilled from childhood. The structure Bourdieu terms 'habitus'; an internalised grammar of practice developed through the lived experiences inscribes meanings onto the body and psyche of the individual. While there are differences in each individual's habitus – unique individuals construct their own – the individual has also been steeped in the specific traditions of a group, embodying all its social codes. Therefore while the habitus has a potentially infinite capacity to produce differences, the actual behaviours brought into active practice are 'constrained':

> ...without violence, art or argument. The group habitus tends to exclude all 'extravagances' ('not for the likes of us'), that is, all the behaviours that would be negatively sanctioned because they are incompatible with the objective conditions. (Bourdieu, 1990: 56)

In fact the primary difference between 'identity' and 'habitus' seems to be that habitus denotes a less conscious level of collective awareness (see Mennell, 1994) whereas according to Goffman and others the presentation of self is much more intentionally stage-managed.

Ethnic identity then is a politically charged field. There is a danger of reification; dominant social codes construct ethnicity as 'other' not 'us'. The fact that 'white English' is possibly an ethnic category may seem odd to a white English person who has come to see his/her identity as 'natural'. Many westerners would see 'Arabs' as a relatively homogenous identity with common interests and broadly similar attributes – while it actually comprises dozens of distinct ethnic groups. Similarly white Australians typically do not differentiate between groups of indigenous 'Aborigines', but that term encompasses over 400 linguistically and culturally separate groups. This everyday essentialism allows for certain groups to be marginalised and made passive; there is no need to examine individual cases or social and historical forces which have shaped relations. This tendency to classify diverse groups of people as homogenous has troubling implications. Stuart Hall in a recent lecture points out the dangers of classification becoming a practice with distorting and belittling consequences:

> ...our identity is partly shaped by recognition or its absence. Often by the misrecognition of others. Non-recognition or misrecognition can inflict harm can be a form of oppression imprisoning someone in a false distorted and reduced mode of being. (Hall, 2000).

Unfortunately it is the distorting perceptions the 'misrecognition' which often seem to persist over generations in the form of stereotypes. Identity is in part a uniquely personal, internal sense of self, but at the same time it relates to that person's place in society and how they are categorised, and the flow of dominant cultural meanings and the power relations contingent on these. Language and other cultural codes are central to our internal identity as well as to our sense of belonging or our collective identity. At a more implicit level, our language with all its cultural baggage has provided us very early in life with a field of restrained expressive possibilities. While there is some freedom of expression, it is constrained by 'available discourses' (Muecke, 1982). The meaning of discourse can be narrowed down to two very influential and particularly relevant aspects of language use. First, the centrality of language in the formation of individual identity; the fact that conversation is perhaps the best medium to express the dialectic between the external and internal worlds of the individual. Second at a more abstract level; social identity is directly related to discourses of power. The Foucauldian (and Lacanian) view that power has no unitary object but is constituted by the matrix of different social knowledge and practices, which have come to be known as discourses. The term 'discourse' has come to mean 'a whole field or domain within which language is used in particular ways' (Loomba, 1998: 38). Subjects are constructed through discourses of, for example, economics, anthropology, psychiatry, racism, literary genres, and the way these regimes of thought influence social reality, through their schemes of classification in different periods of time. As we will see political ideologies produce highly influential discourses which construct very different views of individual and collective identity.

Identity is a work in progress, a negotiated space between ourselves and others; constantly being re-appraised and very much linked to the circulation of cultural meanings in a society. Furthermore identity is intensely political. There are constant efforts to escape, fix or perpetuate images and meanings of others. These transformations are apparent in every domain, and the relationships between these constructions reflect and reinforce power relations. Groups that have suffered marginalisation become acutely politically aware of the politics of identity. Often there is a struggle to reclaim the very terms which had been used to 'other' such identities, for example 'queer', 'wog', 'nigger' are terms stemming from homophobia and racism and have to some extent been reclaimed, parodied and used to highlight awareness of the experience of being objectified and stereotyped.

By studying social identities, we gain insight into the complex range of factors influencing the way we see ourselves, the way we are seen by others and the pressures exerted on individuals to readjust or at least prioritise some social agendas over others. Investigations into social identity show that we have many dimensions. For example, a person is not simply working class. This person may also be defined in terms of gender, ethnicity, sexuality, nationality and adherence to or rejection of particular religious or spiritual views. The social shaping of self-identity operates as a continuous process and will depend upon the specific dynamics of the social context. For example, while an Afro-Caribbean male has a highly complex matrix of identities which compose his habitus, at times certain features will be thrown more sharply into relief. As a single man amongst a large group of women his maleness may be emphasised. At other times his ethnic or religious or political identity may be fore-grounded. Although his other social identities still exist, they will probably have less influence on the way he interacts with the group. But social identity is not only important in understanding the complex nature of the individual. The assumptions made concerning social identity are of central importance in the way we think politically and in the organisation of the political system.

Identity, ideology and class

Politicians and political theorists make assumptions about the nature of the individual when devising their political programmes. It would make no sense to disband the army, reduce the powers of the police, relax censorship and liberalise the education system if you assume that individuals are primarily greedy and untrustworthy. Advocates of social freedom will tend to have faith in the potential of the individual to live a virtuous life. The virtues necessary to create a 'good' society are also often associated with a particular social class. The virtues displayed by the working class are often seen as quite different from those displayed by the aristocracy and by the middle class. A strong sense of class will have a significant impact upon the values we choose as our own from the vast array found within any nation.

Ideological discourse has traditionally revolved around the conflicting claims of different social classes. The modern ideologies that developed in Europe in the years following the French revolution consist in clusters of ideas and deal with fundamental questions about the relationship between individuals and the state. Ideologies contain both an examination of the present and views about possible futures for society. These ideologies are not, however, created in a social and political vacuum. Indeed, social and political theorists are usually driven by sectional interests and almost certainly hold views about the relative importance of various groups in society. They attack or defend divisions and inequalities and aim to establish a social matrix to give order to the social and political demands advanced by numerous social groups. The dominant ideologies in western society (liberalism, conservatism and socialism) contain class views of society.

It is often the case that liberals are viewed as the champions of middle class interests and values. Liberals argue that the individual must be given room to grow and not confined to the class position of his or her parents. Early liberals wrote in opposition to the entrenched class system of the Middle Ages and argued that the new capitalist system needed a more fluid social system. Hierarchies could be allowed to develop, but these should be based upon merit rather than upon the past glories or relative failures of families. The so-called classical liberals of the early nineteenth century believed that we should be seen as isolated individuals pursuing our own interests and that our freedoms depend upon placing limits upon the jurisdiction of the state. They felt that people are dwarfed by large organisations and that the state in particular poses a definite threat to personal freedom. They assume that the common good can be enhanced by allowing everybody the freedom to develop as individuals, to make of life what they will. This rests upon and reinforces the belief that individuals are primarily motivated by the desire for individual betterment and material gain and that we are capable of living according to the dictates of reason. This philosophy of life served the interests of the emerging capitalist class of the late eighteenth and nineteenth century. It made virtues of self help, material acquisition and individualism (Eccleshall, 1994; Barry, 1990: 16–21).

Whereas liberals believe that individuals are capable of listening to reason and therefore have little need for the disciplinary functions of the state, conservatives argue that individuals are flawed, deficient in reason, driven by base motives and therefore need to be disciplined by the moral codes and sense of order enshrined in the modern state. It is argued that too much freedom undermines respect for authority and that the power of the church and the state are necessary to place limits upon the life of the individual. Attempts to break away from the established economic, social and moral order will almost inevitably lead to chaos, violence and social degeneration. From a traditional conservative perspective, we are not capable of controlling our own destinies. We are products of history, carrying personalities shaped by custom and by our sense of belonging to the nation. We must accept the shared moral values of society for these values are necessary for social order and for protecting civilisation. There is little room for permissiveness in this view of the individual. Many conservatives believe that without the refining influences of religion and custom, individuals are apt to become depraved, selfish, arrogant and unrealistic in their aspirations and lifestyle (Eccleshall, 1994b: 62–73; Schwarzmantel, 1998: 116–120; Perry, 1993: 209–211).

Conservatives often argue in favour of maintaining the class system because they think that a cultured (and privileged) elite is best equipped to protect the poor and promote the common good. Whereas liberalism began as the doctrine of the industrial bourgeoisie, modern conservatism began as an aristocratic reaction. This can be seen in its most blatant form in the ideas of the British one nation conservatives who argue that society should be seen as an organic whole in which all people have functions to perform in accordance with their place in the social hierarchy. They argue that the preservation of inequalities can have beneficial social results. Harold Macmillan, for example, claimed that attempts to level the distribution of rewards in society stifles creativity, panders to the spite of the have-nots and fails to give due recognition to the diversity of people in society (Eccleshall, 1994: 73). The class system is thus seen as socially, politically and morally beneficial. From a conservative point of view, social order relies upon us all 'knowing our place' in the social hierarchy. This does not mean that we cannot move between the classes, but the rites of passage are set by custom and by those deemed to be economically successful.

The emphasis upon class identity is also prominent in the writings of key socialist theorists. Socialists since the early nineteenth century have argued that we are products of our environment. Our dominant characteristics are said to be moulded by society and can be altered by transforming the structure of society. Robert Owen, for example, believed that the capitalist system could and should be reformed out of existence by benevolent legislation. He believed that reformers must look beyond class and seek to establish the material and spiritual conditions necessary for the 'harmonious development of all'. This meant instituting anti-poverty programmes and providing education for the workers (Owen, 1927). Owen, a middle class entrepreneur, wanted to improve the living conditions endured by the working class. He saw that poverty damages body and spirit and was therefore unacceptable in a modern 'civilised' society. This reliance upon the benevolent actions of an enlightened minority is criticised by many in the socialist tradition. Marx and Engels, for example, believed that the working class must take control of their own destinies and destroy the capitalist system through revolutionary activity. Marx believed that the capitalist economic system strips workers of their finer qualities by depriving them of a means to express themselves through their work. This process of 'alienation' contaminates society and prevents people from realising their full potential. The abolition of capitalism could only come about once the workers recognise their own degradation and fight for recognition as human beings (Marx, 1977).

The so-called traditional ideologies are dominated, driven and formulated by people advancing the sectional interests of particular social classes, though it is often claimed that the advancement of these particular classes will in turn serve the common good. For example, conservatives often defend the interests of an elite by claiming that all benefit from the guidance of this group, whilst many socialists believe that the common good would be served by abolishing the exploitation of the working class because this exploitation not only harms a significant section of the population but also contaminates relations between the classes. For the traditional ideologies, it is important to establish who holds economic and political power and to determine whether these power relations serve the common good. Each ideology, however, is hemmed in by assumptions about the character and virtues of their favoured class. They define people according to their class positions and attribute identity to these classes. Defenders of aristocrats point to their culture, their role in history and their sense of social responsibility. Defenders of the middle classes point to their entrepreneurial spirit, their independence and their respect for freedom. The working class, on the other hand, are praised

7

for their passion, their hard work and their sense of solidarity. Political debate drawing upon these traditional ideologies will thus bring into play a variety of social identities, all of which are attributed value in accordance with our own political values.

By no means all ideologies are anchored in class identity. The primacy of class politics has been challenged by a range of ideologies including nationalism, feminism and the greens. Nationalists have argued traditionally that we are not isolated individuals and that any loyalty we might feel towards our class is (and should be) superseded by our ties to the nation. The French nationalists of the nineteenth century, for example, believed in line with the spirit of the enlightenment that religion should be replaced by a secular faith in which we pledge allegiance to the nation. This form of 'civic nationalism' defined the nation in terms of territory and political institutions (Perry, 1993: 234; Schwarzmantel, 1998: 188–190; Gamble, 1981; Heywood, 1992: 136–138). For some in the nationalist camp, this view of the importance of the nation does not go far enough. The German romantics of the nineteenth century argued that the French nationalists (indeed, the French in general) assumed too readily that people are capable of being motivated primarily by reason and that this assumption clouded the spiritual significance of the nation. The romantics believed that the nation expressed the so-called spirit of the people and served to bind all members of the nation to each other and to their shared past. For these theorists, the nation is far more important than the individual and individuals can only prosper and recognise their true selves by uniting with others and (if necessary) by sacrificing themselves to the good of the whole (Perry, 1993: 236; Rocker, 1978: 222–223).

Many feminists likewise deliberately cut across class distinctions by looking at the suppression of women and the power relations implicit within gender politics. Feminists are in general united in the belief that women need to liberate themselves from the constraints of patriarchal society. They point out that men tend to have the dominant positions in society and that this does not stem from superior ability but from ingrained and harmful conventions in western society. Feminists point out that the identity of a woman is not determined at birth. They argue that it assumed that men are active and have control over their own destinies, whereas women are seen as passive and thus easily manipulated and moulded according to men's designs. Feminists recognise that gender identities are socially constructed and are influenced by such things as culture and law. Women are encouraged to focus upon their own needs and determine their own destiny rather than allow their futures to be determined by others (Lloyd, 1998: 166; Wilford, 1994).

Whereas feminists argue that class politics serve to obscure the realities of gender inequalities, the greens argue that concentrating upon class does little if anything to challenge the ways in which we destroy the environment. The greens attempt to divert our attention away from the material welfare of different social classes and convince us that the salvation of the human race relies upon looking beyond materialism and adopting a new more spiritual view of humans and their relationship with the planet. The greens tend to reject the traditional ideologies because they are far too uncritical of industrialism and economic growth and far too in favour of the extensive use of technology. Humans are called upon to be more humble and accept that they are merely one of the species living on the planet and that they have a responsibility to live in environmentally-friendly ways. We can only be free to the extent that we live in harmony (rather than try to dominate) the environment. The eco-feminists in particular believe that men need to learn from women the importance of 'mother earth' and that the male ego is responsible for much of the environmental destruction of modern times. People are urged to develop their spiritual sides, cultivate their feminine characteristics and treat the earth as a living entity rather than something to be exploited (Kenny, 1994; Dobson, 1990; Barry, 1998; Dodds, 1988).

These non-class ideologies recognise that class has some importance in shaping our social identities but claim that class should not be seen as the sole or even the dominant influence. They argue that we are united and divided by things other than class and that national characteristics, socially constructed gender codes and our relationship with the environment are of fundamental importance. Proponents of these ideologies will often claim that they are arguing *beyond* class rather than in *ignorance* of class. According to these ideologies, our class positions are of secondary importance in that they denote our place on an economic hierarchy but do not necessarily say anything significant about our dominant characteristics. If we are to understand social identity, we are urged to look beyond the predominantly economic dimensions of class.

The argument does not, however, end at this point. Postmodernists argue that class and non-class ideologies are guilty of *reductionism* in that they attempt to reduce our identities to a single or dominant focal point. Postmodernists argue that individuals select a variety of labels for themselves, that they define themselves using a variety of criteria and that they will inevitably attach different significance to each of the labels (Schwarzmantel, 1998: 189). Postmodernists deny that individuals can be reduced to a single essence and argue that we must be seen as a work in progress, a collection of a multitude of changing influences. Foucault, in a famous end piece of *The Order of Things*, claims that the individual human actor is non-existent, there is no essential meaning to things, he speaks of man the actor being erased 'like a face drawn in sand at the edge of the sea' (Lechte: 111). For postmodernists, identity is a highly complex ceaselessly

9

shifting process. It is fractured and specific to individual social and cultural conditions. Instead of assuming that there is a single reality or essence, they argue that it is impossible to take into account and recognise the importance of difference. Indeed:

> I propose that while it is true that identity 'continues to be a problem' this is *not* 'the problem it was throughout modernity'. Indeed, if the *modern* 'problem of identity' was how to construct an identity and keep it solid and stable, the *post-modern* 'problem of identity' is primarily how to avoid fixation and keep the options open...the catchword of modernity was creation; the catchword of post modernity is recycling. (Bauman, Z in Hall & Du Gay, 18)

This postmodern perspective has also influenced more established ideologies and thereby provided new ways to interpret and challenge oppression in society. Postmodern feminists, for example, claim that it makes sense to replace unitary ideas of a 'woman' with the idea of plural identities '...treating gender as one relevant strand among others, attending also to class, race, ethnicity, age and sexual orientation' (Ross cited in Schwarzmantel, 1998: 188). Postmodern feminists are anti-essentialist. They reject the idea of universal categories and argue that we should embrace the differences between people in general and women in particular. They argue that there are fundamental differences between women and that it is important to take into account a multitude of factors. Indeed, Lloyd points out that '...far from being fixed and static, the category of Woman is fluid, mobile and multiple' (Lloyd, 1998: 176). The postmodernists, like de Beauvoir before them, believe that women need to embark upon an internal journey and they acknowledge the importance of '...subjectivity and an interior exploration by women of their own, individual identities' (Wilford, 1994: 278).

With the development of postmodernism comes the recognition that we do not have a single social identity but a variety of social identities. We belong to different classes, different genders and different ethnic groups. Our sexualities might be complex, our religious views unorthodox or non-existent, our nationalities might likewise be contentious. Nikolas Rose, for example, points out that we are not unified personalities or beings. We are subject to different pressures and pulled in different directions by the needs and demands of our various social functions. He claims that we live in 'constant movement across different practices' and that we are '...addressed as different sorts of human being, presupposed to be different sorts of human being, acted upon as if they were different sorts of human being' (Rose, 1996: 319). For postmodernists, our identities are reflected in differences between people rather than captured in total by rigid categories. Yet a note of caution should be made here. While the recognition of social differences is of vital importance and an essential step in tracing the mechanisms of identity creation and hegemony of dominant meanings, it is also crucial to avoid the pitfalls of reification. For example considering the theorising around 'multiculturalism' Kundnani (2002) suggests that, in academic circles, the popularity of post-modern theories of hybridity has tended to produce a narrow and restrictive concept of culture, rather than inspiring a critical challenge to class and race discrimination.

Conclusion

The papers in this volume recognise the uncertain and fragmented nature of social identity. It is understood that we need to understand the specific sites of identity – their unique histories and the particular dynamics which are manifest in each context, the identity politics with which each form of identity is associated. These contributions to the field of social identity recognise and acknowledge the importance of subjectivity in social analysis. Far from being a 'narcissistic pre-occupation with self and personal experience' (Elliot, 2001: 157) and a retreat from the big issues of patriarchy, capitalism and globalisation, the writers represented here take the opportunity to equip global politics within the local politics of identity. Each contributor addresses a specific dimension of identity and draws us into at least some of the channels cut into the landscape of contemporary society.

Bibliography

Barry, J (1998) 'Green Political Thought' in A Lent (ed.), *New Political Thought*, Lawrence and Wishart: London, 184–200.

Barry, N (1990), *Welfare*, Open University Press: Milton Keynes.

Bourdieu, Pierre, (1989) *Distinction: A Social Critique of the Judgement of Taste*, Routledge.

Bourdieu, Pierre (1990) *In Other Words, Essays toward a reflective Sociology*, Polity Press.

Calhoun, C (1994) *Social Theory & the Politics of Identity*, Blackwell, London.

Coote, A and Campbell, B (1987) *Sweet Freedom*, Basil Blackwell, London.

Craib, I (1998) *Experiencing Identity*, Sage.

Dobson, A (1990) *Green Political Thought*, Unwin Hyman: London.

Dodds, F (1988) *Into the 21st Century*, Green Print: Basingstoke.

Eccleshall, R (1994) 'Liberalism' in R. Eccleshall et al, *Political Ideologies: an Introduction*, Routledge: London, 28–59.

Eccleshall, R (1994b) 'Conservatism' in Eccleshall et al, *Political Ideologies: an Introduction*, Routledge: London, 60–90.

Elias, N (1968) 'Homo clausus and the civilizing process' in Du Gay, P, Evans, J and Redman, P (2000) *Identity: A Reader*, Sage: London, 284–296.

Elliot, A (2001) *Concepts of the Self*, Polity.

Gamble, A (1981) *An Introduction to Modern Social and Political Thought*, Macmillan: London.

Goffman, E, *The Presentation of Self in everyday Life*, 1959, Penguin.

Hall, S and Du Gay, P (1996) *Questions of Cultural Identity*, Sage.

Hall, S (2000) *'The Multicultural Question'*, PERC Lecture (transcript from University of Sheffield).

Hall, S, Held, D and McGrew A. eds. (1992) *Modernity and its Futures*, Polity Press.

Heywood, A (1992) *Political Ideologies*, Macmillan: London.

Jenkins, R (1996) *Social Identity*, Routledge.

Kenny, M (1994) 'Ecologism' in R. Eccleshall et al, *Political Ideologies*, Routledge: London, 218–251.

Kymlicka, W (1990) *Contemporary Political Philosophy*, Clarendon: Oxford.

Lloyd, M (1998) 'Feminism' in A. Lent (ed), *New Political Thought: An Introduction*, Lawrence and Wishart: London, 1998, 163–183.

Perry, M (1993) *An Intellectual History of Modern Europe*, Houghton Mifflin: Boston.

Kundnani, A (2002) *The Death of Multiculturalism*, Institute of Race Relations: Online Resources (visited 12:6:2002).

Lechte, J (1994) *Fifty Contemporary Thinkers*, Routledge.

Loomba, A (1998) *Colonialism/Postcolonialism*, Routledge.

Marx, K (1977) 'Economic and Philosophical Manuscripts' in D. McLellan (ed.), *Karl Marx: Selected Writings*, Oxford University Press: Oxford, 75–112.

Millett, K (1977) *Sexual Politics*, Virago: London.

Muecke, S (1982) 'Available Discourses on Aborigines', in *Theoretical Strategies: Local Consumption*, Series 2/3 Aug. Australia.

Owen, R (1927) *A New View of Society* (edited by GDH Cole).

Rex, J. (1996) *'National Identity in the Democratic Multi-Cultural State'*, Sociological Research Online, vol. 1, no. 2
(http://www.socresonline.org.uk/socresonline/1/2/1.html)

Rocker, R (1978) *Nationalism and Culture*, Coughlin: Minnesota.

Rose, N (1996) 'Identity, Genealogy, History' in Du Gay, P, Evans, J and Redman, P (2000) *Identity: A Reader*, Sage: London, 311–324.

Rowbotham, S (1989) *The Past is before us*, Pandora: London.

Rustin, M (1991) 'Psychoanalysis, racism and anti-racism' in Du Gay, P, Evans, J and Redman, P (2000) *Identity: A Reader*, Sage: London, 183–201.

Sandel, M (1996) *Democracy's Discontent*, Belknap Press: Cambridge Massachusetts, 1996.
Schwarzmantel, J (1998) *The Age of Ideology*, Macmillan: Houndmills.
Smart, B (1995) Michel Foucault, Ellis Horwood.
Wilford, R (1994) 'Feminism' in R. Eccleshall et al, *Political Ideologies: An Introduction*, Routledge: London, 252–285.
Wollstonecraft, M (1982) *Vindication of the rights of woman*, Penguin: Harmondsworth.

Audiovisual material

Brown Britain, Channel 4, 22/08/2001

2. Social Class

Serena Bufton

Interest in social inequality is at the heart of the sociological enterprise and was central to the work of the founding theorists of the nineteenth century, whose analyses of the nature of inequality in industrialised society established the theoretical framework and research agenda for future generations of sociologists. In general, there was agreement between the founding theorists that industrial society marked a qualitative break with the past (Francis, 1987) and that new forms of inequality had emerged. It was around this time that the concept of 'social class' started to be used as a description of the patterned nature of inequality in society. Before the late eighteenth century, differences between groups of people were conceived more in terms of a finely-graded hierarchy of 'ranks' or 'orders' of people (Nisbet, 1966: 174, 176) and the word 'class' simply meant 'group'; we still use it in this way when we speak of a 'class' of children in school.

The perception that industrialisation had brought into being new forms of inequality inspired the work of the early sociologists and Marx and Weber, in particular, devoted a great deal of thought to this area. Although their influence on sociology can still be felt today, changes in the nature of society in the twentieth century (and in the discipline of sociology itself) culminated, towards the end of the century, in a decline of interest in social class and, among some writers, in a rejection of its importance, both as a significant dimension of inequality and as a source of social identity in contemporary society. It is only in the last few years that interest in social class has re-emerged and, as it has done so, there has been a movement away from the ideas of the founding theorists about the nature of social class processes and of class-based identities. This chapter traces these recent developments, situating them within the historical evolution of class theory. Accordingly, the chapter begins with a necessarily brief account of the work of Marx and Weber, moves on to look at the arguments about the 'death' of social class, and finishes with a discussion of recent theoretical work in the area.

Marx and Social Class

For Marx, the most important feature of industrialisation was that it was *capitalist* industrialisation, creating a system in which ownership and control of the means of production was in *private* hands (those of the *bourgeoisie*) and economic activity geared towards *private* profit-making, within the context of a market framework. In a capitalist system, workers (the *proletariat*) neither own nor control the means of production but are free to sell their labour power to any employer for whom they wish to work. In all cases, however, Marx argued that wage labourers are *necessarily* exploited in this system. The reason is that, in a capitalist system, the pursuit of profit is the prime directive: production is a cut-throat business and competition between capitalist producers is intense. Those who make the most profit have the edge: the strong survive and the weak go out of business. Where does this profit come from?

Marx's 'labour theory of value' is the key to understanding how the capitalist system of production works. The idea is that labourers increase the value of raw materials (commodities) such as wood or iron when they work on them to produce new commodities for sale on the market (Crompton, 1998: 27). Indeed, the market price of the labourer – his or her wage – is much lower than the price the employer will receive for the goods that the worker produces (ibid). The difference between the market price of the labourer and that of the goods he or she produces Marx called *surplus value*. Clearly, not all surplus value is profit as the employer has costs associated with production – for example, the cost of the equipment and premises, taxes and so on. Nevertheless, some of the surplus value is profit. For Marx, then, production in a capitalist system inevitably entails the extraction of surplus value from the proletariat, a situation which he described as the *exploitation* of the proletariat by the bourgeoisie.

For Marx, a capitalist system therefore inevitably creates two antagonistic social classes: the owners and non-owners of the means of production. These classes are bound together in a relationship of exploitation; their interests are inevitably in conflict and yet they depend on each other for survival. Marx and Engels (1973: 33) described the dynamics of this relationship graphically in one of their early works, *Manifesto of the Communist Party*. Here, they argued: 'Society as a whole is more and more splitting up into two great hostile camps, into two great classes directly facing each other: Bourgeoisie and Proletariat'. They described these 'two great classes' as involved in a constant battle for survival as the members of the bourgeoisie competed with each other to make a profit, 'constantly revolutionising the instruments of production' in the process' and 'expanding the markets for their goods 'over the whole surface of the globe' (ibid: 36–37). In turn, the members of the proletariat struggle for the means to survive as the competition between employers drives down wages and the inevitable cycle of economic booms and slumps brings with it the constant risk of unemployment.

Marx and Engels argued that the capitalist system was destined to self-destruct:

> Modern bourgeois society with its relations of production, of exchange and of property, a society that has conjured up such gigantic means of production and of exchange, is like the sorcerer who is no longer able to control the powers of the nether world whom he has called up by his spells. (Marx and Engels, 1973:39–40)

Using complex economic arguments, Marx and Engels attempted to demonstrate that, in any capitalist society, the rate of profit will tend to fall, creating fierce competition between producers and the growth of monopolies as smaller, weaker producers are taken over by larger, more successful ones. He predicted a growing gap between rich and poor as the proletariat became increasingly 'immiserated'. Ultimately, they suggested, the system would collapse:

> What the bourgeoisie therefore produces, above all, are its own grave-diggers. Its fall and the victory of the proletariat are equally inevitable. (Marx and Engels, 1973: 49)

Central to Marx's model of capitalist development and collapse is the argument that the members of the proletariat will *inevitably* recognise their shared interests as an exploited social class: they will change from a 'class in themselves' – a group of people sharing the same position in capitalist production but with little shared identity – to a conscious and politically-motivated 'class for themselves'. When this happens, Marx argued, the only outcome could be revolution.

Emerging strongly from the writings of Marx was the idea that groups of people defined by their position in the process of production would inevitably develop a shared class identity and that this would lead to political action. However, not all the founding theorists agreed about this. Max Weber, in particular, put forward views that were rather different.

Weber and Social Class

Weber, like Marx, argued that society was characterised by power struggles although he did not see these struggles as being related exclusively – or even primarily – to social class. In addition, although he agreed with Marx that social classes were *economic* groupings, he differed in his assessment of their nature and their potential for collective action.

Weber argued that classes can only exist in a market economy in which individuals can sell goods or services for money. In such an economy, people bargain for an income on the basis of their ownership of property, skills or qualifications. According to Weber, a 'class' is simply a group of people who share roughly the same position in the market in terms of their bargaining power:

16

> We may speak of a 'class' when (1) a number of people have in common a specific causal component of their life chances, in so far as (2) this component is represented exclusively by economic interests in the possession of goods and opportunities for income, and (3) is represented under the conditions of the commodity of labor markets. (Weber, 1948: 181)

Clearly, ownership of property is an important factor here as property can be used to bring in an income (through rents, for example) but Weber argued that there are significant differences amongst those people who own no property (differences in skills, qualifications and so on). In addition, property owners are divided according to what they own and how they use it for economic ends.

For Weber, then, 'class situation' is simply 'market situation' (ibid: 182) and many different class situations will exist in any market-based society. He contended that *'social'* classes are simply groupings of class situations between which social mobility is easy and commonplace, identifying four major groupings in industrial society: the dominant entrepreneurial and propertied groups; the propertyless white-collar workers; the petite bourgeoisie; and the manual working class. Importantly, however, unlike Marx, Weber did not see social classes as necessarily developing a consciousness of themselves as groupings of people with shared interests, commenting that 'a class does not in itself constitute a community' and arguing that 'however different life chances may be, this fact in itself, according to all experience, by no means gives birth to "class action" (communal action by the members of a class)' (ibid:184).

Nevertheless, Weber conceded that communal action *could* flow from class interests in certain circumstances – for example, when the class enemy is visible and obviously in economic competition, or where large numbers of people share a common class situation. However, the concepts of class and class conflict were not as important for Weber as they were for Marx. Weber accepted that class conflicts had occurred in particular historical contexts and recognised the potential for such conflicts in industrial capitalist societies but, unlike Marx, he did not see such conflicts as inevitable and did not regard them as the motor force of historical change. In addition, Weber believed that class interests were only one possible source of collective identity and struggle.

Weber argued that power struggles in society give rise to status groups as well as to social classes. These are groups of people who attempt to monopolise access to 'social esteem' through a process of *social closure*: by keeping others out. In order to do this, they try to impose criteria of eligibility for membership of their groups, emphasising certain attributes – such as being male, white or privately educated – as necessary for access. The

Freemason society, with its male-only membership and emphasis on mutual help, is an example of such a status group. A point to note here is that status groups, unlike social classes, 'are normally communities' (Weber, 1948: 186): their members are conscious of a shared identity and work to preserve this by excluding others. Weber commented:

> In content, status honor is normally expressed by the fact that above all else a specific *style of life* can be expected from all those who wish to belong to the circle. Linked with this expectation are restrictions on 'social' intercourse...(Weber, 1948:187)

Importantly, Weber contended that 'status honour need not necessarily be linked with a "class situation" (ibid): the two forms of inequality do not necessarily coalesce so that it is possible to have a low status and a relatively high social class and vice versa. The case of the *nouveau riche* in any historical period is an example of this. Nevertheless, Weber conceded that classes and status groups frequently overlap.

The different views of Marx and Weber about the nature of inequality in industrial society can be summarised in the following way. Firstly, for Marx, economic power is the basis of political power and status but, for Weber, power struggles give rise to status groups (and parties) as well as to social classes. Secondly, in Marx's formulation, social classes emerge during the process of production; in Weber's analysis, however, they arise during the process of distribution, in the market. Thirdly, Marx argued that social class is a *relational* concept because classes are defined in terms of their relationship to each other whilst Weber saw it as a *positional* concept: for Weber, a social class is merely a grouping of people who share roughly the same market position. Fourthly, class and class conflict are the motor force of historical change in Marx's theory but, for Weber, merely represent one possible (but not inevitable) site of power struggle. Finally, Marx predicted a polarisation of the class structure as capitalism matures whilst Weber anticipated its fragmentation and diversification.

Assessment of the Classical Legacy

Marx's ideas on social class have been subject to much debate and a number of major issues have been noted. Importantly, his insistence that relationships in the system of production underpin social differentiation and shape human activities has been challenged by those who assert the importance of non-economic sources of differentiation and identity, such as gender and ethnicity. In addition, doubt has been cast on Marx's claim that class-consciousness is crucial to the identification of a class – a point which Weber had already made (Crompton, 1998: 32). The problem is that Marx appeared to suggest that class position would inevitably lead to class consciousness and class action; indeed, this was central to his model of social change. Yet he also identified circumstances that might lead to class consciousness – conflicts over material resources, de-skilling and alienation, for example – implying that such consciousness was a *contingent* rather than a *necessary* condition of class position (as Weber had argued) (ibid: 37). Following this line of reasoning, it is clear that the relationship between class position and class-consciousness is one which has to be examined *empirically*.

Much work on class in the second part of the twentieth century was based on the assumption that class structure (the 'objective' dimension of class) is analytically and empirically separate from class consciousness (the 'subjective' dimension of class) (ibid). This mirrored the structure-action dualism in sociology generally and led to two rather different approaches to the study of social class (ibid: 44). Firstly, there are 'theoretical' or 'relational' employment-based class schemes. Drawing on the work of both Marx and Weber, a number of writers have attempted to identify the various groupings that make up the class structure. Those working within a neo-Weberian framework (such as Lockwood [1958] and Dahrendorf [1959]) used the 'work' or 'market' situation of occupational groups to identify their position in the class structure (Crompton, 1998: 39). On the other hand, neo-Marxist theorists, such as Wright (1985, 1997), have been motivated by the need to update and extend Marx's ideas to accommodate the growing complexity of the class structure in the twentieth century.

In addition to these theoretical ('relational') class schemes, there have been historico-cultural ethnographies of social class drawing upon historical and anthropological approaches. These focused on the nature of class consciousness and on the cultural, rather than the structural, dimensions of social class. The work of the historian E. P. Thompson was particularly influential here. Although writing from a (humanist) Marxist position which gave central place to relationships in the process of production, he argued that social classes are not simply economic groupings but also have distinct *cultural* features so that people in the same class share a system of symbolism, meaning and practices:

> ...class happens when some men [sic], as a result of common experiences (inherited or shared), feel and articulate the identity of their interests as between themselves, and as against other men whose interests are different from (and usually opposed to) theirs. The class experience is largely determined by the productive relations into which men are born – or enter involuntarily. Class-consciousness is the way in which these experiences are handled in cultural terms: embodied in traditions,

19

value-systems, ideas and institutional forms. (Thompson, 1980:8–9)

In addition to social history writers such as Thompson, academics working within cultural studies have examined the cultural features of social classes, conducting ethnographic studies into the symbolism, meanings and ways of life of people in them – particularly those in the working class. However, it is in the work of these writers that deep-seated problems with social class theory began to emerge. These problems, *inter alia*, culminated in the rejection of social class as either an empirical reality or a fruitful theoretical tool for sociological analysis.

4. The death of social class?

Although social class is now starting to reappear on the academic agenda, there has been little interest in it in recent years, many writers denying its relevance as a source of social cleavage or identity and rejecting its centrality in social science analysis (see, for example, Lash, 1990; Bauman, 1992; Giddens, 1990). Paradoxically, this rejection of the relevance of class occurred at a time when the gap between rich and poor was widening, the levels of education, housing, health and lifestyle experienced by different social groups were being shown to correlate very strongly with measures of social class (Adonis and Pollard, 1998) and talk about the effects of class proliferated in the media. The debate about the 'death' of class is complex and cannot be fully explored here but a brief account can be given.

It was argued above that one of the enduring features of the classical legacy has been the fragmentation of class studies along the structure/action divide: whilst some writers have been interested in the 'objective' identification of social classes, for example, as groupings of occupations, others have been more concerned with the 'subjective' dimensions of social class as revealed in class consciousness and identity. Those adopting an 'objective' focus may follow Marx and see classes as groups defined in terms of their position in production, which gives rise to different interests. Alternatively, Weberian-inspired writers may identify classes as groupings of people sharing similar positions with respect to income, occupation and education. In contradistinction, those adopting a 'subjective' view of social classes tend to see them either as (conscious) socio-political actors – groups of people who challenge existing social arrangements – or as (conscious) socio-cultural groups – groups who share a common system of values and norms and a collective identity (Pakulski, 1996: 62–3). Given this difference in perceptions of the nature of social class, it is not surprising that arguments about its continuing relevance have been dogged by semantic confusion and have very often involved people talking at cross purposes. However, beneath this semantic confusion there lie real problems of both an empirical and conceptual nature.

The empirical case against class rests on a number of claims. Firstly, widespread economic and social changes in the last half of the twentieth century have been argued to have contributed to the progressive fragmentation of the class structure and eroded its centrality in systems of inequality. These changes include the decline of mass production industries, the growth of new, information technologies and forms of production, and the proliferation of small property ownership. These and other changes, it is claimed, have fragmented the working and middle classes, blurring old class boundaries and sources of solidarity and contributing to a process of *individualisation* as workers are forced to negotiate paths through an increasingly diverse and unstable employment market (Crompton, 1998: 18–19). Secondly, processes of economic restructuring have been associated with social and cultural changes of such magnitude that many commentators have argued that 'modern', industrial capitalist society has now given way to a new social form described, among other things, as 'post-modern', 'post-industrial' or even 'post-capitalist' society. A prominent idea here is that the transition has been from a 'modern', production-based society to a 'post-modern', consumption-based one (Bauman, 1992) in which social classes are replaced by rather different kinds of social distinctions centred on consumer life styles, giving rise to a multiplicity of fragmented groupings (Scott, 1996:15).

With the decline of 'objective' class interests and of collective class identities, individual biographies are seen today to be more about *choice* than about class processes (see, for example, Beck, 1992; Giddens, 1990). Accordingly, non-class-based 'imagined communities' of people with shared interests and concerns are seen as being increasingly important (Pakulski, 1996: 66). These 'imagined communities' derive their identities from a variety of sources, including gender or ethnic origin, 'consumption-sector cleavages' (for example, Saunders, 1986) or 'new social movements' (for example, Offe, 1985). In support of this claim, research in Australia by Emmison and Western concluded that '...the discursive salience of class for identity is minimal' (Emmison and Western, 1990: 241). Other studies, however, have revealed a less certain and more complex picture.

Evidence for the Existence of Class Identity

Two major studies have concluded that class is still an important source of identity. In a national, large-scale survey in the 1980s, Marshall and his colleagues showed that around sixty percent of their respondents thought of themselves as belonging to a particular social class and over ninety percent could place themselves in a specific class category (Marshall et al, 1988: 143).

The conclusion of the survey was that 'class consciousness is rather widespread in British society' and that 'social class is the most readily available and commonly employed source for constructing social identities' (ibid: 156).

However, this study has been criticised in a number of ways. Saunders (1990), for example, argued that the research was biased as the respondents were asked a number of questions about social class – so sensitising them to it – before they were asked about their class identity. In addition, Marshall et al themselves noted an ambivalence in the class consciousness they found, which did not involve a consistent or rigorous interpretation of the world. Many of their respondents held conflicting views about society and their places within it and did not have a '...developed class consciousness comprising class identity, class opposition, class totality and the conception of an alternative society' (ibid: 190). Marshall et al therefore concluded:

> ...the 'class consciousness' of the majority of people in our sample is characterised by its complexity, ambivalence and occasional contradictions. It does not reflect a rigorously consistent interpretation of the world with an underlying ideological rationale rooted in perceived class interest alone. (ibid: 187)

Devine's study of thirty-two affluent, manual-working couples in Luton produces similar findings to those of Marshall. Devine's research indicated that there was a high level of class awareness amongst her respondents, including a view of society as polarised between 'us' and 'them', but that they held a variety of identities which shaped the way they saw themselves, their beliefs and attitudes, and the ways in which they interacted with others. One of the most important sources of identity for Devine's interviewees was region of origin: people with common regions of origin tended to socialise with each other and to identify themselves explicitly with their geographical origins and the 'subcultural differences associated with them' (Devine, 1992b: 236). Similarly, being a native Lutonian was an important source of identity for some interviewees. Regional identity, then, shaped individual identities and the way people viewed and interacted with others. In addition to region, nation was a common source of identity, evidenced by the divisions that were seen to exist between white residents and those with different cultural backgrounds.

Nevertheless, Devine noted that class was still an important source of identity, bringing people together even when their regional or national identities differentiated them. All of the interviewees in Devine's study identified with a class – mostly the working class, although they also referred to themselves as 'average', 'ordinary', 'ordinary working people' or 'lower middle class' (1992b: 240). When asked to describe their social class, all spoke of a large class of 'ordinary' families who had to work and had similar standards of living, distinguishing this class from an upper class which did not necessarily have to work to enjoy a high standard of living (ibid: 240–241). The interviewees generally made no distinction between the middle and working classes, pointing to their similarity of incomes and standards of livings, although they sometimes reluctantly identified people such as doctors and other professionals as middle class, indicating that their awareness of social class was not fully developed (ibid: 241).

In Devine's study the perception of a divide between 'us' and 'them' emerged strongly in relation to politics, with all of the interviewees identifying the two main political parties with particular social classes (ibid:246). She noted that it was in discussions about politics that the interviewees were most ready to describe themselves as 'working class' rather than 'ordinary working people' (ibid). However, their support for the Labour Party appeared to be motivated by the desire for a fairer redistribution of money and did not signify a deep loyalty to this party, the effectiveness of which they remained sceptical (ibid: 246–7). Devine concluded that her interviewees demonstrated 'a high level of class awareness', although this existed alongside other social identities' (1992b: 249). However, more recent research has cast doubt on this conclusion.

Evidence that Class Identity is Minimal

Skeggs (1997) studied 83 women on caring courses in a college of further education. She argues that class was central to the identities of these women but not as a source of identification. Instead, the women were at pains to dis-identify with their working-class origins, distancing themselves from these because they saw them as a source of stigma and a threat to their *respectability*. Skeggs contends that, historically, the working class has been pathologised and seen as poor, deprived, dangerous and degraded. For this reason, she argues, the women in her study, acutely aware of the popular representations of working-class women as 'rough', 'common', 'tacky' and 'tarty', were at pains to distance themselves from these representations. As Skeggs comments: 'Who would want to be seen as working class?' (Skeggs, 1997: 95).

In a parallel study, Savage, Bagnall and Longhurst (2001) conducted in-depth interviews between 1997 and 1999 with two hundred people living in four different areas of Manchester. In the interviews, Savage and his colleagues only asked two questions about social class and these were right at the end of the interviews. However, a third of their respondents spoke spontaneously about class before this, when talking about the kinds of people who lived around them. Nevertheless, the research by Savage and his colleagues indicated that, although two thirds of the respondents could define themselves in class terms, this identification was '... usually ambivalent, defensive and hesitant' (reported in Savage, 2000: 36). Significant numbers said they had never thought about class before and others switched during the interview from one class to another.

Supporting the findings of Skeggs, Savage et al found that those identifying with social class – either middle- or working-class – tended to do so by *distancing* themselves from other social classes, stressing their 'ordinariness' and 'normality'. Savage (2000: 35) notes that this is consistent with results from the British Attitudes Surveys, which show that people tend to avoid the 'extreme' classes at the top and bottom of the scales. Savage argues that this may explain the relatively high rate of identification with the working class found in Britain: the 'working class' may be seen as the 'mainstream category', lying between the 'poor' or 'lower working class' and the 'middle or upper middle class'. Identification in surveys with the working class may therefore constitute an indirect 'refusal' of class identity (ibid).

Savage et al (2001) note a class difference in the way that respondents spoke about social class. Young, professional men, often with degrees (whom Savage et al describe as having 'cultural capital') were able to think confidently and reflexively about how class labels might apply to them. Such respondents were able to 'try on', reject and even invert class labels. Older professional males – the most privileged respondents in the sample – seemed to find it easiest to put themselves into classes. Similarly, some working-class men had an inverted pride in their unequivocal working-class status.

Although the majority of the respondents were ambivalent about their class location, most of them did not believe that society was becoming classless and used the language of class when describing political conflict in society. Savage et al claim that people '...have little difficulty in talking about class "out there", but do not like to think about class closer to home, with respect to their own sense of identity' (Savage et al, 2001: 880). Savage et al explain this inconsistency by arguing that, unlike other sources of identity, such as gender, ethnicity or locale, social class bridges the divide between individual and society, anchoring identity in social structures. The idea of class therefore challenges individuality and '...pollutes the idea of individuality, since it challenges people's autonomy by seeing them as the product of their social background'. (Savage et al, 2001: 882). Indeed, the '...stress on 'ordinariness' can therefore be seen as a defensive strategy used by people to evade categorisation in social class terms' (ibid: 889).

Savage et al conclude that classes are used to make sense of society but are not generally drawn upon to define personal identity. The majority of their respondents were defensively ambivalent about their class identities, although there were minorities who did identify with these in a straightforward fashion or were 'reflexive class identifiers' (2001: 886). However, class appears to provide a set of external benchmarks against which one's personal trajectory through life, one's life history, can be measured. Indeed, Savage et al note that their respondents used the language of class more readily when talking about their life histories. They conclude that the ambivalence that the majority of their respondents demonstrate in relation to class identity should not be taken as evidence that class is no longer important and that class '... does not determine identity, but it is not irrelevant either. It is a resource, a device, with which to construct identity' (ibid: 888). The stress that many of the respondents in the study by Savage et al laid on being 'ordinary' can be seen as significant because, to be 'ordinary', there has to be a contrast with people who are not 'ordinary'. In other words, the respondents were defining their identities in relation to others, so that class is implicitly invoked.

The evidence from research into class identities therefore shows a number of clear trends:

- Class is not a strong source of individual or social identity for most people.
- Even for those who do identify with social class, there is no well-developed consciousness involving the idea of class opposition, conflict and notions of an alternative society (i.e., no sense of structure-consciousness-action in the Marxist sense).
- Dis-identification with social class is widespread, indicating that, for some people at least, class is seen as a threat to individual identity.
- There are differences in the way people see themselves in relation to social class. These differences are structured along class and, probably, gender lines.
- Dis-identification with social class does not generally mean a rejection of the idea that society is class-based; people are more willing to talk about class as a social and political issue than they are to identify themselves in class terms.

Clearly, class is still an important part of the mental landscapes of many people although class identities are generally ambivalent. What is needed is a theoretical framework through which the nature of social class processes in contemporary society can be explored and many writers have argued that the development of this framework needs to take into account the *cultural* as well as the economic dimensions of social class. In the last section of this chapter, some of these recent theoretical approaches will be explored and evaluated.

Class and Culture

It was argued above that the questioning of the importance of social classes as discrete, *empirical* groupings providing sources of identity and value systems has been paralleled by a *conceptual* critique and a rejection of class as a central concern in the social sciences today. The debate involves an engagement with the classical tradition and centres on a re-evaluation of, *inter alia*, the work of Marx and Weber. Following this debate there has been an emergence of new, theoretical frameworks for class analysis, many of which draw on the work of Pierre Bourdieu.

Underlying much debate about class consciousness is the claim that, *pace* Weber, social classes are more than statistical aggregates or potential sources of identity. Instead, they are viewed as economically-structured groupings with distinct *cultural* features: in other words, a social class is argued to be a group of people sharing a system of ideas, values and practices. A number of traditions in sociology have focused on these class cultures: the 'neo-Weberian industrial sociology' exemplified by the work of David Lockwood (1958, 1966); the social history of writers such as E. P. Thompson (1963, 1980); and the cultural studies of Richard Hoggart (1957), Raymond Williams (1977) and the Centre for Contemporary Cultural Studies (1982).

The relationship between value orientations and economic and social context was drawn out in early work by Lockwood (1958, 1966), who argued that images of society, forms of social consciousness and value orientations vary according to work and community relationships. Lockwood identified three distinct forms of working-class consciousness related to three ('ideal typical') structural positions: proletarian traditionalist (mining communities); deferential traditionalist (farming villages); and privatised (new industrial towns). A brief consideration of the first of these will serve to illustrate his argument.

Proletarian traditionalists – thought by Lockwood to be dying out even in the 1950s and 1960s – were associated with industries such as mining, docking and ship-building. Lockwood argued that proletarian traditionalists had a high degree of job involvement and distinctive occupational culture involving feelings of comradeship and pride in doing 'men's work'. They tended to live alongside their fellow workers in traditional working-class communities characterised by low rates of social and geographical mobility. The shared leisure time and mutual system of support which grew up in such communities fostered a sense of cohesion and a common identity so that these communities became highly integrated and rather inward-looking.

Lockwood argued that proletarian traditionalists generally held a view of society as polarised between two conflicting groups: 'us' and 'them' – the latter being the bosses, managers, white-collar workers and larger society in general. The power of 'them' was well understood and there was a feeling of being subject to a 'distant and incomprehensible authority' (Lockwood, 1966: 251–2).

For Lockwood, then, the material conditions of life – employment and living arrangements – formed the basis of cultural attitudes and values which distinguished the social classes from each other. The genesis of cultural studies in the 1960s, and the writings of Richard Hoggart (1957) and Raymond Williams (1958) in particular, developed this idea of social classes as cultural groups. These writers used autobiographical material to present a picture of working-class life and the values and beliefs, or 'structures of feeling' (Williams, 1977: 128), that informed it. Hoggart (1957) wrote nostalgically of life in working-class communities in the middle of the twentieth century. With its roots in the concrete and the local, it produced a feeling of 'groupness' and identity with 'an all-pervading culture' (ibid: 32) which involved 'living intuitively, habitually, verbally, drawing on myth, aphorism, and ritual' (ibid: 33). This way of life was argued to be grounded in the concrete and the particular and one's place in the social world was to seen as ascribed rather than achieved.

The work of Lockwood and the early cultural studies writers contributed to the emergence of the idea that structural position in society creates a distinctive outlook and value system and leads to certain types of social action (the 'structure-consciousness-action' argument). This argument was subsequently criticised both for its economic reductionism and for its emphasis on the solidarity and continuity of working-class communities (Savage, 2000: 33). It has been argued that idea of solidarity in working-class communities is an idealised view of the past. Bourke (1994), for example, in her social history of the working class in Britain, contends that the working-class community is a 'retrospective construction' which did not survive the individualism emerging in the period following the Second World War: 'A shared identity as "working class", even if rooted in a single geographical space, could not surmount the difficulties inherent in a competitive society' (Bourke, 1994: 169). The social networks in post-war working-class communities were, Bourke argues, discordant and ad hoc and did not provide either a unified outlook or consistent social identity (ibid).

By the 1980s, attention in cultural studies had turned away from social class to focus on issues around feminism and ethnicity. Later, in the work of Giddens (1990) and Beck (1992), the concept of working-class culture, historically-generated and based on notions of collectivism, was replaced by the idea of the rise of individualized cultures which were argued to work against the development of class identities (Savage, 2000: 33). The subsequent period marked a low point in class analysis and it is only in recent years that attention has started to focus again on class. Attempts to rescue class as a *cultural* phenomenon have led to an increased interest in the writings of Pierre Bourdieu. In particular, there has been a move to re-orient class theory to:

- Avoid economic reductionism, giving the cultural dimensions of social class more autonomy.
- Avoid structural determinism, allowing a role for he creative social actor in social class formation.

Bourdieu: Class and 'Habitus'

Bourdieu's ideas about class are part of his wider model of society. Essentially, he argues that social life is inherently conflictual as individuals and groups struggle for the control of desirable resources in the different 'fields' which make up the social space – the economic field, the academic field, the cultural field etc. The position of individuals or groups in these various fields, and their opportunities for advantage in them, depend upon the nature and extent of the 'capital' they possess. Bourdieu identifies three main forms of capital:

- economic capital (command over economic resources)
- cultural capital (legitimate knowledge, language use, manners, dispositions and orientations)
- social capital (social networks of support which can be mobilised through, for example, family connections).

These forms of capital are not evenly distributed in society so that some groups are relatively advantaged whilst others are relatively disadvantaged. The differential distribution of capital gives rise to social classes, which Bourdieu defines as:

> ...sets of agents who, by virtue of the fact that they occupy similar positions in the social space (that is, in the distribution of powers), are subject to similar conditions of existence and conditioning factors and, as a result, are endowed with similar dispositions which prompt them to develop similar practices. (Bourdieu, 1987: 6)

Bourdieu uses the concept of 'habitus' to describe both the material conditions of existence and the related set of attitudes and predispositions which characterise the positions of individuals and groups in the social world. A social class can therefore be seen as a group of people who share the same habitus.

Bourdieu's model of social class represents an attempt to move beyond the economic reductionism of earlier, cultural models of social class. He argues that classes are not narrowly-defined economic groupings. Brubaker explains Bourdieu's view of social classes in the following terms:

> Class divisions are defined not by differing relations to the
> means of production, but by differing conditions of existence,
> differing systems of dispositions produced by differential
> conditioning, and different endowments of power and capital.
> (Brubaker, 1985: 761)

These 'conditions of existence' clearly include position in the process of
production but also involve other, less tangible things such as area of residence,
network of friends and acquaintances (social capital), level of education
(cultural capital) and so on. Savage (2000) argues that the distinction
made by Bourdieu between different kinds of capital – economic, cultural,
social etc – is crucial for a non-reductive conceptualisation of culture as it
implies that class formation occurs along more than one axis (ibid: 106).
Savage therefore argues:

> Culture is not a product of class relations but is itself a field in
> which class relations operate. Cultural battles are therefore
> recursively involved in class formation. (Savage, 2000: 106)

Classes work at a cultural level to reproduce their advantage, attempting to
ensure the recognition of other groups of the superiority of their cultural style.
(Bourdieu describes this process as 'symbolic violence'). Those with
economic capital do not always have cultural capital and work to achieve it
through, for example, education. Similarly, groups can struggle to establish a
positive valuation of their cultural capital thereby hoping to see this converted
into economic capital. In this way, Bourdieu focuses on class formation as
a dynamic and fluid process: he is interested in the way in which conflict and
the search for 'distinction' in social life creates changes in the class structure
as new groups emerge and try to consolidate their advantage across a range of
different 'fields'.

Bourdieu's ideas can be drawn upon to explain the relative absence of class
consiousness: class habitus impresses itself on people at an unconscious level
so that they do not necessarily recognise that their experiences of social life,
and their attitudes, values and dispositions, are linked to their social class. Our
feelings about our place in the social world are, according to Bourdieu, 'closer
to a class unconscious than to a "class consciousness" in the Marxist sense'
(1991: 235). In this way, he explains the relative absence of class consciousness
in a society which is characterised by class-based attitudes and actions.

An Application of Bourdieu's Ideas

In his book *Distinction*, written in the 1960s but not published in Britain
until the 1980s, Bourdieu began his analysis of the cultural dimension of social
class, focusing on the active processes of class formation and re-

formation which take place as groups struggle for positions within the social space. As noted earlier, the rapid pace of social change has produced a large and fragmented middle-class which spans a range of different occupational groups, including low-level service employees, new service professionals (social workers, librarians etc.), traditional professional, managerial and administrative groups, and newer occupational groupings such as computer experts and psychotherapists (Crompton, 1998: 150). The sheer size and diversity of this 'middle class' has frequently been cited as evidence of its conceptual redundancy as a social class.

Nevertheless, the work of Bourdieu provides a useful framework to help us understand what is happening in the middle class. Bourdieu (1984) argues that it is possible to identify the constituent groupings in terms of the volume and types of capital they possess. For example, there is a general distinction between the bourgeoisie (high on economic capital, low on cultural capital) and the intellectuals (relatively low on economic capital but high on cultural capital) (Crompton, 1998: 152). Bourdieu draws on an enormous body of empirical evidence to describe, in minute detail, the differences in lifestyles and tastes between different occupational groupings (which he takes, loosely, as indices of social class position) and the processes of struggle over time as new groupings challenge the cultural dominance of older ones. For example, he describes the cultural differences between the 'old' and 'new' bourgeoisie in the following way:

> Whereas the juniors of the dominant class and the new bourgeoisie denounce the 'up-tight', 'stuffed-shirt' rigour of the old bourgeoisie and preach 'relaxation; and a 'laid-back' lifestyle, the old bourgeoisie condemns the 'sloppy' life-style of the new bourgeoisie and calls for more restraint in language and morals. (Bourdieu, 1984: 311)

What is at stake here is more than an aesthetic struggle over types of 'taste' and lifestyle. Bourdieu argues that cultural struggles – especially those in the middle classes, where new groups are arising and the 'positions' that can be occupied may be relatively undetermined – can result in tangible changes in the economic position of occupational groupings (Bourdieu, 1984: 344). What is at stake, then, in 'conflicts over art or the art of living' is 'securing the best conversion rate for the type of capital with which each group is best provided' (ibid: 310).

Assessment of Bourdieu's Arguments

Brubaker (1985: 763) argues that Bourdieu's model of social class represents an attempt to unite the theories of Marx and Weber by viewing classes as economically-grounded status groups with shared dispositions and practices.

These shared dispositions and practices may be positively or negatively evaluated by others and lie at the heart of the power struggles through which class advantage is legitimised and reproduced. Bourdieu therefore gives social class a central place in his model of society. Through his twin concepts of class and habitus, the material conditions of existence and their reflection in dispositions and practices become the 'universal explanatory principle' underlying all aspects of social inequality (Brubaker, 1985: 762). However, a number of weaknesses in this approach have been identified.

Firstly, there is the problem of the relationship between the economic and cultural dimensions of social class. Savage contends that 'culture and class are inextricably bound together in specific material practices' (Savage, 2000: 193–4): they are clearly linked in some way and 'cultural outlooks are implicated in modes of exclusion and/or domination' (Devine and Savage, 2000: 195). But how far does economic position determine cultural outlook through the habitus, and how far is this cultural outlook independent of material circumstances? Significantly, to what extent can power struggles at the cultural level change the economic position of groups? A linked problem is the extent of creativity and innovation allowed for in Bourdieu's model. Are people cultural dopes, at the mercy of their habitus, or can they change things? Bourdieu argues that social practice is not shaped simply by the influence of the habitus but is the outcome of the meeting of the habitus with a specific field. This, he argues, can produce innovation. But is this a convincing argument? Weight seems to be behind the forces of reproduction rather than those of change in social life.

A further problem is whether social class, as a collective actor, has survived the individualizing tendencies of modern life. Savage (2000) recognises that there has been a decline of classes as self-conscious collectivities and a growth of individualism in contemporary society. Nevertheless, he believes that individualization is '...a cultural process involving differentiation from others' (ibid: 104) and that class cultures are inevitably implicated in this, although they now operate as 'modes of differentiation' rather than 'types of collectivity' (ibid: 102). Class processes, therefore, 'work through the individual' (ibid: 95). This argument rests on a conception of identities as 'relational constructs in which individuals develop a sense of their own selves by comparing themselves with "meaningful others"' (ibid: 117). Savage argues that class is a 'benchmark' against which people interpret their lives: 'class is salient in terms of constructing an idea of difference, not in terms of defining a class which one belongs to' (ibid: 113). This explains why research consistently shows that knowledge of social class is well developed among respondents but that personal identification with it is much more qualified and ambivalent. Savage concludes:

31

> If we recognize the individualized role of class formation, and see class formation as related to the identification of trajectories rather than as an attachment to fixed positions, then a rather different perspective on class formation and social mobility is suggested.... (Savage, 2000: 95)

A problem here is the tendency for class to become specified almost entirely at the ideal level, as a mental pattern of the social landscape which we carry around in our heads and use to interpret and orient our (individualized) paths through the social world.

Conclusion

What is clear is that reports of the death of social class are premature: although attacked as both an empirically and theoretically obsolete tool of social science analysis, it refuses to go quietly. The problem is that class cannot be identified as just one thing: it is an enduring, structured system of inequality, a cultural outlook, a mental landscape of the social world and a measure of individual, biographical change. At the structural level, class can be viewed as a *real* economic and cultural phenomenon with generative mechanisms of which social actors may not be aware. At the level of social action, however, class processes are implicated in the struggles for distinction in social life – material, cultural and symbolic – of purposive and active social agents, although social classes at this level may now operate more as modes of differentiation than as forms of collectivity (Savage, 2000). It is suggested here that the relationships between the structural and cultural dimensions of social class, and between each of these and social agency, are contingent upon historical and social circumstances; these relationships can therefore only be specified in concrete, empirical contexts. Following this, it is argued that the generative mechanisms of social class affect what happens in a contingent (rather than a necessary) way so that the outcomes of the struggles for distinction in social life are not fixed.

Bibliography

Adonis, A. and Pollard, S. (1998) *A Class Act*, London: Penguin.
Bauman, Z. (1992) *Intimations of Postmodernity*, London: Routledge.
Bourdieu, P. (1984) *Distinction: A Social Critique of the Judgement of Taste*, London: Routledge.
Bourdieu, P. (1987) 'What Makes a Social Class?', *Berkeley Journal of Sociology* 32: 1–17.
Bourdieu, P. (1991) *Language and Symbolic Power*, Cambridge: Polity Press.

Bourdieu, P. and Passeron, J. C. (1979) *The Inheritors: French Students and their Culture*, London: University of Chicago Press.

Bourke, J. (1994) *Working-Class Cultures in Britain, 1860–1960: Gender, Class and Ethnicity*, London: Routledge.

Brubaker, R. (1985) 'Rethinking Classical Theory: The Sociological Vision of Pierre Bourdieu', *Theory and Society* 14 (6) 745–775.

Centre for Contemporary Cultural Studies (1982) *The Empire Strikes Back*, London: Hutchinson.

Crompton, R. (1998) *Class and Stratification*, 2nd ed., Cambridge: Polity Press.

Crompton, R., Devine, F., Savage, M. & Scott, J. (eds) (2000) *Renewing Class Analysis*, Oxford: Blackwell.

Dahrendorf, R. (1959) *Class and Class Conflict in an Industrial Society*, London: Routledge.

Devine, F. (1992a) *Affluent Workers Revisited: Privatism and the Working Class*, Edinburgh: Edinburgh University Press.

Devine, F. (1992b) 'Social identities, class identity and political perspectives', *Sociological Review* 1992: 229–252.

Devine, F. (1998) 'Class Analysis and the Stability of Class Relations', *Sociology* 32 (1) 23–42.

Emmison, M. and Western, M. (1990) 'Social Class and Social Identity: a comment on Marshall et al', *Sociology* 24 (2) 241–253.

Francis, D. (1987) 'The Great Transition' in R. J. Anderson, J. A. Hughes & W. W. Sharrock (eds) *Classic Disputes in Sociology*, London: Unwin Hyman Ltd.

Gerth, H. H. & Mills, C. Wright (1948) *From Max Weber*, London: Routledge and Kegan Paul.

Hoggart, R. (1957) *The Uses of Literacy*, London: Penguin (1992 Edition).

Joyce, P. (ed) (1995) *Class*, Oxford: Oxford University Press.

Lash, S. (1990) *Sociology of Postmodernism*, London: Routledge.

Lockwood, D. (1958) *The Blackcoated Worker: A Study in Class Consciousness*, London: Allen and Unwin.

Lockwood, D. (1966) 'Sources of Variation in Working Class Images of Society', *Sociological Review* 14 (3) 249–267.

Marshall, G. A., Newby, H., Rose, D. and Vogler, C. (1988) *Social Class in Modern Britain*, London: Unwin Hyman.

Marx, K. & Engels, E. (1973) *Manifesto of the Communist Party*, Beijing, China: Foreign Language Press (originally published in 1848)

McLellan, D. (1977) *Karl Marx: Selected Writings*, Oxford: Oxford University Press.

Milner, A. (1999) *Class*, London: Sage.

Nisbet, R. A. (1966) *The Sociological Tradition*, London: Basic Books.

Offe, C. (1985) *Disorganised Capitalism: Contemporary Transformations of Work and Politics*, Oxford: Basil Blackwell.

Pakulski, J. (1996) 'The dying of class or of Marxist class theory?' in D. J. Lee & B. S. Turner *Conflicts about Class*, Harlow, Essex: Longman.

Reay, D. (1998a) 'Rethinking Social Class: Qualitative Perspectives on Class and Gender', *Sociology* 32 (2) 259–275.

Saunders, P. (1986) *Social Theory and the Urban Question*, 2nd ed, London: Hutchinson.

Saunders, P. (1990) *A Nation of Home Owners*, London: Unwin Hyman.

Savage, M. (1995) 'Issues in Class Analysis and Social Research' in T. Butler & M. Savage (eds) *Social Change and the Middle Classes*, London: UCL Press.

Savage, M. (2000) *Class Analysis and Social Transformation*, Buckingham: Open University Press.

Savage, M., Bagnall, G. and Longhurst, B. (2001) 'Ordinary, Ambivalent and Defensive: Class Identities in the Northwest of England', *Sociology* 35 (4) 875–892.

Savage, M., Barlow, J., Dickens, A. & Fielding, T. (1992) *Property, Bureaucracy and Culture: Middle Class Formation in Contemporary Britain*, London: Routledge.

Scott, J. (1996) *Stratification and Power*, Cambridge: Polity Press.

Skeggs, B. (1997) *Formations of Class and Gender*, London: Sage.

Thompson, E. P. (1980) *The Making of the English Working Class*, London: Penguin (first published in 1963).

Weber, M. (1948) 'Class, Status, Party' in H. H. Gerth & C. Wright Mills (eds) *From Max Weber*, op cit.

Williams, R. (1977) *Marxism and Literature*, Oxford: Oxford University Press.

Wright, E. O. (1985) *Classes*, London: Verso.

Wright, E. O. (1997) *Class Counts*, Cambridge: Cambridge University Press.

3. Gender

Lorraine Green

This chapter analyses the relationship between identity and gender. The first part of the chapter briefly reviews social science literature on identity and outlines and justifies the theoretical position that will be adopted in relation to gender and identity. Following this, the importance of analysing gender in relation to identity will be elucidated. The ways in which identity is both gendered and linked to issues of power will then be described and evaluated.

Identity: A Contested Concept?

As du Gay et al (2000: 1) and Hall (2000: 15) have argued, identity has become both a major and a continuously contested theoretical concept within social science over recent years. This has resulted in the once accepted centrality of class as a master identity being increasingly challenged by the development and expansion of new social movements, which have included feminisms and black and ecological pressure and identity groups. The growth of national and sub-cultural identities and identities based upon consumerist principles have also been important. These developments seem to have contributed to the proliferation of theorisation and debate around identity, emanating from a number of different standpoints.

Both structuralist and post-structuralist accounts of identity are problematic when adopted unequivocally and without reference to other perspectives. In structuralist approaches, the individual becomes a product of macro forces, – a cultural 'dope' – an approach which has attracted criticism for presenting the individual as determined by social forces and denying individual agency (see e.g. Wrong, 1979). One example of a critical structuralist theory might be the economic determinism of Marx in his writings on class and class inequalities. Another might be the gendering of individuals being produced in a top down manner, via a process of *internal colonisation* that operates in and through a monolithic patriarchy (Millett, 1972) or via patriarchal and capitalist forces, as traditionally explicated by radical and dual systems feminists.

Macro structuralist theories can also be criticised on essentialist grounds because they pre-suppose all people in a certain perceived position, e.g. black people, women, the working or upper class, are all subjugated or privileged in a certain, homogenous manner and experience this positioning in the same way. Macro theories, therefore, tend to embrace universalist conceptions of certain groups of people. Macro critical or conflict theorists additionally posit people as being trapped by their structural positions and through dominant ideologies, which they subscribe to, often via a position of *misrecognition* (Gramsci, 1971; Althusser, 2000).

The individual is alternatively heralded by post-structuralism as free-floating and dynamically and temporally positioned between various shifting discursive strategies. According to this viewpoint, genealogies of subjectification assume the individual is constituted within and by diverse strategies, tactics and practices which are historically and socially contingent and variable (Foucault, 1979; Rose, 1989). The emphasis in post-structuralist approaches is on flux and change. Post–structuralist perspectives veer away from macro, modernist, universal conceptualisations and ground the individual in a specific historical contingency. Power, according to Foucault, can only ever be exercised, never possessed, and resistance and reversal are always possible. Power is also not always exercised coercively and unidirectionally, nor is it always negative in its effects. Although post-structuralism seemed to overcome many of the over-generalising facts of macro structural theories by deconstructing concepts and insisting on genealogical practices and historical specificity, it has brought with it problems of its own. For example, although Foucault describes webs of power as operating in a capillary-like and multi-directional manner, his accounts of disciplinary practices, including self-surveillance and the production of docile bodies suggest that individuals have minimal spontaneity and agency. Therefore, post-structuralists can be accused of not resolving the very problem of over-determinism for which they repudiate meta-narratives, by presenting the person as a mere blank slate to be inscribed upon by discourse (Sibeon, 1997; Layder, 1993).

As Hall (2000), has argued, although post–structuralist theories adopt a deconstructive critique and hence challenge the essentialism and stasis often prevalent within structuralism, they are difficult to utilise in a constructional theoretical manner because they put key constructs 'under erasure' (Hall, 2000: 16) without replacing them with alternative operational constructs. However socially constructed, contingent and in flux, categories of 'woman', 'black' and 'gay' are, they are still the ways in which people identify themselves and others and construct identities that are 'real' and have meaning for them. To totally deconstruct categories important to marginalised groups, renders group identification difficult to argue for and may lead to further disempowerment and de-politicisation of these groups (Spivak, 1994; Cohen, 1996). Identification with a particular group or identity does not, however, mean each view the group's identity in an identical manner and it is important these differences be studied.

Although psychological and psychoanalytic perspectives problematically rely upon an invisible and latent unconscious, their advantage lies in their ability to try and explore and describe how identities are constructed from within, not necessarily withstanding the influence wider societal forces have upon their production. As Hall succinctly puts it:

> If we are not to fall directly from an economistic reductionism into a psychoanalytic one, we need to add that ideology is effective because it works at *both* the rudimentary levels of psychic identity and the drives *and* at the level of the discursive formation and practices which constitute the social field. (Hall, 2000: 20)

Certainly when looking at social theory, one of the key unresolved dilemmas is the micro/macro agency/structure debate. Society and the individuals within it can not be understood nor theorised solely by examining micro interactions but neither can they be fully understood by resorting to macro structural theories. A number of theorists (e.g. Giddens, 1984, 1987; Habermas, 1981; Bourdieu, 1977, 1979 – most of whom have not seen gender as a central issue) have addressed this problem. In a multitude of different ways they have attempted to bridge the two spheres but this Manichean divide of social theory has, as of yet, not been satisfactorily resolved (Layder, 1993). Post-modernism and post-structuralism can also be accused of glossing over the agency vs. structure predicament rather than addressing it (Layder, 1993; Sibeon, 1997).

One of the key questions that remains in relation to identity is whether the individual has any choice or power in relation to their identity, and if so, to what extent? And following from this, are identities stable, coherent and concrete self constructs, or are they inherently unstable and subject to fluctuation or change, dependent upon context and social and historical contingency? If identities are continuously in flux, can identity therefore be seen as a useful or utilisable theoretical concept? Or does the fact that people may assume shifting, insecure and contradictory gender positions, that may manifest themselves in different ways, contexts and time periods, even within the same individuals, render identity an eternally elusive and slippery concept? Hall evidently sees identity as important but not immutable when he refers to it as 'not fixed' but 'not nothing either' (Hall, 1997: 33).

This brief theoretical exploration of the term 'identity' highlights the problems in trying to define and explain it. This problem is exacerbated further when attempting to apply it to the notion of gender, itself also a highly debated and challenged term. What does seem important though, is the need to acknowledge that both micro and macro factors influence the construction of identity, that identities may change or transform themselves in different situations and that one person may have many identities rather than one.

The next section will examine how important gender is in relation to identity, drawing on a combination of both micro (the private, domestic and personal) and macro (wider societal structures, ideas and discourses) perspectives, indicating that the interaction between these is important. Following this three different theories of gender identity will be presented and evaluated and the way in which gender formation and identity is achieved will be tentatively outlined. The idea of dichotomous gender linked to dualistic sex, i.e. whether gender and sex are the same or interchangeable, will be analysed, alongside questions of whether gender is something we 'have' by virtue of biological predetermination, acquire through socialisation and other processes or do/perform. These questions will be explored taking into account the concepts of the psyche and the unconscious, micro interactions between individuals or small groups of people, notions of socialisation, wider societal structures and constraints (e.g. legislation, education etc.) and the influence of discursive practices.

The Importance of Gender as Identity and Identifier

Following on from Hall's earlier warning about not being reductionist or limited when trying to explain identity formation, there have certainly been calls for the integration of sociology and psychology, often with specific reference to gender (Connell, 1987). An interest in, and burgeoning theorising in relation to, the sociology of self, identity, intimacy and emotions appears to have fuelled and been made intelligible by such calls (Macinnes, 2001).

Glick and Fiske (1998) embrace theoretical coalition in their chapter on gender, power dynamics and social interaction, when they argue that social psychological processes such as identity need to be embedded within social structural realities to be understood. It is only through doing this, they argue, that we can begin to understand why dichotomous gender identity is so important, why sex/gender ambiguity is not tolerated, and why love and domination can co-exist simultaneously within the same relationship and be premised on gendered grounds.

One example they give is from an episode of the fictional drama ER, in which a baby is born of indeterminate sex, although it is subsequently found to be chromosomally male. This baby would need considerable reconstructive surgery for male genitalia, but with simple surgery and hormones could be reconstructed as a non-reproductive female. The sad culmination of this fictional tale is that the father decides to give the baby up for adoption because he does not want an impotent, infertile son, or a daughter whose appearance is maintained by hormones.

This unfortunate and unsettling fictional episode is however not too far distant from what may have happened in reality. Fausto-Sterling (1998) drawing on published articles in respected American medical journals, documents that it has often been common practice to castrate baby boys, who possess statistically very small penises and to reallocate them as female, with corresponding reconstructive surgery and lifelong hormone treatment. This sex/gender reassignment has even occurred in situations where there was no indication these baby boys were hormonally or chromosomally inter-sexed or would be impotent and infertile as adults (Kessler, 1990; Griffin and Wilson, 1992).

Following on from this, there is now much justified criticism aimed at the medical profession from groups of American inter-sexuals. These groups are protesting against being subjected to, in their eyes *unnecessary*, prolonged, painful and long-term surgery on their genitalia, which often produced long-term physical damage and eradicated sexual feeling. Intersexuals are people born of indeterminate sex, often-possessing chromosomal or hormonal abnormalities or conditions, such as hermaphroditism or Klinefelter's syndrome. The medical profession have justified their interventions in terms of paternalism and have claimed they tried to ensure these individuals' genitalia resembled that of one sex or the other so that they would fit into society and be accepted as either men or women (Hird and Germon, 2001). Gordo Lopez (1996) in his study of gender identity and gender dysphoria clinics for transsexuals (people who are not born of indeterminate sex, but nevertheless subjectively feel they were born in the body of the wrong sex) also highlighted how health and welfare professionals in these clinics effectively silenced the voices of individuals occupying multiple and ambiguous gender positions. He additionally observed that in order to obtain gender reassignment surgery and/or hormone treatment, patients had to conform to very stereotypical notions of male and female behaviour and identity.

The sex we attribute to an individual is therefore tremendously important in determining how we see, understand and respond to them. If we are unable to tell the sex of an unknown person we are interacting with, this can lead to tremendous discomfort. Woodhouse (1989) recalls that she was at a transvestite/transsexual group when she was unable to tell if a particular individual was a 'real' woman or a transvestite. She describes being unable to approach and talk to this person until she knew 'what' she was; and through analyses, shows that the ways we interact with people are intrinsically and inextricably linked to them displaying congruent sex/gender norms in terms of language, non verbal communication and dress codes. Similarly Glick and

Fiske (1998) argue that sex is the primary category through which people identify and subsequently gender stereotype others and that this is often done both automatically and unconsciously. People are also typically classified according to sex faster than any other forms of categorisation (Zarate and Smith, 1990).

A fictional tale of two parents, in conjunction with scientists, trying to bring up a baby, referred to as X, as both non-sexed and non-gendered, reveals the dilemmas associated with non-sexist child rearing (Gould, 1978). This tale documents the hostility faced by the parents and the child from a range of other people who were unable to cope with not being told or able to ascertain the sex of the child by haircut, clothes, characteristics or preferences. The fictional X enjoyed the company of both boys and girls and could play and master the skills associated with boy's activities equally as much as girls' activities. The parents, however, experienced tremendous problems in buying non-sexed clothes and toys for X. Interacting with other people, who were embarrassed, rude and finally ostracised them when they refused to disclose the sex of X to anyone, even their closest relatives, was also difficult for X and its parents. The school additionally had problems in accommodating an X as all the students had to line up in rows of boys or girls and all the toilets were marked for one sex or the other. However the school agreed to X using the Head's toilet that was only marked 'bathroom' and children were subsequently asked to line up alphabetically, rather than by sex. The parents of the other children at school also became defensive and aggressive, once their children had stopped teasing X for doing and enjoying both boys' and girls' activities they then began to emulate X's non-gender stereotyped behaviour, seeing the potential for choice it generated. These other parents were extremely threatened by such activities as their little boy pushing a pram around and their little girl refusing to wear pink dresses.

These examples illustrate just how important binary, polarised and dichotomous notions of gender are within our society and how well policed they are. The first words often relayed to the parents of a newly born baby are those of – 'Congratulations you have a beautiful baby boy or girl'. From the very moment a child is born, even though most trained observers cannot distinguish the sex of a clothed baby, babies are treated differently by many men and women and even identical behaviours are interpreted and responded to differently according to sex allocation. If it was either unimportant to know the sex of a child or a simple process, parents would not have to dress boys and girls in different coloured and motifed clothing. This process carries on throughout childhood into adulthood and throughout a person's life. Individuals, both within the private sphere of the family and the public sphere of work, politics and organisations, are treated very differently and expected to behave very differently according to whether they are designated male or female. One's sex and corresponding socially constructed gendered identity are often seen by the general public as being one and the same thing, i.e. that gender follows naturally given the attribution of biological sex.

Such a simplistic, essentialised and deterministic conception of gender is pervasive throughout society and often seen to be reinforced by accounts of gender in socio-biology and evolutionary psychology (Wilson, 1975; Dawkins; 1989; Moir and Jessell, 1989). These accounts claim men and women are fundamentally and irrevocably different by virtue of different genes, brains, hormones and bodies. The fact that there are many masculinities and femininities, operating in different societies and in subcultures within the same society, as well as in different historical periods, appears to invalidate these determinist notions of gender and to lend support to socially constructed notions of gender. In some societies there is even acceptance of third or fourth gender positions. However, pop psychology books, which claim men and women are fundamentally so different that they can scarcely communicate with each other, such as Gray's *Men are from Mars Women are from Venus*, as well as more accepted academic works such as Tannen's (1990) book on gender, language and communication, seem to be tremendously popular and almost unanimously accepted as depicting an accepted reality.

Contemporary theorists agree, femininity and masculinity in different cultures may vary considerably (Grosz, 1990; Lorber and Farrell, 1991) but they often extend the argument by demonstrating many different types of masculinities and femininities within one society (Hearn, 1991; Connell, 1995). These are significantly affected by dimensions of class and race/ethnicity (Ferree et al, 1999). White middle class hegemonic masculinities are exalted, celebrated and naturalised, while those subordinated masculine identities; black, working class and gay, as well as all types of femininities, are negated and marginalised (Connell, 1995). Men enacting femininities and women enacting masculinities are also negated or marginalised because their gender is seen as dissonant and disconnected from their biological sex (Green et al, 2001).

Research has, however, shown considerable cross-cultural consistency in relation to gender stereotypes. In a study of 25 countries that were significantly different economically and culturally, men were frequently perceived as being more active, aggressive and dominant and women as more passive, weaker and more nurturing (Best and Williams, 1993). Although gender stereotypes may not be that closely linked to people's actual behaviour or identities, they do tend to have an influential effect on how people are seen and expected to behave in relation to sex and gender and to hierarchies of power and prestige. The notion of sex role theory or gender as the product of childhood socialisation has also become increasingly unpopular in gender theorising and it now tends to be seen as lifelong 'work in progress' (Ferree et al, 1999). Hence it is more common to see gender as dynamic and to talk of 'doing gender' (West and Zimmerman, 1987) rather than being a gender (Butler, 1990, 1993) or possessing a gender, although such a conception seems to diverge completely from common sense naturalised beliefs about gender.

Analysing Gender Identity: Evaluating Different Perspectives

Psychoanalytic Theories

If one looks at feminist psychoanalytic theories of gender identity, identity arises from the primacy of women rearing children and males needing to separate emotionally from the mother and become independent and girls associating with and remaining bonded with the mother (Chodorow, 1978; Dinnerstein, 1991). This results in women being more emotional and nurturing and identifying with a caring role and men becoming more independent and detached. Gilligan (1978) argues that because of this, children learn to apply rules of morality differently, girls apply it relationally and looking at possible impacts of their decision on the people involved and boys make moral decisions based on abstract and detached principles of justice. Psychoanalytic feminists such as Chodorow have therefore been subject to the criticism of essentialising or naturalising processes of gender identity. Young (1997) also points out, in relation to her critique of Chodorow's psychoanalytic theory of gender and others' appropriations of it, that to argue that this is the cause of male domination is flawed and illogical. Chodorow not only assumes an ethnocentric, sexist and essentialist view of childrearing, but ignores the fact most societies are organised around gender differentiated power structures, modes of address, gender symbolism and associated legitimating ideologies and the impact this might have on individuals' self perceptions and behaviour (Young, 1997: 27). Although psychoanalytic theories may help us to understand processes that seem not fully comprehensible when trying to understand gender identity, they are problematic because they rely on an invisible unconscious and are thus not amenable to empirical validation. They also often tend to either ignore or privilege the micro over the macro.

Socialisation Theories

Seeing gender identity exclusively as the internalised self-fulfilling product of childhood socialisation is equally problematic, as this model assumes little agency, or the potential for resistance or transgression and essentially allies itself with a structural approach.

Most early socialisation theories, whether gender aware (Wehrenreich, 1978) or sexist and gender blind (Parsons and Bales, 1956) assume that children are effectively socialised into society's norms and values via a process of internalisation (which is not described) and that any transgressions are anomalies or dysfunctional (Stanley and Wise, 2002). Socialisation theories are therefore deficient because they privilege societal structures and the macro over the micro, including the psyche. Gender blind socialisation theories assume effective socialisation is productive for the whole of society, whereas feminist accounts see the socialisation process in western society as disadvantaging females as they are socialised into passivity, nurturing roles and inferiority.

However, as Thorne (2002) shows in her research, the oft-prevailing thesis that boys and girls inhabit different cultures and ways of being can be challenged. She found some girls and boys do play in mixed sex groups, not exclusively single sex conglomerations, and that some girls are not always exclusively found in intimate dyads and triads and boys in large, competitive gangs. Girls also used threats, insults and physical violence both towards their own sex and also to males and many did not fit neatly into the stereotypical view of girls as caring and kind. Even when such direct confrontation was not obvious, Thorne noted many examples of girls overtly pretending to be co-operative whilst being manipulative and/or aggressive. Therefore a simple, linear model of gender acquisition is not possible, as has been traditionally advocated by many radical and Marxist/socialist feminist theories and by functionalists. The very fact some of the girls researched by Thorne tried to disguise manipulative or aggressive behaviour (under the mantel of pretended co-operation) does seem to suggest they were very aware of how their sex were expected to behave and that sanctions could be imposed if they overtly (rather than covertly) flaunted gender stereotypical behaviour.

Post-structuralists and Queer Theorists

In recent years, the notion that sex is a purely biological and undisputed category and gender is socially constructed has been contested. Two seminal pieces of work, which question the demarcation between sex as a biological fact and gender as a socially constructed facet, are Laqueur's 'Making Sex' and Butler's Foucauldian influenced 'Gender Trouble'. Laqueur (1990) shows through historical analysis of diagrams and writings, how medical discourse and its representation of the sexual organs shaped conceptions of there being two distinct sexes. Prior to this the one sex model existed, whereby women and men were thereby thought to be relatively similar, both physically and mentally and women were thought to possess an internal rather then an external phallus. Butler (1990; 1993) also questions the 'naturalness' of binary biological sex and argues:

> If the immutable character of sex is contested, perhaps this construct called "sex" is as culturally constructed as gender, indeed perhaps it already was gender, with the consequence that the distinction between sex and gender turns out to be no distinction at all. (Butler, 1990: 7)

Butler's analysis also brings into question not only, whether there can be clear demarcation lines between sex and gender, but also, whether it is possible to separate out sexuality from sex and gender. This is because desire is heterosexualised and is produced within binary and asymmetrical oppositions between masculine and feminine, which are understood to emanate from one's status as male or female (ibid: 17). Therefore identities in which gender does not follow from sex or where desire does not link to sex or gender are seen as anomalous or unintelligible. In Butler's analysis of subverted and trangressive categories, such as the act of 'camp' or 'drag' by gay men, she shows how, in their farcical and parodied representations of womanhood, they expose gender as socially constructed, and as 'copy to copy' rather than 'copy to original'. One cannot copy an original if it is a chimera or denotes 'hyperreality' in the age of the simulacrum (Baudrillard, 1983, 1987), by functioning as a copy of an object or an event that no longer or never actually existed (Seidman, 1994).

It can therefore be argued that sex, gender and sexuality are so intermingled they are virtually inseparable (Green, 1998). The interconnections between the three concepts help to construct and consolidate a very influential naturalised patriarchal edifice, whereby sexuality is incomprehensible without linking it to preconceived essentialist notions around gender and sex. The two sexes, genders and sexualities are then incorporated into one of two apparently seamless, yet dichotomised entities, the hierarchically heterosexual, masculinised man or sexually hetero passive feminised woman. These entities and the symbolism associated with them (Gherardi, 1995) are however, problematic, unstable and precarious and incorporate numerous ambiguities and inconsistencies (Butler, 1990). These sexualised, sexed and gendered binary constructions are, however, not separate entities in their own right as they continually refer and defer to each other. Each is in essence meaningless without the reference point of *the other*, as Derrida (1978) has demonstrated with his concept of *differance*.

When analysing the relationship between gender and identity one must therefore be aware of the precarious, unstable and continually negotiated nature of gender identity, whilst at the same time acknowledging that gender is a primary and fundamental way of categorising, and identifying self and others within society. It is also important to be aware of the way in which gender is constructed from, and dependent upon, socially constructed notions of both sex and sexuality and hence cannot be seen in isolation from them.

It is additionally important that when looking at gender identity one does not automatically conflate the acquisition of a gender identity with either a gender role (Pleck, 1976; Clatterbaugh, 1990) or with power inequalities within society. One may assume a gender role within society or perform a gender play that seems congruent with sex attribution, but not simultaneously acquire the corresponding gender identity, as gender dysphoric and ambiguously gendered transsexuals seem to show (Gordo Lopez, 1996). Jan Morris for example, enjoyed a very successful journalistic career as an ambitious male, married and reproduced before embarking on gender reassignment surgery.

Post–structuralist theories are therefore very successful in deconstructing essentialist notions of sex, gender and sexuality and thereby exposing and destabilising their espoused naturalism and inevitability. However, they can be criticised for not fully acknowledging the material constrictions and power structures that shape people's lives. As Hall points out, they also effectively minesweep the known semantic and conceptual ground from under people's feet, by theoretically demolishing key concepts, without replacing them with alternatives.

The Merging of theories

Following on from the three previous sections which have explored and analysed different perspectives on how we come to acquire our gender identity, the next three sections will look at the writings of three of the key theorists who try and explain gendered identity by incorporating and merging, micro, macro and post-structuralist theories: Smith, Butler and McNay.

Dorothy Smith is known as a standpoint feminist and her writings attempt to explain the experience and subordination of women by linking the micro interactional sphere with macro-structural features (1987, 1990 a and b). She draws on Marx's materialism, feminist theory, critical theory and Garfinkel's ethnomethodology. In her elucidation of the 'relations of ruling' she claims the public spheres of society are dominated by men and are a product of both patriarchal and capitalist forces and that increasingly the private/domestic sphere has become colonised, regulated and placed under surveillance by the public sphere.

Her analysis of how social practices (which may disadvantage women) become ingrained, normalised and institutionalised over time, such as falling

45

in love, getting married, and looking after children, seem very similar to Giddens' explanation of social practices in his representation of structuration theory (1985; 1987). However, Giddens in many ways seems to imbue individuals with more potential for changing themselves and the social order than Smith does. Additionally, although she does acknowledge there are many spheres and levels at which power operates she does not concur with Foucault's position in terms of the de-centring of power. Smith, despite theorising both the macro and the micro, prioritises the micro sphere and argues that sociologists should start from the everyday life experience of women as authentic (standpoint feminism) and then proceed to look at their everyday practices and beliefs and how wider social relations create and impinge on these. However, standpoint feminism assumes women experience a bifurcated consciousness and are able to understand and theorise their disadvantage and patriarchal objectification. This may be very unlikely if they are either enchained by discourse or an alternative consciousness is silenced and prevented from developing, before any embryonic utterances of dissent are heard, by the persuasive power of ruling class, patriarchal ideologies.

Smith's work therefore assumes that gender identity is problematic in that women's experiences may depart from and contradict how they are textually represented by dominant capitalist and patriarchal forces. Her weakness is she presents little evidence to substantiate this and by privileging the micro sphere over the macro sphere she claims it is not possible to evaluate objectively the way society operates.

Judith Butler synthesises a Foucauldian influenced theory of gender with Lacanian derived psychoanalytic concepts (Hall, 2000). Her view of the acquisition of gender is that it is performative and reiterative and becomes repetitively, but not necessarily voluntarily or painlessly, inscribed upon one's corporeality and psyche. However, one of the main problems with Lacanian theory is that it relies on linguistic signifiers, where the signified, the penis, is always denoted by and has its potency increased by phallic signifiers. This results in women always being defined in a phallocentric culture by lack and as the inferior Other; whilst men, oppositely, are represented as the taken for-granted agentic Subject. It has also been argued that Lacan's account of subjectification is ahistorical and 'forecloses a satisfactory account of agency' (McNay, 2000: 7).

Butler (1990,1993), however, argues that transgressive sex/sexuality and gender performances and identities indicate resistance and the potential for social change. Unfortunately, these minority performances frequently seem to reinforce, defer to, or be framed within, conventionally accepted gender performances, rather than act to contest them (Evans, 1993; Gordo Lopez, 1996; Cooper, 1995). Although Butler has argued that the phallus as signifier can be appropriated by women and is transferable in terms of the power it bestows in the context of men and gendered hierarchic masculinity, such a claim has been disputed and the phallocentric social order as theorised by Lacan also throws such a possibility into doubt. Butler can be criticised for locating gender and desire within the domain of significatory performance and glossing over questions of human 'needs' and inequitable material positions (Morton, 1995).

Although Butler has successfully deconstructed essentialist and naturalised notions of gender, sex and sexuality and exposed their intrinsic inextricability, her vision of successful subversion is doubtful. Her claim therefore that transgressive performativity can lead to a transversal of and destabilising of power relations can be questioned, unless of course large numbers of the populace engage publicly and in a prolonged fashion with gender resistant performances and publicly pronounced non-gendered identities. Her reliance on Foucauldian concepts of discourse also results in the agency of her subjects/objects remaining questionable and her theory being subject to the same criticism of the de-centring of power, levelled at Foucault more generally. In terms of the acquisition of gender identity, Butler posits a more fluid and transgressive ideal than seems possible. However, her description of the performative, reiterative nature of gender illuminates its socially constructed nature and her elucidation of the interconnections between sex, gender and sexuality also exposes, deconstructs and enables us to trace the processes through which gender is constructed and consolidated.

McNay's project attempts to link the macro structures of power to theories of agency and gender identity, drawing on a variety of different feminist and non-feminist social theorists. She claims that the recent dominant influence of Foucauldian and Lacanian theory on feminist theorising is problematic. This is due in her eyes to it resulting in either a negative or a one-dimensional account of identity. The subject elides into passivity in Foucauldian theory because of the often implicit but assumed passivity of the subject and the way in which Foucault has concentrated much of the time on how the privilege of dominant groups has been sustained by excluding, derogating and marginalising subjected groups (McNay, 2000: 9). In Lacanian theory, the individual is constituted in the phallocentric order and thus agency is construed negatively and seems always linked to a struggle to appropriate the phallus and little else. These limitations, according to McNay, subsequently result in the potential for accommodation and adaptation in relation to gender identity generally being ignored, with the focus being highlighted on subversive resistance and denial. McNay, however, acknowledges some forms of identity (such as gender identity) are more durable than others and must be contextualised and within their historical and social formations.

47

Gender identities are not free-floating: they involve deep-rooted investments on the part of individuals and historically sedimented practices which severely limit their transferability and transformability (McNay, 2000: 18).

Despite this, she still sees it as possible to reconfigure notions of agency in feminist social theory. She does however, concede limitations and constraints on the breadth and pace of change. McNay's contribution to reformulating a more substantive, generative and creative agency within feminist theory has been to examine the work of three theorists, whose work has been to some extent neglected within gender theorising, Pierre Bourdieu, Paul Ricoeur and Cornelius Castoradis.

Bourdieu is a social theorist who attempts to bridge the macro micro divide through his notions of fields (different forms of social structure – economic, social, cultural educational, aesthetic etc.) and his idea of corporeal dispositions – *habitus* which is influenced by the fields. Bourdieu claims that the identity and practices of the body are not natural but culturally achieved and inscribed through a somatisation process he names bodily *hexis*. Via the *sens pratique*, individuals acquire cultural knowledge about how to behave. These skills are seen as a mastered at a pre-reflexive level, which cannot be overtly articulated or consciously understood. Bourdieu has been interpreted as being over deterministic and as not according the individual any social agency – merely showing how class relations are reproduced over time.

However, McNay argues that his work may be more productive than Foucauldian inspired work for understanding generative forms of gender identity because it replaces 'discursive determination' with 'a more dialogical temporal logic' (McNay, 2000: 72). This takes into account not only the sedimentary effects of power but also the embodied potential for agency. The coupling of habitus and field also allows comprehension of how material relations gives meaning to and constructs the body's actions. Although McNay's suggestion that Bourdieu's theories open up the possibility of more generative and creative forms of identity in relation to gender, this possibility is introduced at a purely theoretical level and until some attempt is made to link the theoretical with empirical research it is not possible to evaluate how successful it might be.

McNay then attempts to incorporate Ricoeur's work on narrative and coherence of the self (Ricoeur, 1983, 1988, 1992) into a feminist theorisation of agency. To argue that the self has some continuity through narrative but this can change over time as long as some coherence is retained, overcomes the idea of the constructed self being static, or completely fragmented and in flux and as post- structuralist theory posits. It may also help to explain why people can tolerate ambiguities in their conceptions of self. Joas (1988) argues that violence, marginalisation and denigration can help stabilise identities but these are not sufficient in themselves to explain identity formation. Similarly Hollway (1988) argues that some constructionist accounts appear unidimensional and are incapable of explaining why individuals cling on passionately to oppressive and seemingly irrational gender identities. The idea of narrative can, however, be incorporated into a social constructionist account because it deals well with the temporal dynamics of identity whilst simultaneously suggesting that there might be significant constraints on the extent to which identity may change. This appears to be very much the case with gender, perhaps far more than for national or religious identities. This is because it is hard to conceptualise alternatives to gendered identities or have non-gendered role models or examples to emulate or suggest an alternative direction. As Butler rightly says:

> If human existence is always gendered existence, then to stray
> outside of established gender is in some sense to put one's very
> existence into question. (Butler, 1987: 132)

Ricoeur's work is also useful because it demonstrates how post and pre events imagination can be used to pre-empt action or alternatively to understand, rationalise and give it coherence. McNay therefore suggests that the link between self and other, when one looks at gender identity, interaction and relationships between men and women, does not always necessarily have to be predicated on a negative, deficit paradigm of subjectification, in the ways she suggests Lacanian and Foucauldian theorising tends to lead (McNay, 2000: 100).

The third theorist that McNay analyses and attempts to herald as useful in terms of gender and agency is Castoriadis (1987). Castoriadis is a psychoanalyst who unusually attempts to take into account the socio-historic realm in his theorising and argues that creative action cannot be reduced to either the psyche or society and that they both inhere to each other. McNay again claims this opens up a more active notion of agency than the negative representation of subjectification posited by Lacan. This also overcomes a criticism levelled at many psychoanalysts, namely that they are ahistorical and ignore or give little credence to the impact society has on the development of the individual (see Young's criticism of Chodorow).

Analysing the work of three prominent gender theorists, who draw on combinations of macro, micro and post-structuralist perspectives on gender identity and formation does not appear to have led to a significantly greater understanding of how this occurs. Butler's work is highly theoretical and although her concept of the performative has significantly advanced understanding of gender, she underplays the importance of wider societal structures because of her reliance on Foucault. Notwithstanding her examples of transgression via minority individuals, she does not seem able to account for acts of accommodation and adaptation and more subtle rejections of gender norms.

McNay's work is again highly complex and theoretical, but is also significantly more confusing and disjointed than Butler's. Although she aims to open up an agentic theoretical space where women are not the gender cloned cultural dopes of socialisation theory or the discursively determined yet free floating and fragmented individuals post structural theory describes, it is not clear she has achieved this. Her utilisation of Ricoeur's work on narrative and cohesion of the self suggest a promising route for trying to understand gender identity, particularly in relation to how individuals cope with ambiguities and adapt and accommodate gender stereotypes within their identities. However, it is not clear how Castoraidis and Bourdieu's theory can be applied to previous empirical research or inform new empirical inquiry. Many of her suggestions therefore remain at the level of abstract and to some extent inchoate theorising.

Smith's work is to some extent more empirically grounded and she does give more concrete examples to substantiate some of her claims about patriarchal and capitalistic power and domination. However, her position of being a standpoint feminist theorist, who privileges the words and experiences of subjugated groups, such as women, over a more 'objective' macro analysis is problematic. This is because there appears to be no conclusive empirical evidence that most women possess a *bifurcated consciousness* or are able to examine and analyse their disadvantage and how their everyday lives may contradict with how women and femininity are represented within patriarchal texts and the relations of ruling.

We therefore at this point need to dispense with the elusive search for a perfect theory that explains gender identity and concede there is immense debate and disagreement. Perhaps the best way to deal with such problems is to use a toolkit approach, as Foucault advocates, drawing on theories, only as and when they appear useful or applicable. The next section will therefore attempt to look at gender identity taking into account both external pressures and wider social structures and how they may or may not appear to interconnect with the psychological formation of identity. The validity of post-structuralist accounts, which attempt to theoretically destabilise sex/gender/sexuality norms and normative gender identities, will also be considered. This section will therefore attempt to provide a tentative explanation of how gender identities might be formed through looking at specific areas such as childhood socialisation, language, education, the workplace and sexuality. It will also try and explain how resistance may manifest itself and its consequences, as well as looking at accommodation and adaptation in relation to gender identity.

Becoming gendered and acquiring a gendered Identity

As previously mentioned, from the moment a child is born and often even before, it is designated as one sex or the other. This simple and seemingly unproblematic labelling results in a dichotomous life or even death trajectory. In some countries, such as China and India where sex preference for a boy child is very strong, gendercide is common and girl children are often selectively aborted or killed after birth (Renzetti and Curran, 1999). A 1993 survey found that in India, despite infanticide being outlawed over a hundred years ago, 30,000 baby girls every year were actively murdered or left to die through neglect (Burns, 1994). In westernised countries sex selection before birth is also increasingly seen as morally acceptable (Koller and Burke, 1992).

After a child is born, even parents who claim they treat their or other children no differently according to sex will treat their children in significantly different ways. There is a large body of research that shows mothers and fathers are likely to stereotype girls as softer, prettier and more sensitive than boys; and boys as more active, fearless and exploratory than girls. Adults therefore tend to interpret and respond to the same behaviour differently according to the child's sex. For example Fagot et al (1985) showed that even though 13/14 month old babies of both sexes attempt to communicate in the same ways, adults were more likely to responded to boys if they 'forced attention' by being aggressive or crying and screaming. Girls conversely were ignored if they displayed the same behaviour and were more likely to be acknowledged if they used gentle touching or gestures or talked. Parents also engage in rougher more physical play with boys (MacDonald and Parke, 1986) and fathers tend to engage in more physical interactive games with boys that encourage the development of visual psychomotor skills and alternatively promote verbal interaction with girls (Bronstein, 1988). Other research suggests that parents feel and act on the basis that girls require more help than boys, therefore reinforcing the message at a very early age that boys are and should be more able and independent than girls (see Renzetti and Curran, 1999).

By the age of two or three children have heard themselves referred to as a good or bad girl or boy, hundreds, if not thousands of times and are quite aware they belong to one category or the other (R4, 1999). However they are at this time still in the process of acquiring cognitive awareness of the fixity of sex and its socially constructed relationship with gender, often assuming sex is based on characteristics such as girls wearing dresses and having long hair. Hence when, playing with a friend's three-year-old daughter, I was assured I was a boy when I had a baseball hat on and my long hair tied back in a pony tail so it could not be seen. Yet two minutes later when I took the baseball cap off and let my hair down, I was told I was a girl again. However, at the same time that children think sex is a reversible category, many are often very troubled by transgression of sex and gender categories and try and ignore ambiguities and uncertainties.

In her research with pre-school children, Davies (2001) gives the example of one boy who chooses to wear a dress but gets teased by the other children. Another boy she researched angrily refused to acknowledge men ever wore dresses, despite the researcher showing him pictures of priests and Greek men wearing clothing that was identical to dresses in all but name and his Malay father customarily wearing sarongs. Similarly, a friend of mine now in her forties, recently recounted an incident when at the age of seven, the gas meter reader mistook her for a small boy and greeted her by saying 'Hello sonny'. She remembers being very upset and disturbed by this mis-recognition and running into the house crying. Pre-school children are also far more likely to accept and initiate play with other children who engage in gender stereotyped behaviour than those who transgress it. Similarly Delamont's (2001) extracts from the problem pages of popular women's magazines exposed just how concerned and inflexible parents were when their children, particularly boy children, transgressed the 'appropriate' gender roles and behaviour. This seems to reflect how the male sex role and men are valued above femininity and women and the acceptance of tomboyish behaviour in young girls is sometimes accepted but not the converse.

So sex and associated gendered characteristics are reinforced and encouraged by both adults and peers at a very early age. Even toys in children's bedrooms are still distinctly gender stereotyped, girls toys distilling an ideology of domesticity, motherhood and nurturing (dolls houses, Barbies, miniature house appliances etc.) and boys toys (Batman, Lego, guns military trucks, sport games etc.) being more concerned with independence, aggression, adventure and exploration. Studies over the last thirty years show very little has changed in America in relation to the toys that boys and girls have (e.g. Rheingold and Cook, 1975; Stoneman et al, 1986). A perusal of contemporary toy catalogues in America (Renzetti and Curran, 1999) and in England (Delamont, 2001) also demonstrates that toy marketing and consumption is still extremely gendered.

Similarly the media continues to impart the message that men and women are very different creatures, men often being portrayed as powerful, ingenious and fearless and women as passive, needing protection, depicted in subordinate stances and as frequently as not working, mothers, or doing gender stereotyped jobs. By the age of four, children in America will have watched over 400 hours of television and are thus subject to the message that men are 'tough guys' and that women 'use exceedingly large quantities of shampoo' (Hodson, 1984). The media also continually propound messages that 'sex/gender 'differences' are biological and have been proved by evolutionary psychology to show 'men cannot do the ironing or change babies' nappies' (Delamont, 2001: 5).

Education continues to contribute to gendering individual by giving children stereotypes about the type of jobs men and women should and are capable of doing. Hence most dinner time supervisors and classroom assistants are female and a very high proportion of heads and deputy heads, particular in high schools are male. School materials are also often gendered, for example maths problems being presented in a way that is more likely to appeal to boys than girls. Teachers also often unconsciously treat children in sexist ways, giving boys more attention for being more vociferous and forceful and often ignoring girls who behave in the same way. A hidden gendered curriculum therefore also operates (Thorne, 1992) alongside the formal curriculum, which seems to offer equality of treatment and opportunity.

Language is additionally gendered in many ways and is a key medium of socialisation. The generic male pronoun, whereby words denoting one sex are used to describe both e.g. he/man, mankind, and history, is problematic, because women are rendered invisible and the words are often used, particularly by men, in a non-generic, unisex manner (Gibbon, 1999). Words used to describe women that were previously positive or neutral are often subject to semantic derogation and frequently take on negative sexual overtones, whereas their male equivalents do not. Examples might include master/mistress, patron/madam, and bachelor/spinster (Renzetti and Curran, 1999). The way men and women interact in conversation is also gendered, previous studies finding men tending to talk more in mixed sex conversation and that men tend to interrupt women more than women interrupt them (Renzetti and Curran, 1999). However, more recent research indicates one should be cautious about over-generalising and that male/female communication differs considerably and is situation specific (Cameron, 1990). Non-verbal communication is also gendered with women tending to avert their eyes more when men talk to them than vice versa and also smile more at men, regardless of their state of mind, characteristics that can be regarded as indicating submissiveness (Bartky, 1997; Henley, 1977).

Much identity and bodywork is centred on creating differences, rather than revealing natural divergences. Bartky (1997) in her Foucauldian examination of femininity and the modernisation of patriarchal power reveals how through disciplinary practices involving surveillance of self and other, women create bodily femininity. They do this by restricting their movements, taking up as little space as possible in public places, concentrating on physical appearance, make-up and dieting, and signalling their difference from men in terms of lack of bodily hair by continual plucking of eyebrows and shaving of legs and underarms. Men in contrast are rarely interested in restricting their movements and open themselves up to take up as much space as possible. Bodily hair and the development of musculature and strength are considered masculine and indicative of virility, so this is encouraged rather than discouraged, as with women. The image of the 'body beautiful' has entered men's vocabulary in the eighties, nineties and the millennium with media representations of the 'new man' and 'new laddism' (Beynon, 2002). It, however, still appears that women are almost pathologically concerned with appearance and dieting (Bordo, 1990). The image of the 'new man', in terms of changed and more equal and nurturing behaviour therefore appears to be more of a chimera and a capitalist consumer ploy than a reality for most men (Edwards, 1997).

The dichotomous roles, abilities and 'natures' of men and women are seemingly reflected in both private and public spheres. Research continually shows that women are taking the key domestic and childcare roles, within the family, even when both parents are working full-time (Connell, 2002). Men and women are also vertically and horizontally occupationally segregated. This means that men possess most of the key authority roles in all occupations and professions (vertical segregation), even in those, such as social work, nursing and primary school teaching, numerically dominated in rank and file positions by women (Hugman, 1991; Grimwood and Popplestone, 1993). Women tend to be dominant in occupations associated with caring and servicing others such as the hospitality and catering industry, secretarial work and in care work such as social and residential work, but only in the lower and manual and managerial echelons (horizontal segregation). Jobs associated with a caring or servicing roles also command less prestige and less financial remuneration than other jobs that may require as much or as little skill but are stereotyped as men's jobs. Men's jobs are those associated with technical skills such as computing and engineering, physical strength and prowess and those requiring authority and supervision skills. It is significant that men inhabit most key national and international decision making positions in politics, the military and in the corporate capitalist financial worlds. On the basis of recent statistics, 93% of all cabinet ministers in the world's governments are men (Connell, 2002). Studies have also shown that both men and women have more trust and conviction in males than in females and see men as more able.

When women do attempt to break through the occupational *glass ceiling*, (Glass Ceiling Commission, 1995), they are often doubly disadvantaged and stigmatised and occupational performance does not necessarily denote promotion and recognition and may result in denigration and harassment. The infamous Hopkins vs. Price Waterhouse legal case involved Ann Hopkins appealing against her application for a partnership being turned down, despite the fact she had brought more money into the company than any other applicant (Reskin and Padavic, 1994; Benokratis, 1998). The basis for her being denied promotion was that she was seen as being too aggressive and not dressing femininely enough or wearing make-up or perfume. Ann Hopkins won her case but most women do not take their cases to Equal Opportunity tribunals and often the sexism involved is too covert, subtle and hidden to challenge legally (Benokraitis, 1997). Similarly even when women are subject to sexual harassment they often blame themselves and try and cope with the problem at an individual level by avoiding the perpetrator, changing jobs or dressing in as unattractive manner as possible (Cockburn, 1991).

In relation to sexuality and sexual behaviour, gendered norms and double standards still apply. A large body of research has shown girls have very little agency and ability to explore sexuality in terms of their own pleasure and desire (Lees, 1997; Halson, 1991; Holland et al, 1998). Their behaviour is often dictated by the necessity of having a steady boyfriend to dispel notions of a bad reputation and being labelled as worthless and a 'slag', 'tight' or a lesbian by male and female peers alike. Female sexuality is expected to conform to notions of accepted passive femininity and behaviour that expresses desire and challenges notions of a hierarchic male dominated, compulsory heterosexuality (Rich, 1997; Hearn, 1987) is subject to peer and parental sanction and negatively labelled as unfeminine. Hence many teenage girls fear asking men to use contraception or to carry it themselves because they are worried about being seen as planning for sex or as a 'slag'. This severely affects their choices and agency, as well as their safety in relation to pregnancy and STD's. Sexuality throughout the life span is therefore subject to essentialised norms and expectations (see next chapter).

Conclusion

What does all this mean in relation to gender identity and to analysing how micro and macro spheres interact and the implications of this? Certainly at the micro level of face to face interaction, children and adults are relentlessly bombarded with messages about the naturalness of dichotomous gender and are rewarded for conforming to gender stereotypes and punished for transgression. At the macro level of social structures, male power is in evidence and men are at the helm of most decision making bodies.

Gendered ideologies and practices are also embedded within organisational norms and modes of operation and are evident in the media. If one accepts that power is not always possessed, coercive or operates with the threat of force, then post-structuralist notions of discourse and the multi-directional and capillary nature of power are also important (Foucault, 1979, 1981).

55

Discourses are regimes of truth and knowledge that operate at a number of different levels, and through different technologies, tactics and strategies, for example, through language, micro interactions and social structures. As Foucault claims, power may be at its most effective when it is productive and creates pleasure, even when ultimately that pleasure may be disadvantageous. So, for example, one student I was teaching on a course about sex and sexuality claimed 'This stuff about male power in relation to sexuality is codswallop. I like sex with my husband and enjoy being passive and penetrated and I talked to my friend and so does she'. So the disadvantages and unequal power structures in relation to masculine and feminine sexuality are often ignored and disregarded, particularly if they are imbued with ambiguity.

Very few people publicly and visibly transgress gender stereotypes and identities but this does not necessarily mean they subscribe to them and believe them wholesale. As McNay has claimed, accommodation and adaptation may be far more common than resistance, possibly because people are aware of how men and women are expected to behave and the possible negative consequences of challenging this. Interestingly, Wilkes (1995) in her research into women who had undertaken caring careers noted that many of the women made a distinction between 'doing caring' and 'being caring'. They were very ambiguous about the 'care' aspect of being in a caring career or had chosen it because they saw it as being a socially acceptable career for a woman that would not be questioned by others. Her research therefore indicates that choosing a caring career does not necessarily equate with women identifying caring as an intrinsic part of their feminine identity. Similarly some married yet professional female students of mine in their late thirties and forties said they would always behave in a public forum as if their husband was the head of the household and would defer to his decision, even though both they and their husbands did not really behave in this manner in the confines of their own homes.

Although individuals may acquire a gender identity, whose public face and performance is more apparent than its private one and be aware that conforming to gender identity is important, there is a lack of overall difference in many attributes and types of behaviour between men and women. This is surprising considering how differently the sexes are treated and expected to behave. Connell (2001) in his examination of *sex differences research* from the 1970's to the present day concludes that it was misnamed and should really be called *sex similarity research*. This is because no significant sex differences could be found in both individual studies and meta analyses to show men and women are really that different in terms of intelligence, sociability, physical skills and a range of psychological and personality characteristics. As Thorne's research into gender in schools shows, children do engage in cross-sex play and activities and do not always correspond to rigid gender roles and identities. Even when differences are found their significance may be over-exaggerated. For example there is a slight sex difference favouring men as more aggressive in situations of non-provoked aggression, and some boys engage in more rough and tumble play than girls, although significantly most boys and girls fall within the same range (Connell, 2002).

The fact that there are few significant differences between men and women despite differential socialisation and the different familial and occupational roles they undertake in adult life, pays testament to gender identity being both socially constructed and performative, but never fully achievable. Structural aspects of society are also important because discursive strategies may not be fully effective. As Walby (1994) has shown coercive legislation at certain times, such as that criminalising abortion, contraception and male homosexuality and denying custody to lesbian mother, whilst offering legal support for the state of marriage, has been used to police and regulate certain configurations of gender and sexuality. Therefore individuals seem often to conform to and invest in gender identities because of both discursive positioning and structural and micro interactional sanctions, rather than being fully convinced of their naturalness.

The evidence put forward therefore suggests people accommodate to and adapt to gender identities to varying degrees, but are not totally bound by them. However, the potential for change is limited unless a large number of people are prepared to publicly and consistently resist gender categorisation and identification and transverse and transgress dichotomous gender categories. It must also be acknowledged that patriarchal, hegemonic power significantly limits and constrains individual agency and self actualisation, particularly that of women, whose significantly reduced life chances in comparison to men, are reflected in gendered inequalities in poverty (Glendinning and Millar, 1992), health (Doyal, 1995), and in various other spheres such as employment. Even when women do 'break through' the glass ceiling and manage to attain significant occupational positions, they are often still found juggling childcare and domestic roles with work commitments, in a way men rarely do or are expected to do (Observer, 28.04.02).

Bibliography

Ahmed, S. (1994) 'Theorising Sexual Identification: Exploring the Limits of Psychoanalytic and Postmodern Models' paper presented to the BSA annual conference, *Sexualities in a Social Context*, University of Central Lancashire, Preston, March, 1994.

Althusser, L. (2000) 'Ideology Interpellates Individuals As Subjects' in P. du Gay., J. Evans and P. Redman (eds.) *Identity: A Reader*, London: Sage/OUP.

Bartky, S. L. (1997) 'Foucault, Femininity and the Modernization of Patriarchal Power' in Tietjens Meyer, D. (ed.) *Feminist Social Thought: A Reader*: London: Routledge.

Benokraitis, N. V. (ed.) (1997) *Subtle Sexism: Current Practices and Prospects for Change*, London: Sage.

Best, D. L. and Williams, J. E. (1993) 'A Cross-Cultural Viewpoint', New York: Guildford in A. E Beall and R. J. Sternberg (eds.) *The Psychology of Gender*, New York: Guildford.

Beynon, J. (2002) *Masculinities and Culture*, Buckingham: OUP.

Bourdieu, P. (1977) *Outline of a Theory of Practice*, Cambridge: Cambridge University Press.

Bourdieu, P. (1979) *Distinction: A Social Critique of the Judgement of Taste*, London: Routledge, Kegan and Paul.

Bordo, S. (1992) 'Anorexia Nervosa: Psychopathlogy as the Crystallisation of Culture' in H. Crowley and S. Himmelweit (eds.) *Knowing Women:feminism and knowledge*, Cambridge: Polity Press.

Bronstein, P. (1988) 'Father-Child Interaction' in P. Bronstein and C. P. Cowan (eds.) *Fatherhood Today: Men's Changing Role in Family Life'*, New York: John Wiley.

Burns, J. F. (1994) 'India Fights Abortion of Female Fetuses', *New York Times*, August 27, 1994.

Butler, J. (1987) 'Variations on Sex and Gender: Beauvoir, Wittig and Foucault, M. in S. Benhabib and D. Cornell (eds.) *Feminisms as Critique: Essays on the Politics of Gender in Late Capitalist Societies*, Cambridge: Polity Press.

Butler, J. (1990) *Gender Trouble: Feminism and the Subversion of Identity*, London: Routledge.

Butler, J. (1993) *Bodies that Matter: On the Discursive Limits of Sex*, London: Routledge.

Cameron, D. (ed.) (1990) *The Feminist Critique of Language*, London: Routledge.

Castoriadis, C. (1987) The *Imaginary Institution of Society*, Cambridge: Polity Press.

Chodorow, N. (1978) The *Reproduction of Mothering*, Berkeley, University of California Press.

Clatterbaugh, K. (1990) *Contemporary Perspectives on Masculinity: Men, Women and Politics in Western Society*, Boulder, Co: Westview Press.

Cockburn, C. (1991) *In The Way of Women*, Basingstoke: Macmillan.

Cohen, C. J. (1996) 'Contested Membership: Black, Gay identities and the Politics of AIDS' in S. Seidman (ed.) *Queer Theory/Sociology*, Oxford: Blackwell.

Connell, (1995) *Masculinities*, Cambridge: Polity.

Connell, R. W. (2002) *Gender*, Cambridge: Polity.

Connell, R. W. (1987) *Gender and Power: Society, the Person and Sexual Politics*, Cambridge: Polity.

Cooper, D. (1995) *Power in Struggle: Feminism, Sexuality and the State.* Buckingham: Open University Press.

Davies, B. (2002) 'Becoming Male or Female' in S. Jackson and S. Scott (eds.) *Gender: A Sociological reader*, London: Routledge.

Dawkins, R. (1989) *The Selfish Gene* (revised edition), Oxford: Oxford University Press.

Delamont, S. (2001) *Changing Women, Unchanged Men? Sociological Perspectives on Gender in a Post-Industrial Society*, Buckingham: Open University Press.

Dinnerstein, D. (1991) *The Mermaid and the Minotoar: sexual arrangements and human malalaise*, London: Harper Collins.

Derrida, J. (1978) *Writing and Difference*, Chicago: Aldine.

Doyal, L. (1995) *What Makes Women Sick: gender and the political economoy of health*, London: Macmillan.

Du Gay, P., Evans, J. and Redman, P. (2000) 'General Introduction' in P. du Gay., J. Evans and P. Redman (eds.) *Identity: A Reader*, London: Sage/OUP.

Edwards, T. (1997) *Men in the Mirror: men's fashions, masculinity and consumer society*, London: Cassell.

Evans, D. (1993) *The Material Construction of Sexualities*, London: Routledge.

Fagot, B.I., Hagan, R., Leinbach, M.D. and Kronsberg, S. (1985) 'Differential reactions to Assertive and Communicative Acts of Toddler Boys and Girls, *Child Development*, 56: 1499–505.

Fausto-Sterling, A. (1997) in R.N. Lancaster and M. Di Leonardo (eds.) *The Gender/Sexuality Reader: culture, history, poltical economy*, London: Routledge.

Ferree, M, M., Lorber, J. and Hess, B.B. (1999) (eds.) *Revisioning Gender*, London: Sage.

Foucault, M. (1979) *Discipline and Punish*, London: Penguin.

Foucault, M. (1981) *The History of Sexuality Volume 1: an Introduction*, Harmondsworth: Penguin.

Gherardi, S. (1995) *Gender Symbolism and Organizational Cultures*, London: Sage.

Gibbon, M. (1999) *Feminist Perspectives on Language*, Harlow: Pearson Education/Longman.

Giddens, A. (1984) *The Constitution of Society*, Cambridge: Polity Press.

Giddens, A. (1987) *Social Theory and Modern Sociology*, Stanford: Stanford University Press.

Gilligan, C. (1982) *In a Different Voice: Psychological Theory and Women's*

Glass Ceiling Commission (1995) *Good For Business: Making Full Use of the Nation's Capital, The Environmental Scan*, Washington DC: Federal Glass Ceiling Commission.

Glick, P. and Fiske, S. T. (1999) 'Gender, Power Dynamics and Social Interaction' in Ferree, M, M., Lorber, J. and Hess, B.B. (1999) (eds.) *Revisioning Gender*, London: Sage.

Glendinning, C. and Millar, J. (1992) *Women and Poverty in Britain: the 1990's*, revised edition, Sussex: Harvester Wheatsheaf.

Gordo Lopez, A. (1996) 'The Rhetoric of Gender Identity Clinics: Transsexuals and other Boundary Objects' in E. Burman., G. Aitken., P. Alldred., R. Alwood., T. Billington., B. Goldberg., A. Gordo Lopez., C. Heenan., D. Marks and S. Warner (eds.) *Psychology Discourse Practice: From Regulation to Resistance*, London: Taylor and Francis.

Gould, L. (1999) X: A Fabulous Child's Story' in Kourany, J. A., Sterba, J. P. and Tong, R. (eds.) *Feminist Philosophies* (second edition), Upper Saddle River, New Jersey: Prentice Hall.

Gray, J. (1993) *Men are from Mars, Women are from Venus: a practical guide for improving communication and getting what you want from relationships*, Thorsons.

Green, L., Parkin, W., Hearn, J. (2001) 'Power' in E. Wilson (ed.) *Organizational Behaviour Reassessed: The Impact of Gender*, London, Sage.

Green, L (1998) *Caged by Force, Entrapped by Discourse: A Study of the Construction of Control of Children & Their Sexualities Within Residential Children's Homes*, unpublished PhD thesis, University of Huddersfield.

Griffin, J.E. and Wilson, J. D. (1992) 'Disorders of Sexual Differentiation' in P.C. Walsh., A. B. Retik., T.A. Stamey and E.D. Vaughan (eds.) *Campbells Urology*, Philadelphia: Saunders.

Grimwood, C. and Popplestone (1993) *Women, Management and Care*, Basingstoke: BASW/Macmillan.

Grosz, E. (1998) 'Inscriptions and Bodymaps: Representations and the Corporeal' in T. Threadgold and A. Grany Francis (eds.) *Masculine, Feminine and Representation*, Sydney: Allen and Unwin.

Habermas, J. (1981) *The Theory of Communicative Action, Vol 1: Reason and the Rationalization of Society*, Cambridge: Polity Press.

Hall, S. (1997) 'Interview on Culture and Power' *Radical Philosophy*, 86:24–4.

Hall, S. (2000) Who Needs Identity? In P. du Gay., J. Evans and P. Redman (eds.) *Identity: A Reader*, London: Sage/OUP.

Halson, A. (1991) 'Young Women, Sexual Harassment and Heterosexuality: Violence, Power Relations and Mixed Sex Schooling' in P. Abbott and C. Wallace (eds.) *Gender, Power and Sexuality*, London: Macmillan.

Hearn, J. (1987) *The Gender of Oppression: Men, Masculinity and a Critique of Marxism*, Sussex: Wheatsheaf.

Henley, M.N. (1977) *Body Politics*: New Jersey: Prentice Hall.

Hird, M. J and Germon, J. (2001) 'The Intersexual Body and the Medical regulation of Gender' in K. Backett-Milburn and L. McKie (eds.) *Constructing Gendered Bodies*, Basingstoke: Palgrave/BSA.

Holland, J., Ramanozoglu, C., Sharpe, S. and Thompson, R. (1998) *Male in the Head: Young People, Heterosexuality and Power,* London: Tufnell Press.

Hollway, W. (1984) 'Gender Difference and the Production of Subjectivity' in J. Henriques et al (eds.) *Changing the Subject: Psychology, Social Regulation and Subjectivity*, London: Methuen.

Hugman, R. (1991) *Power in Caring Professions*, London: Macmillan.

Kessler, S. (1990) 'The Medical Construction of Gender: Case Management of Intersexed Infants, *Signs*, 16: 3–26.

Kolker, A. and Burke, B.M. 'Sex Preference and Sex Selection: Attitudes of Prenatal Diagnosis Clients, paper presented to *the Annual Meeting of the American Sociological Association*, Pittsburgh, PA.

Laqueur, T. (1990) *Making Sex: Body and Gender: From the Greeks to Freud* London: Harvard University Press.

Layder, D. (1993) *Understanding Social Theory*, London: Sage.

Lees, S. (1993) *Sugar and Spice: Sexuality and Adolescent Girls*, London: Hutchison.

MacDonald, K. and Parke, R. D. (1986) 'Parent-Child Physical Play: The Effects of Sex and Age on Children and Parents, *Sex Roles*, 15:367–378.

Macinnes, J.(2001) 'The Crisis of Masculinity and the Politics of Identity' in S. M. Whitehead and F. J. Barrett (eds.) *The Masculinities Reader*, Cambridge: Polity.

McNay, L. (2000) *Gender and Agency: Reconfiguring the Subject in Feminist and Social Theory*, Cambridge: Polity.

Millett, K. (1972) *Sexual Politics*, London: Abacus.

Moir, A. and Jessel, D. (1989) *Brain Sex: The Real Differences between the Sexes*, London: Mandarin.

Morton, D. (1995) 'Birth of the Cyberqueer, *PMLA*, 11: 369–381.

Parson, T. And Bales, R. (1956) (eds.) *Family, Socialization and Interaction Process*, London: Routledge.

Pleck, J. H. (1976) 'The Male Sex role: Problems, Definitions and Sources of Change, *Journal of Social Issues*, 32: 155–164.

Radio 4 (BBC R4) 01.03.99 *Turning into Children: Gender and Sexuality*.

Renzetti, C. M. and Curran, D. (1999) *Women, Men and Society*, fourth edition, Needham Heights, Boston: Allyn and Bacon.

Rich, A. (1997) 'Compulsory Heterosexuality and Lesbian Existence' in S. Kemp and J. Squires (eds.) *Feminisms*, Oxford: Oxford University Press.

Reskin, B. F. and Padavic, B. (1994) *Women and Men at Work*, USA: Pine Forge Press.

Ricoeur, P. (1983) *Time and Narrative, vol 1*, Chicago: University of Chicago Press.

Ricoeur, P. (1988) *Time and Narrative, vol 3*, Chicago: University of Chicago Press.

Ricoeur, P. (1992) *Oneself as Another*, London: University of Chicago Press.

Rose, N. (1989) *Governing the Soul: The Shaping of the Private Self*, London: Routledge.

Seidman, S. (1994) *Contested Knowledge: Social Theory in the Postmodern Era*, Oxford: Blackwell.

Sibeon, R. (1997) 'Power, Agency/Structure and Micro/Macro: An Excursus into Anti Reductionist Sociology', Paper presented to *the BSA annual conference, Power and Resistance*, University of York, April, 1997.

Smith, D. (1988) *The Everyday World as Problematic: A Feminist Sociology*, Boston: Northeastern University Press.

Smith, D. (1990) *Texts, Facts and Femininity: Exploring the Relations of Ruling*, London: Routledge.

Smith, D. (1990) *The Conceptual Practices of Power: A Feminist Sociology of Knowledge*, Boston: Northeastern University Press.

Spivak, G. C. with Rooney, E. (1994) 'What's in a Word?' in N. Schor and E. Weed (eds.) *The Essential Difference*, Bloomington: Indian University Press.

Stanley, L. and Wise, S. (2002) 'What's Wrong with Socialisation? in S. Jackson and S. Scott (eds.) *Gender: A Sociological reader* London: Routledge.

Tannen, D. (1990) *You Just Don't Understand: Men and Women in Conversation*, New York: Ballantine books.

Thorne, B. (2002) 'Do Girls and Boys Have Different Cultures' in S. Jackson and S. Scott (eds.) *Gender: A Sociological reader*, London: Routledge.

Walby, S. (1994) 'Towards a Theory of Patriarchy' in *The Polity Reader in Gender Studies*, Cambridge: Polity.

Wehrenreich, H. (1978) 'Sex Role Socialization' in J. Chetwynd and O. Hartnett (eds.) *The Sex Role System*, London, Routledge.

West, C. and Zimmerman, D. (1987) 'Doing Gender' *Gender and Society*, 1: 125–51.

Wilkes, J. (1995) 'the Social Construction of a Caring Career' in C. Burc and B. Speed (eds.) *Gender, Power and Relationships*, London: Routledge.

Wilson, E. O. (1975) *Sociobiology: The New Synthesis*: Cambridge USA, Harvard University Press.

Woodhouse, A. (1989) *Fantastic Women*, London: Macmillan.

Wrong, D. (1979) *Power: Its Forms, Bases and Uses*, Oxford: Blackwell.

Young, I. M. (1997) 'Is Male Gender Identity the Cause of Male Domination?' in Tietjens Meyer, D. (ed.) *Feminist Social Thought: A Reader*: London: Routledge.

Zarate, M. A. and Smith, E. R. (1990) 'Person Categorization and Stereotyping', *Social Cognition*, 8: 161–85.

4. Sexuality

Julia Hirst

Sexuality is one of the prime sites for the expression of identity. Yet, there is little consensus over what it is the term sexuality describes or its significance for the ways in which individuals experience and organise their lives. Nevertheless, there are defining features that unite particular perspectives. Commonplace usage in lay and popular discourse refers (simplistically) both to sexual practice ('having sex') and sexual identity (in making the distinction between hetero-, homo-, and bi-sexuality). Academic perspectives with origins in medicine, psychiatry, psychology, religion and sociobiology focus on the extent to which sexual identity and sexual behaviour are biologically and genetically determined as products of 'normal' and 'natural' instincts and drives. This emphasis on sexuality as a physically determined phenomenon is oft referred to as the *essentialist* view.

The essentialist approach is problematised by social scientists (in sociology and critical social psychology) who argue that the biological basis of sexual expression is less important than the impact of society and processes of power in constructing particular identities and regulating sexual practices, choices and life chances. Debates in this arena are loosely labelled under the umbrella of *social constructionist* accounts of sexuality.

By distinguishing the essentialist and social constructionist viewpoint I am not suggesting they occupy single theoretical or political positions. Broad assumptions certainly foreground how each sees the sexual as constituted and expressed but each span various perspectives, agendas and research approaches. Therefore, essentialist and constructionist accounts are best seen as occupying relative positions along a continuum if understanding of sexuality (and its implications for identity) is not to be constrained (Schwartz and Rutter, 1998).

Focusing on biological or evolutionary (genetic) imperatives without acknowledgement of social processes is arguably as reductionist as social constructionist viewpoints (ibid.) that negate the place of the physical body in expressions of sexuality and desire. For instance, compared to previous generations, the average age of puberty begins at a younger age for females and males (Hill, 2000) hence rendering an enhanced potential for earlier sexual activity among young people. Having said this, the inference is not that the process of inscribing a sexual identity begins at puberty or that sexuality only becomes expressible at the onset of puberty. Children have a sexuality and act in sexual ways long before puberty (Jackson, 1982).

Biology, therefore, has its place but the sexual body has to be understood as socially embedded and it is this embeddedness in cultural, political, historical and institutional settings that social constructionist accounts deconstruct and make salient the implications for identity and practice (Weeks, 1985).

This chapter begins by looking at views on sexual identity and practice from the perspectives of essentialism, sexology and early psychoanalysis. These ideas are then problematised in arguing that they have contributed to enduring assumptions concerning norms for sexual identity and practice that marginalise or make invisible some identities and practices, underestimate the various impacts of gender, ethnicity, heterosexism, social class and disability, and render some identities as deviant. This provides a context for social constructionist responses wherein firmer linkages are made between sexual identity and social, cultural, political and historical factors. The relationship between gender and sexuality is then explored before moving on to reviewing notions of compulsory sexual identity and practice that are said to result from entrenched and powerful ideas about permissible identity and practice. Discussion of critical thinking on female heterosexuality and homosexuality brings the effects of constraints on authentic expressions of sexual identity into sharp relief. Up to this point the chapter deploys theories and research evidence that reside more or less in the domain of the micro and the point at which lives interconnect with the structural and macro mediators of identity. The latter part of the chapter moves on from these micro and middle ground ideas to consider the macro workings of power, and focuses in particular on the work of Foucault and the mass regulation of identities and practices. Critiques on Foucauldian thought are summarised in brief before concluding the chapter with a brief consideration of current policy initiatives.

Essentialism and sexology

Essentialist perspectives on sexuality have a long history. Sexual identity as synonymous with biological pre-determinants was borne out of the post-enlightenment period and the concomitant primacy of scientific and medical thinking to define sexual normality and its corollary, sexual deviance (Segal, 1994). Sexual behaviour and identity were explained on the basis of fixed and inherent, hormonally and genetically induced drives that predicated 'normal' and 'natural' expressions of sexual identity for female and male behaviour. In essence, to ensure the survival of the human species, the genetic predisposition of males 'programmed' them to select young fecund females who were in turn programmed with desires to procreate with older males who could provide guarantees of security and protection. Within this construction men are the active sex-seeking agents, that is, the *givers* of sex, whereas women are the passive recipients (or *receivers*) of men's 'natural' biological urges. This established views that have had enduring influence throughout twentieth century western theorising on sexuality (Harding, 1998).

These ideas were afforded greater potency by developing within a framework of Christian thought that gave (and still gives) primacy to marriage and reproduction, and rendered non-marital sex as sinful or unnatural (Fulcher and Scott, 1999). Hence the negative reactions to contraception and prostitution (see Smart, 1995) because they provide(d) mechanisms for sexual expression and behaviour outside marriage and without the desire for procreation.

Powerful secular medical and psychiatric discourses in the eighteenth and nineteenth century transformed religious convictions on sinful sexual activity to ones of perversion and abnormal pathology (Foucault, 1979). Furthermore, nineteenth century scientific discourse not only established heterosexuality as the accepted and natural form of sexual identity, it established male homosexuality as a deviant identity – a primary perversion said to result from abnormalities in biological functioning (Foucault, 1979).

By the end of the nineteenth century the foundations of the essentialist case were laid and they informed studies of sexual behaviour undertaken by so called sexology authors between the period 1890–1980 (Gagnon and Parker 1995). Early sexology, under the auspices of science and medicine, made claims to objectivity and impartiality that intended to make the study of sex respectable (Bland, 1998). Despite varied methodological approaches, sexologists since this time have been united in believing that 'sex' has a natural essence (driving force), and that it is 'discoverable' through the collection of empirical evidence. Jeffrey Weeks (1989) argues that most sexologists adopt a 'naturalistic' approach which aims to describe and classify sexual practices and preferences, that is, sexual forms as they exist in nature. From this, sexologists deduce that different biological functioning can explain, and hence be used to define female and male sexuality differently. For example, Havelock Ellis (1913) spoke of the powerful male sex drive, and women's pleasure was taken as derived from men; and the Kinsey reports (Kinsey et al, 1948, 1953) were consistent with medical discourse in focusing on the 'naturalness' (i.e. biological imperative) of 'sexual outlets'. Within this, men are depicted as experiencing uncontrollable urges that should not be repressed and women are seen in relation to men as passive, reactively gaining pleasure from satisfying men, and ultimately reproducing. It should be noted, however, that Kinsey was emphatic in avoiding judgmental distinctions between sexual 'normality' and 'abnormality'. His alleged sexual experiences with men perhaps go some way to explaining this.

While adopting different methodologies and explanations for the basis of sexual 'drives', Ellis and Kinsey are united in constructing sexuality as an internally induced and *essential* aspect of individuals; and the individual (not society) is the focus of research because the drive (whether biological or psychological) is accepted as embedded in the individual (Harding, 1998). These approaches are evident in more recent studies of sexuality such as Hite (1976, 1981, 1987), Hutt (1972), and Masters and Johnson (1966, 1970, 1975). Sheer Hite (1987) was critical of the previous stances on female sexuality but appeared still to be concerned with describing and categorising sexual behaviour (Thomson and Scott, 1990) rather than offering explanations for diversity or changes in attitudes to sexuality. In this way Hite's work reflects the 'sex as nature' approach of sexology researchers entrenched in the essentialist perspective (Segal, 1994).

It is important to note that essentialist explanations for sexuality are used to support different political and ideological opinions. As Weeks (1995) observes, essentialist perspectives unite both the controllers and liberators of sexuality: the moral right justify the primacy of heterosexual procreative sexuality on the basis of the biological 'naturalness' of heterosexual identity and practice; and liberal (and some gay and feminist) thought argues that by the same token, if sexuality is natural, then one is born homosexual and does not become gay through choice, pathological deviation or poor psychological maturation.

Psychoanalysis and the sexual

Psychoanalysis, as the invention of Sigmund Freud, developed at the dawn of the twentieth century, and reflected the interests of sexologists in seeking explanations for the origins or 'cause' of the sexual impulse. Freud (1953) accepted biology as having some role but also explored the previously unacknowledged role of the unconscious mind in expressions of sexual desire.

Freud made similar claims to sexologists in declaring himself an objective and scientific observer of the 'sexual'. Based on clinical practice involving relatively few 'patients', he theorised extensively on the saliency of the psyche on sexual drives. Freud maintained the tradition set by his sexological counterparts by theorising female sexuality as different to male sexuality. He argued that sexuality originates in infants and 'normal' sexual instincts evolve in the process of development of mental and physical functioning. Freud referred to homosexuals as a 'third sex', 'perverse' people and 'inverts' who, he alleged, break the distinction between the sexes because their 'sexual life *deviates* in the most striking way from the *usual* picture of the *average*' by choosing people of the same sex as the 'object choice' (Freud in Saraga 1998: 146; my emphasis). The possibility of procreation provides another marker to distinguish normal from abnormal sexuality. Freud's use of language distinguishes homosexuality from the 'norm' (of the usual, the average) and undermines his claim (Freud, 1953) that homosexuals should be seen on an equal footing to heterosexuals.

Freudian psychoanalytic theorizing has been influential in psychiatry but his ideas on sexuality have been criticised by those who question the validity of the empirical basis for his theoretical claims and the tendency to reinforce essentialist constructs of women as the weaker sex. This said, psychoanalytic theories on sexuality were reasserted in the 1970s with the work of Jacques Lacan and Juliet Mitchell. I will return to their ideas later.

Deconstructing sexology and essentialism

As sexology and psychoanalysis developed, so did feminism. Since the early twentieth century, feminists have questioned essentialist constructs of female sexuality (Segal, 1994). Margaret Jackson (1994) argues that the emphasis on heterosexual identity and expression as both natural and fulfilling, with penetration defined as the essential sexual act, subordinates the position of women to the necessity of male penetration and leaves the power of men over women unrecognised in sexological research and Freudian psychoanalysis. For this reason, Jackson, together with other feminists such as Vance (1984), Harding (1998) and Segal (1994, 1999), insist that sexuality has to be seen through the lens of gender. The patriarchal nature of research on sex and sexual identity undermines its claims in failing to recognise the different discourses that frame women and men's sexuality, and in obfuscating the inequalities in power between the sexes. In a similar vein, the objectivity and lack of bias claimed through allegiance to scientific methods is questioned by feminists (e.g. Smith 1988, Stanley and Wise 1993, Ramazanoglu, 1992) who stress the importance of problematising positivistic methodology in terms of what researchers and research tools do or do not see. The emphasis in sexology and psychoanalysis on white populations and the heteropolarity in essentialist accounts are notable examples of this methodological and ideological failure to see the spectrum and complexity of sexual identity and behaviour. Similarly, homosexuality is either made invisible or rendered abnormal by positioning it as a deviation from the norm of heterosexual procreative identity and practice (Watney, 1987; Jackson, 1999).

These absences in representation are arguably not accidental. Thomson and Scott (1990), and Weeks (1985), note that studies of sexual behaviour provide access to current forms of knowledge and ideologies which exist (or existed) in particular cultures and historical epochs. We have seen that the biological reductionism embraced by early sexology created a system of bipolar opposites to explain sexual identity: the male as aggressive, forceful and 'active'; the female fragile, responsive and 'passive', with no desire in her own right (Fine, 1988). Each of these is then understood in relation to a second dyadic of heterosexual/homosexual subjectivity (Rubin, 1999). In Victorian England these biological metaphors were useful to endorsing calls for social reforms (Griffin, 1993) to prevent poverty, violence, crime and disease that were linked to non-procreative activities and sinful 'unnatural pleasures', and masturbatory 'self-pollution' (Segal, 1999: 192).

Stuart Hall (1997) positions these ideologies in relation to the hegemony of the white race (and concern to control the sexual behaviours of white men) that was reinforced against a backdrop of sexualised racist metaphors for Asian and African people. 'Black' bodies were coded as corruptive, promiscuous and animalistic, at the mercy of uncontrollable raw sexual energy (Segal, 1990). Negative and punitive discourses fuelled the Darwinian eugenics movement and remain evident in the racist 'othering' practices of sexual purist agendas (Gilroy, 1999). For example, Saraga (1998) points to studies by Dollard (1949), Marshall (1996) and Frankenberg (1993) that evidence sexuality as gendered and racialized and which places black people in the category of the deviant or sexual other. Disclosures from white people illustrate perceptions of black men and women as naturally and pathologically more sexually voracious and uncontrolled than white people (a perception Dollard argues is fuelled by myths of larger genitalia among black men). This legitimises ideas of black men as dangerous to white women, of black women as sources of illicit sex for white men, and of sexual relationships that cross racial boundaries as degrading and unacceptable. By voluntary association with black men, white women automatically default to the category of deviancy, inadequacy or perversion (Saraga, 1998). Underpinning these ideas is the essentialist notion that both race and sexuality are premised on biology. Such views become hegemonic because they are reinforced both by the institutionalised ideology of the day and by lay perceptions in providing explanations for subjective feelings and prejudices by giving them a clear and unavoidable cause.

This hierarchical ordering of gendered and racialised men and women is not separable from norms for reproduction and the family (Thomson and Scott, 1991). This has consequences for all unmarried mothers (Hudson and Ineichson, 1991) but black young mothers in particular regarding their 'fitness' as parents. Ann Phoenix (1991) highlights current UK political rhetoric that scapegoats black single mothers with a concomitant string of negative associations seen as arising out of cultural predisposition to early sexual behaviour, single parenthood and welfare dependency.

In sum, despite a questioning of the essentialist view, norms for sexuality based on a biological or psychological pre-given have prevailed and continue to inform constructions of sexuality and its intersections with gender, social class, race and ethnicity (see also Davis, 1982 and Mac an Ghaill, 1996). Disability (see Thomas, 1999) and age (Clark and Hirst, 1996) are also used to construct notions of 'normal' sexuality, with the physically and mentally able, and the youthful vigorous body privileged at the expense of the disabled or infirm body.

None of the views critiqued so far are based on statements of fact. Rather, they are constructions emanating from a particular set of assumptions. Another feature of essentialist writing is that it often lacks a definition of sexuality. McFadden (1995: 2) cites Padgug's (1979) observation of sexuality presented as obvious and as '...a thing, a universal given, an essence – implicitly understood, assumed by all, not requiring definition'. This reinforces the accusation that proponents of this view do not question the nature of their assumptions and the failure to problematise this lack of definition derives from failing to question heterosexual ideology and the biological origins of identity and practice. It also leads to a failure to acknowledge the diversities of sexual expression and a reductionist approach to the varying impacts of gender, culture, age, disability, ethnicity and social class (McFadden, 1995).

It is timely, therefore, before discussing social constructionist perspectives, to offer a definition of sexuality. This definition acknowledges a plurality of influences and embraces the views of proponents adopting different approaches to explaining the social construction of sexuality: Sexuality encompasses psychological, biological, socio-cultural, political, historical and moral issues. It is unfixed and dynamic in the ways it expresses sexual identity. There is a mutable relationship between sexual behaviour and identity. Bodily experiences are given meaning by their situation within social relationships, ideas and values. Sexual activity with, and attraction to, the same or opposite sex does not dictate a homosexual or heterosexual identity, and neither should it be reductively represented as such.

Social constructionist responses to essentialism

Before elaboration of social constructionist ideas it is important to appreciate that they have a dual purpose. First, to reiterate a previous point, essentialist explanations for sexuality and sexual identity are questioned and indeed regarded as social constructions. Second, sexuality is itself taken as socially constructed. Sexuality and sexual identity are not seen as inevitable and unchanging, or entirely premised on sexual behaviour, but as the outcome of various social, cultural, political and economic phenomena and viewpoints. So, the aim is not to categorise behaviours, but to enquire about the meanings and attitudes that construct sexuality and the effects of these on the ways in which individuals experience their lives and construct their identities (Weeks, 1995).

Sociology's interest in the social construction of sexuality did not develop until the 1960s and attention focused on theorizing rather empirical investigation. Nickie Charles (2002) comments this may be due to a reluctance to sanction socially oriented research. She cites the Mass Observation survey of 1949 that looked at the meanings and significance of sex but was not published until 1995 (Stanley, 1995) and the withdrawal of funding by the then Conservative government for the national survey of sexual attitudes and lifestyles. Subsequent funding by the Wellcome Trust brought the latter to fruition (see Wellings et al, 1994). The reticence by the state to support research on sexuality says as much about its social research priorities as the ideological prerogatives which underpin the decision making process – attending to epistemological gaps in knowledge might at the same time problematise the central tenets of rhetoric and policy that promotes the hegemony of heterosexuality, marriage and the traditional nuclear family. The occurrence of HIV and AIDS provided a justification to widen empirical understanding of sexuality, in all its forms, and in relation to the specific mores of contemporary historical and socio-cultural contexts. But, how far these data will succeed in changing the *status quo* that privileges heterosexuality remains to be seen.

Critics of the essentialist and sexological view adopt different theoretical approaches. As Carol Vance asserts, social constructionism is not a unitary and singular approach, constructionists have '...arguments with each other, as well as with essentialists' (Vance, 1989:19). Middle ground constructionist theory accepts a biological basis to the sexual impulse but sees the expression of this impulse as contingent on society's constructions of sexual identity, behaviours and choices. Purist social constructionist theory, like that developed by Foucault, regards the sexual impulse itself as socially constructed; Weeks positions himself within the Foucauldian tradition but argues we should not underestimate the role of the psyche in expressions of sexuality and choice (1995).

The interactionist work associated with Ken Plummer (1975, 1995) and Gagnon and Simon (1973) situates the social construction of sexuality at the level of individual social actors. Sexuality is constructed through the learning of sexual roles and identities (Plummer) and in the social, political and cultural 'scripts' that mediate ideological constructs for sexual and gender identity (Gagnon and Simon). In essence, the argument is that, our sexuality follows from socialisation processes that give us a language and norms for sexual identity and behaviour. How we locate ourselves in these scripts varies and has implications for our resultant subjectivity. Sexual subjectivity builds on the foundations of gender socialisation (established at

71

an earlier age, and as discussed in the previous chapter) so that girls and boys follow gender and hetero specific scripts that hold different implications for females and males (Jackson and Scott, 1996). The power of essentialist ideas is evident here in that 'acceptable' female sexual behaviour is discursively predicated on passivity and receptivity while the male norm is assumed as active and aggressive. As Holland et al (1996) suggest sexual reputations are also constituted through these normative constructs for femininity and masculinity so that adolescent girls learn of the need to conceal sexual activity if they are to safeguard reputations and boys learn of the pressures to demonstrate sexual achievements.

Staying at the level of the individual but positioned within the Freudian psychoanalytic tradition, Jacques Lacan (1977) looks at how the subject is positioned by the linguistic order (Bristow, 1997) and Juliet Mitchell resurrected Freudian psychoanalysis with the theme of gender difference and more explicit links between the psyche and the social. Stepping beyond the individual, social constructionists like Foucault and Jeffrey Weeks look for explanations in the processes of history, wider society and discourse.

Foucault's and Week's views span continents and centuries and provides sharp contrasts with Plummer's micro perspective. The emphasis on language and scripts in Lacan's psychoanalytic perspective has some similarities with Foucault's and Weeks' emphasis on discourse; and Mitchell draws on Foucault's notion of power but points to the absence of a gendered sense of power in Foucault's work. Despite the differences and convergences, these approaches ultimately agree in their rejection of the autonomous 'naturalness' of the sexual and acknowledge (to different degrees) the social, linguistic, historical and political sources of sexual definition (Bristow, 1997). As Rubin notes, once sex is '…understood in terms of social analysis and historical understanding, a more realistic politics of sex becomes possible' (Rubin, 1999: 150).

However, as Parker et al (1999) point out, because sources of sexual definition and regulation emerge from both informal micro cultures and macro sociocultural institutions and there is interplay between the micro and the macro, analysis at both levels is essential for a comprehensive account of sexual culture and identity. Interactionists focus on the micro but tend to negate the impact of structure and processes of power and, as we shall see later in the chapter, ideas that focus on the macro and power (e.g. Foucault) tend to ignore the impact of informal cultures and everyday worlds. I will now explore ideas concerned with factors that operate in and between the individual level (informal cultures or 'private' micro worlds) and macro level. These ideas are sometimes referred to as middle ground constructionist theory and some intersect with those in the previous chapter on theorising gender.

Sexuality and gender

While gender is often taken as a prime site for the expression of sexuality, there is no consensus on theorising the relationship between them but it is usual to conceptualise sexuality as distinct from but related to gender (Jackson, 1998). This prevents over-deterministic theorising that has potential to subsume gender under sexuality and risk universalising female and male subjectivity.

Drawing on the work of Foucault, Wendy Hollway (1998) argues that sexual and gender roles and behaviour derive, in part, from the ways we position ourselves within particular discourses related to sex. She identifies three main discourses that have a profound impact on perceptions of gender differences, power relations and the production of subjectivity. First, the 'male sexual' discourse assumes that men have a 'natural' need for regular sexual gratification and it is women's role to satisfy this need. Second, the 'have/hold' or 'romantic' discourse assumes that females aim to secure a male partner for protection and procreation. And, third, the 'permissive' discourse values sex and pleasure for its own sake; it can be experienced by either sex with no obligation from either party to enter into any form of commitment.

While the 'male sexual' and 'have/hold' discourses enhance perceptions of gender differences and naturalistic notions of males and females, the 'permissive' discourse positions men naturally (as active) and the female unnaturally (in refuting her naturally passive role). While the 'permissive' discourse is available to women, its use is contingent on other scripts for gender and sexual behaviour particularly those based on women protecting their reputation. Hollway suggests that individuals draw on one or more of the discourses (often simultaneously) to describe or explain their actions, and readily switch between discourses if circumstances change. Therefore, context is significant to deciding where one gets located or locates oneself within one or more of the discourses. Among other constraining factors, this depends on the aspect of sexual and/or gender identity that the individual actor is seeking to 'perform' (Butler, 1990), that is, it depends on who it is being displayed to. This reinforces notions of social identity as embedded in social practices.

Not all or the same scripts are available to each individual. Cultural inscriptions of gender and hetero/homosexuality have different signifiers for the variation in scripts available to women and men, and heterosexuals, lesbians and gays. For example, Hirst (2001) found that young women and men routinely used different ascriptions of gender in making predictions for the nature of their future identities: young men and women both wanted independence, but females, unlike male peers, hoped for security, romance and parenthood in future relationships. Also, for females, impending

73

domestic responsibilities were seen as axiomatic to future subjectivities, whilst male participants did not include domestic roles in their constructions of identity.

The suggestion is not that individuals are positioned mechanistically by traditional scripts for gender (Measor et al, 2000) or sexuality, because material factors and biographical traditions place additional and different constraints on an individual's choices (Simon, 1996; Evans, 1993). Not withstanding these social constraints, Hirst's (2001) observation that female respondents selected different culturally available themes and constructs to male contemporaries in efforts to legitimise their experience and aspirations raises the issue of whether gender is something that we 'have' or 'are', or whether it is something that we 'do'. Adopting the view that gender is socially constructed (and not based purely on biological differences between sexes), theorists (notably Davies, 1997; Connell, 1996, 1987; Butler, 1990; and Morgan, 1992) contend, albeit in different analytic modes, that gender does not provide a template for how to 'be'. Individuals perform or 'do' gender by employing symbolising discourses and actions in making claims to femininity or masculinity (Butler (1990) suggests that the performance of gender is also reiterative in that the forms displayed are not innate or original but are copies of copies available from a plurality of scripts and discourses emanating from education, culture, literature, medicine, media etc.).

These authors see gender in relation to a system that delineates the masculine from the feminine, a 'two-sex model' (Davies, 1997: 11) of binary opposites that define males and females differently as opposite and distinct (Butler, 1990). The concept of gender is inherently relational, as Connell argues that masculinity '...does not exist except in contrast with "femininity"' (1996: 68). Hence one of the ways in which female participants in Hirst's study articulated their current and future identity was via constructs of gender that differentiated them from male counterparts. Relatedly, Hirst (2001) and Hirst and Selmes (1996) comment that school sex education positions male and female behaviour and roles differently and in relation to each other.

The observation that women and men display different forms of the self in different contexts and under different pressures can appear as contradictions. But these performative selections and shifts in identity are more appropriately seen as what Morgan refers to as a 'Goffmanesque presentation of self' (1992: 47) wherein individuals pick and choose from the ascriptions available to them. But, as several respondents in Hirst's study confide, experiencing oneself in contradictory ways can be problematic (Hollway, 1998). Weeks (1985) reminds us that psychoanalytic theory recognises the impact of the subconscious and experiences that are more routinely hidden from view. As Hollway (1998) suggests, discourses stemming from the historical, cultural and biographical, can have an impact at an emotional and psychological level that influence actions more than rational choices or conscious knowledge of the choices available (Morgan, 1992). Perhaps it is these psycho-emotional elements which were surfacing when female respondents reticently anticipated slipping into more traditional gendered roles as in the example above. (There are other instances in the data (Hirst, 2001) where females seemed happier to take on the feminine mantle of 'caring' and the 'emotion work' (Hochschild, 1983) involved in facilitating relationships with male peers. Jennifer Mason (1996) suggests that acting in the feminine role can be enjoyable for women as it endorses their subjectivity and a sense of 'safe' femininity.) Hirst comments that female respondents were unhappy with this recognition of gendered subjectivities since it symbolised the circle of reproduction that was felt to undermine previous claims to resistance.

But there are also problems for males. Hirst (2001) documents that while some male interviewees were uncomfortable in their recognition of the power and privilege bestowed by patriarchal socialisation processes (Arnot, 1984), they were unable (or unwilling) to discuss the implications for their masculinised identity and practices. Nancy Chodorow (1994) offers insight here. She argues that while women face conflicts concerning feminine identity and the choices created by being socialised in the context of male power, at least there exists a clarity regarding the constructs and constraints they are operating within. 'Femininity' is ascribed, whereas 'masculinity' has to be achieved, so on a day-to-day basis, there is a less firm sense of what it is that males want to be or how to act. This is increasingly so in an age which routinely points to men as 'possessing a problematic masculinity' (Giddens, 1994: 247). In practice, Chodorow suggests this manifests in males fearing anything feminine, for this is the point at which male subjectivity is defined, that is, in the bipolar and oppositional relationship to feminine identity and practice. This might account for the observation in Hirst's (2001) data that males were more eager to state their actions than explain them. Where girls' experiences were retold as stories, boys' talk on sex was not in narrative form and rarely connected to an envisaged future. To do this would mean entering the realm of constructs of gendered identity, intimacy and emotionality which females so readily engaged with. In the context of research interviews, males shied away from this because they were unequipped to justify their own actions without responding to the version that young women disclosed from the female perspective. This non-contributory stance, that gives little away, is a means by which young men do not threaten their ontological security, but neither do they actively defend it. This might stem as much from the fear of femininity (Chodorow, 1994) as insecurity regarding what it is they are trying to defend. In contrast to females, males are not only unconfident of what to speak of, but how to speak it. Thompson (1989) argues that female teenagers' narratives of self are more fluent than males because they have been rehearsed in numerous conversations in subcultures and as part of the female socialisation process. Hirst's findings also suggest that feminist thinking has permeated young women's discourse and this facilitates an articulation of the female standpoint. An equivalent has not been provided for young men. This has implications for sexual health promotion if men are to be supported in expressing themselves more openly with the longer-term goal of assisting more egalitarian and non-sexist relations. This requires a more radical sex education agenda for work with boys which has been recognised in the DoH (2001) 'National Strategy for Sexual Health and HIV.'

In conclusion, over-deterministic readings of identity are avoided by acknowledging the multiplicity of discourses and constructs that position females and males in manifold ways, together with creating differences between groups of the same sex. Ethnicity, social class, family biography and other social divisions also create different opportunities for constructions of identity. Within this there are different degrees of passivity and resistance to normative constructs of gender and sexuality that have varying implications for individual agency and subjectivity.

Compulsory sexual identity and practice

Another aspect salient to sexuality and expressions of sexual identity is that differences in relation to gender, age and ethnicity have to be seen in relation to a matrix of heterosexuality and the characteristics of heterosexual desire which provide scripts for appropriate sexual practices (Butler, 1990; Rubin 1989). Numerous studies (Hirst, 2001; Hirst and Selmes, 1996; Wight, 1996; Whately, 1992; Ward and McLean Taylor, 1994; Trenchard and Warren, 1984, and Thomson and Scott, 1991) evidence knowledge of a dominant heterosexual ideology that fashions learning about sexuality in both formal and informal settings and in turn influences feelings about permissible sexual identity and practices. Sexual discourses are scripted for both sexes in exclusively heterosexual terms so that attraction to the opposite sex is assumed and reinforced, whereas attraction to the same sex rarely features in either discourse or representations. This creates a hierarchy of identities scaffolded in place by the power of heteropolar ideology.

In seeking to understand the mechanisms by which these regulative powers operate Gayle Rubin (1989) in *Thinking Sex* arranges beliefs about 'good' and 'bad' sexuality into a diagram that identifies degrees of social acceptability and unacceptability among a range of social and sexual institutions and practices (see Rubin, 1989: 281). 'Good', normal, natural (i.e. 'desirable') sexuality is at the top of the hierarchy and includes (among several typifications) sex between heterosexuals, in couples, those who are married and have sex in private, and for a procreative purpose. Rubin refers to this as the 'inner charmed circle' of identity and practice. These practices are reinforced or 'blessed' by professional discourses and institutionalised ideologies in numerous forms (to be discussed below). By contrast, at the lower end of the hierarchy, or in the 'outer limits' of the circle, is bad, abnormal, 'damned' sexuality or those practices involving the unwed, non-monogamy, homosexuals, bisexuals, and other non-legitimised identities and practices.

Hirst (2001) applies Rubin's model to data on young people's experience of sex education and sexual health provision. A comparison of teenagers' sexual discourses and practices with the discourses and representations used by sexual health professionals (the official view) reveals significant anomalies between the two. The 'official view' codes sexual identity as white, heterosexual, married, and monogamous. Sexuality is reduced to sexual practice and concerned with vaginal penetration for the purposes of procreation. The context is the home and privacy, and in the absence of alcohol. This is the ideal or acceptable identity and practice. Teenagers' sexual identity and practices meet few of these ascriptions for 'good' identity and practice and hence violate the normative expectations of the proscribed model for sexual conduct. This relegates young people's identity and practice to the 'outer' or non-sanctioned realm of the 'charmed circle'. The significance for identity is not lost on young people, particularly females:

> ...if you're *always* doing the exact opposite to what they're [teachers] telling us is right you're bound to feel bad (Maisie)
> ...if sex is meant to be being married or being in love, and you aren't any of those things then what are you? Bad, bad, bad, wrong, wrong, wrong (Millie).

Compulsory female heterosexuality

While there are implications for the sense of self of anyone who does not conform to the norms for sexual identity and practice, the notion of an institutionalised heterosexuality that renders heterosexuality particularly compulsory for women has fuelled debate among feminists since the 1970s. In 1980, drawing on the work of Kathleen Gough (1975) and Catharine Mackinnon (1979), Adrienne Rich (1998) analysed the invisibility of lesbian identity by questioning the 'naturalness' of women's attraction to men. She argues that women are not born heterosexual but coerced into a heterosexual identity by various discourses, representations and dogmas that idealise heterosexual romance and marriage and stigmatise non-heterosexual identity. In addition, because men hold the most economic and political power, women are forced into heterosexual relations by their material dependence on men. Rich stresses the threat of emotional and physical violence as a means of controlling women's behaviour, but, more controversially, Susan Brownmiller (1986) argues rape is the ultimate heterosexual sanction that maintains the hegemony of male power over women. All in all, there is no political, emotional or economic incentive to step outside the boundaries of heterosexuality, and society punishes those who make the 'wrong' choices. Hence, Rich problematises the idea of a biological divide between heterosexual and lesbian women in arguing that women's experience is structured by heterosexual ideology and economic dependence but where women position their sexual identity depends on their location on what she terms a 'lesbian continuum'. The 'lesbian continuum' includes not just sexual experience with another women but a range of 'women-identified experience' (1998: 135) that includes celebrating womanhood, giving practical and political support, resistance to male power and the rejection of a heterosexual way of life. Rich believes that if we entertain the possibility that all women '...exist on a lesbian continuum, we can see ourselves as moving in and out of this continuum, whether we identify ourselves as lesbian or not' (1998: 136).

Heterosexuality, therefore, becomes less compulsory when it is not constrained by economic security based on relationships with men, thus the potential for lesbian existence is intimately connected both to the desire for sexual experience with women and economic autonomy. It follows then, that in the second millennium as women achieve greater independence from men and same-sex relationships become more acceptable, then heterosexuality will shed its compulsions and free more women to live out the sexual identity of their choosing.

Reconfiguring homosexuality

Just as lesbianism has been obfuscated or pathologized as abnormal in essentialist accounts, representations of male homosexuality have been underscored by similarly negative discourses and constructions that were premised on deficit models of identity. Theoretical challenges came in the 1960s and 1970s with Mary McIntosh's (1968) highly influential paper on the 'The Homosexual Role' and the foundations this provided for subsequent gay and lesbian studies and activism. In looking back through history and comparing different cultures McIntosh observed two types of homosexuality, the 'institutionalised homosexual role' and the liaisons between males who are otherwise heterosexual. She asked whether the two patterns could be understood as expressions of the same biological drives because they seemed to hold different social meanings – the first constructs homosexuality as a type of person, the second involves homosexual behaviour but not homosexual identity. McIntosh asserted that, in modern societies (from the beginning of the eighteenth century) the homosexual facilitates a specific social role. While homosexuality is acknowledged as widespread it is also reinforced as a social danger and debates that perpetuate the 'cause' of homosexuality serve to reinforce the stigmatising and much publicised distinction between permissible and impermissible behaviour. She argues that researching the aetiology of homosexuality is meaningless in itself but hugely significant in creating and maintaining the stigmatised category that functions as a mechanism to separate the pure from the impure. A homosexual identity, therefore, is mediated not solely through same sex activity *per se* but through an individual's willingness or ability to deal with being labelled as homosexual. Whether one is 'out' as a homosexual or in the 'closet' (maintaining heterosexual identity but with desire and/or sexual involvement with the same sex) depends not so much on biological drives but on the individual, social and political circumstances that will or will not support the chosen identity. Mcintosh's work also challenges the bifurcated construct of homosexuality and heterosexuality as oppositional and writings since this time develop this (see Weeks, 1989; Vance, 1989) in pointing to convergences that unite sexual identities because of ubiquitous processes of power that regulate desires, attitudes, practices and subjectivities.

In a similar vein to the authors above, Michel Foucault analysed sexuality and the privileging of heterosexuality in relation to the working of power and innovated constructionist perspectives in radical ways. However, while his work attracted great interest it also aroused controversy, particularly among proponents of a feminist analysis of sexuality because Foucault dedicates little time to gendered power relations and to the manifestations of power imbalances in the private and micro sphere. Rather, he focuses on the broader machinations of power and the mass control of populations through discourses that permeate the social body as a whole. In this way Foucault bypasses the impact of power on individual experience. This moves the discussion on from middle ground to macro theory.

Foucault and neo-Foucauldian theorising

Foucault (1979) rejected biological essentialism in proposing that there is no innate form of sexuality to be expressed, repressed or emancipated. Rather, there are '...ideas about sexuality which are put into words – discourses' (Harding, 1998: 18). Discourses are multiple and complex, and produced by 'a whole series of mechanisms operating in different institutions' and over different historical epochs (Foucault, 1979: 33). While individuals are positioned variably in relation to these discourses, and there are choices involved (Weeks, 1985), some discourses hold greater power. For instance, Weeks (1989) echoing Foucault (1979), suggests that discourses in the media, medicine and education have been particular instrumental in 'normalising' some identities and practices and 'abnormalising' others. So, procreative, heterosexual sexual practice within the confines of marriage is legitimated by some dominant discourses, whereas sexual behaviour between other groups such as teenagers and gay people is condemned (Wilton, 1997).

The mass regulation of sexuality, as one of the processes of 'biopower' (Foucault, 1979), involves both explicit and implicit mechanisms of control. We see explicit forms of regulation in laws that sanction marriage between heterosexuals but not homosexuals; in tax reductions, and residency, pension and tenancy privileges for married but not unmarried couples; in Section 28 (repealed 2003) of the Local Government Act 1988 (DES, 1988) that forbade 'the promotion of homosexuality as a pretended family relationship'; and until 2002, unequal ages of consent for heterosexuals and homosexuals. Medicine (particularly psychiatry) has viewed and represented homosexuality as an abnormal deviation from the norm (Foucault, 1973) until very recently. The workplace is on one hand asexualised but on the other inherently heterosexist and patriarchal in its policies and procedures (Hearn and Parkin, 1987). Educational doctrine and schooling promotes heterosexuality and renders gay and lesbian identity invisible in explicit ways such as in the teaching of heterosexist sex education, and in implicit ways such as the non-representation of gay authors and political and historical role models. Discourse, imagery and literature virtually ignores disabled people and older adults (Clark and Hirst 1996) and disabled gay men and lesbians are invisible in sexual health promotion and literature (Shakespeare et al, 1996).

On the other hand, as Wilton (2000) observes, gay men are referenced with disproportionate frequency in HIV/AIDS literature where the context of illness enhances perceptions of homosexuality as inherently unhealthy. Similarly, teenage sexuality rarely appears outside the confines of popular polemic on sexual risk taking or government strategies to reduce rates of pregnancy or sexually transmitted infections (see for example SEU, 1999). While there is a real need to address the problems posed by early pregnancy and STIs (including HIV) for teenagers and the disproportionate rates of HIV among gay men, the lack of representation in other mainstream discourses serves to reinforce the dominant ideology that constructs these identities as deviant.

While discourse, policy and representations are crucial to maintaining norms for identity and practice and influencing subjective notions of identity, Foucault argues that norms become internalised through 'capillary action' (Grbich, 1999: 39) which manifests in individuals self-regulating themselves and others. Those who do not match the norms also self-regulate by concealing or fabricating authentic identities and behaviours and discourses. This process of self-regulation and/or fabrication can be analysed as a regulative agent in maintaining the *status quo* of the normative discourse. Because actual behaviours and discourses are concealed, they are not acknowledged in official/ public discourses, so the dominant framework is not challenged and hence has enhanced potential for reproduction. Therefore, the role of the state in reinforcing normative ideology becomes more comprehensive and complex with its multiple sites and mechanisms of power that operationalise the '...biopolitics of the population' (Foucault, 1979: 139).

The methods and discourses used in the teaching of sex education and in sexual health clinics (see Hirst, 2001; Hirst and Selmes, 1996) can be used to illustrate Foucault's analysis (1979, 1980) of power, knowledge and discourse. The power of language is particularly significant in these contexts. The knowledge and resources that young people have access to can be limited by the language and wider discourse of the cultural context in which sex education and communication on sexual issues occurs (Wilton, 1997). This can constrain views of sex and sexuality to a particularly scientific and impersonal framework (Watney, 1991). Hirst (2001) found that technical and medical terms alienate teenagers because of stylistic inaccessibility and by emphasising the chasm between formal (that is, acceptable) language and that used informally between peers or sexual partners (Aggleton and Kapila, 1992). There is no evidence to suggest that young people use a formal discourse in their everyday lives, and whether this is due to unwillingness or inability is not the issue. Rather it is the *effect* of internalising a discourse that is not theirs that is significant. Discourses used by teachers and clinicians create definitions of 'normality' and deviance that contribute to 'bad' or 'good' norms for action and behaviour (Hirst, 2001). The social construction of sexuality by professionals, in this case, stands alongside essentialist constructions in replacing one reductionism with another. For those who are aware that they do not meet the criteria for 'normality' laid out in ideology and 'official' discourse, there is great potential for alienation and marginalisation (Wilton, 2000).

Reclaiming power

So far, I have presented only those aspects of Foucault's work that construct power in negative terms. But, because Foucault (1979) conceptualises power not as something that is possessed but exercised, there is the potential for production as well as reproduction. In his later work, Foucault (1987, 1988) acknowledges that micrological strategies of power (i.e. not the individual as possessed of power) can resist hegemonic and normalising discourse and counter the imposition of decreed identities. It is only in societies that adopt a repressive relationship between sex and power, Foucault (1979) argues, that emancipation from silence and/or condemnation is necessary. Under these conditions, merely speaking about sex can appear as deliberate defiance of the prevailing power. This is particularly relevant to analysing contemporary representations of sexual identity which appear as deliberately transgressive in naming and describing an alternative discourse and form of the sexual. For example, social movements such as the Gay Liberation, Feminism, and Black Activism have consciously challenged dominant morality and definitions of norms and conventions relating to sex, gender, and family relations (Clark and Hirst, 1996). Queer and black activism has reclaimed appropriations such as 'faggot', 'queer' and 'nigger' that have been used to denigrate the identity and adopted them as positive terms (Pini, 1997). In this way oppressed identities have begun to be legitimised (Foucault, 1988).

However it is relevant to note that the impact of any challenge to dominant discourses can have both positive and negative repercussions, as Harding argues that they may '… help to constitute and reinforce a boundary between public and private domains, even as they appear to erase it' (Harding, 1998: 19). Context is important here. The situational specificity of *where* one *speaks out* in opposition to the dominant position may influence the outcome. Take for example the experiences of teenagers in the domain of the classroom or home environment (Hirst, 2001). Counter discourses are rarely or never declared in these public realms for fear of reinforcing negative perceptions of youth and/or incurring punitive sanctions, such as restrictions on freedom.

Evaluating Foucault

Foucault's ideas have been influential in postmodern theorizing on sexuality, but, as mentioned above, there are ambiguities and omissions that have led to criticisms of his work. Foucault was preoccupied with the structural level and he did not satisfactorily explore the relationship between the macro and micro, or the effects of power imbalances in the microscopics of everyday life (Layder, 1994). This prevents the necessary nuanced appreciation of differences and inequalities between classes, ethnicities, genders and sexual orientations. Poster suggests that this is explained in part by Foucault's emphasis on discourse which leads him 'to a totalising view of the history of sexuality' (Poster, 1984: 136) that does not allow comprehension of sexuality in ways other than collectively. Foucault (1979) stresses that different social groups are constituted on the basis of discursive codes for ethnicity, culture, gender, sexual orientation and social class, but as other chapters in the book demonstrate, identities cannot be fully explained on the basis of discourse, other resources and factors come into play.

Regarding social class, Poster (1984) argues classes differ more than they are alike and their sexuality cannot be explained on the basis of one unifying discourse. Thus he calls for a more adequate theory of class sexuality. Foucault is also accused of inattentiveness to issues of racial difference because his discursive formations make it difficult to give priority to the influence of ethnicity, race and racism (Stoler, 1995). Similarly, feminist critiques of Foucault call for a more explicit appreciation of the influence of gender inequalities on identity. Foucault's work has contributed to understanding the social construction of female sexuality, and hence lent more fuel to the feminist project than that of essentialising constructs that render women passively and immutably repressed (Jackson and Scott, 1996). However, there is considerable scope for a more sophisticated reading of gendered power and its regulation of female sexuality, with a feminist critique now well established which debates the various interpretations of Foucault's reading of gender (see Ramazanoglu, 1993; McNay, 1992; O'Farrell, 1989; McHoul and Grace, 1995; Bordo, 1999). Furthermore, Penelope (1992) highlights Foucault's emphasis on male homosexuality and his omission of lesbian sexuality, which contributes to making lesbian identity and practice invisible.

Conclusion

This chapter has reviewed various contributions to essentialist and social constructionist thinking on sexuality. I have argued that recent theorising and empirical evidence on the social, cultural and political construction of meanings that define and regulate sexuality, attitudes and beliefs, are more persuasive in explaining the diversity and complexity of sexual subjectivities, practices and discourses, than that learnt from categorising sexual behaviour and preferences as in a majority of essentialist accounts. We have seen that representations of heterosexuality as 'natural' and 'normal' stem from the dynamics of power and institutionalised ideology.

Though academic thinking on sexuality has undoubtedly become more sophisticated in the last thirty years, and attitudes to sexual morality have become more liberal, it is arguable that these more enlightened, critical and reflexive views have not crossed over to the domain of UK government policy initiatives. Recent publications, such as the National Strategy for Sexual Health and HIV (DoH, 2001), adopt a reductionist position that emphasises sexual behaviour as both the primary code for sexual identity and mediator of ill health and moral hazards, such as early and lone parenthood. The Teenage Pregnancy Strategy (DoH, 1999) is ostensibly concerned with social justice and equal rights but the emphasis on reducing conceptions and increasing the rates of return of pregnant teenagers and parents to education, training and ultimately employment, suggests a financial not equality incentive (Bullen and Kenway, 2000) in that such outcomes would reduce dependency on state welfare. While those affected by early parenthood should be supported in actualizing their potential and human rights, such policies infer a lack of interest in wider understandings of the place of the sexual, power, pleasure, desire and situation in determining subjectivities, life chances and achievements. For example, the discourse of 'moral panic' that stigmatises teenage sex (Griffin, 1993) and constructs teenage mothers as deviant is as crucial to social exclusion as the fiscal hardships that can accompany early parenthood. State policy pays little heed to these considerations. Moreover, current policy confirms a lack of interest in those who are not heterosexual, pregnant or young but who may be equally 'at risk' from having their sexuality denied or illegitimated by the enduring preoccupation with maintaining the dominance of a 'natural' and 'normal' form of sexuality. The alienation and marginalisation that can result is rarely acknowledged beyond the orbit of those directly affected and hence it is left to minority group activists to continue to reassert the rights of those not privileged by heterosexist and patriarchal workings of power. This state of affairs is all too reminiscent of debates that should be seen as anachronisms in the contemporary age but still have saliency, and must, therefore, continue to be challenged if discrimination and vilification of identities on the basis of sexual behaviours is to be curtailed.

Bibliography

Aggleton, P. and Kapila, M. (1992) 'Young people, HIV/AIDS and the promotion of sexual health', *Health Promotion International*, 7, 1: 45–51.

Arnot, M. (1984) 'How shall we educate our sons?' in R Deem (ed.) *Co-education Reconsidered*. Milton Keynes: Open University Press.

Bland, L. (1998) 'Gender and sexual difference', in L. Bland and L. Doan (eds.) *Sexology Uncensored*. Cambridge: Polity Press.

Bordo, S. (1999) 'Feminism, Foucault and the Politics of the Body' in J Price and M. Shildrick (eds.) *Feminist Theory And The Body*. Edinburgh: Edinburgh University Press.

Brownmiller, S. (1986) *Against our will: men, women and rape*. Harmondsworth: Penguin.

Bullen, E. and Kenway, J. (2000) 'New Labour, Social Exclusion and Educational Risk Management: the case of "gymslip mums"', *British Educational Research Journal*, 26, 4: 441–456.

Butler, J. (1990) *Gender Trouble: Feminism and the Subversion of Identity*. London: Routledge.

Charles, N. (2002) *Gender in Modern Britain*. Oxford: Oxford University Press.

Chodorow, N. (1994) 'Gender, Relation and Difference in Psychoanalytic Perspective' in *The Polity Reader in Gender Studies*. Oxford: Polity Press in association with Blackwell Publishers.

Clark, D. and Hirst, J. (1996) 'The Conundrum of Sex and Death: Some Issues in Health Care Practice' in J Weeks and J Holland J (eds.) *Sexual Cultures: Communities, Values and Intimacy*. London: Macmillan.

Connell, R. W. (1996) *Masculinities*. Cambridge: Polity Press.

Davies, B. (1997) 'Constructing and deconstructing masculinities through critical literacy', *Gender and Education*, Vol. 9, no. 1: 69–87.

Davis, A. (1982) *Women, Race and Class*. London: The Women's Press.

DES – Department of Education and Science (1988b) *Local Government Act 1988: Section 28*. Circular 88/90. London: HMSO.

DoH – Department of Health (2001) *The National Strategy for Sexual Health and HIV*. London: HMSO.

DoH (2001) *Teenage Pregnancy Strategy*. http://www.cabinet office.gov.uk/seu/index/more.html.

Dollard, J. (1949) *Caste and Class in a Southern Town* (2nd ed.) New York: Harper and Brothers.

Ellis, H. (1913) *Studies in the Psychology of Sex Vols, 1–6*. Philadelphia: Davis.

Evans, D. (1993) Sexual Citizenship: The Material Construction of Sexualities. London: Routledge.

Fine, M. (1988) 'Sexuality, schooling and adolescent females: the missing discourse of desire', *Harvard Educational Review*, 58, 29.

Foucault, M. (1988) 'Technologies of the self' in L. H. Martin, H. Gutman and P. H. Hutton (eds.) *Technologies of the Self*. London: Tavistock.

Foucault, M. (1987) *The Use of Pleasure. The History of Sexuality Volume Two*. London: Penguin.

Foucault, M. (1980) *Power/Knowledge: Selected Interviews and Other Writings 1972–1977*. Edited by Colin Gordon. New York: Pantheon Books.

Foucault, M. (1979) *The History of Sexuality. Volume One: An Introduction*. London: Penguin.

Foucault, M. (1973) *The Birth of the Clinic*. London: Tavistock.

Frankenberg, R. (1993) *White Women, Race Matters*. London: Routledge.

Freud, S. (1953) *'Three essays on the theory of sexuality'*, *Standard Edition VII*, London: Hogarth Press.

Fulcher, J. and Scott, J. (1999) *Sociology*. Oxford: Oxford University Press.

Gagnon, J. H. and Parker, R. G. (1995) 'Conceiving Sexuality', in R. G. Parker and J. H. Gagnon (eds.) *Conceiving Sexuality: Approaches to Sex Research in a Postmodern World*. London: Routledge.

Gagnon, J. H. and Simon, W. (1973) *Sexual Conduct: The Social Sources of Human Sexuality*. London: Hutchinson.

Giddens, A. (1994) 'Men, Women and Romantic Love', in *The Polity Reader in Gender Studies*. Oxford: Polity Press in association with Blackwell Publishers.

Gilroy, P. (1999) 'Diaspora and the detours of identity' in K. Woodward (ed.) *Identity and Difference*. London: Sage/The Open University.

Gough K. (1975) cited in A. Rich (1998) 'Compulsory Heterosexuality and Lesbian Existence' in S. Jackson and S. Scott (1996) (eds.) *Feminism and Sexuality*. Edinburgh: Edinburgh University Press.

Gough, B. and McFadden, M. (2001) *Critical Social Psychology: An Introduction*. Basingstoke: Palgrave.

Grbich, C. (1999) *Qualitative Research in Health*. London: Sage.

Griffin, C. (1993) *Representations of Youth: the Study of Youth and Adolescence in Britain and America*. Cambridge: Polity Press.

Hall, S. (1997) 'The spectacle of the "Other" ' in S. Hall (ed.) *Representation: cultural representations and signifying practices*.

Harding, J. (1998) *Sex Acts. Practices of Femininity and Masculinity*. London: Sage.

Hearn, J. and Parkin, W. (1987) *'Sex at Work': The Power and Paradox of Organisation Sexuality*. Brighton: Wheatsheaf.

Hill, A. (2000) 'One girl in six hits puberty by age of eight', *The Observer*, 18 June: 1–2.

Hirst, J. (2001) 'Identity, Discourse and Practice: A Qualitative Case Study of Young People and their Sexuality'. Unpublished PhD thesis, Sheffield: Sheffield Hallam University.

Hirst, J. and Selmes, S. (1997) *How was it for you*? Sheffield: Health Research Institute, Sheffield Hallam University.

Hite, S. (1987) *Women and Love*. London: Penguin.

Hite, S. (1981) *The Hite Report on Male Sexuality*. New York: Knopf.

Hite, S. (1976) *The Hite Report*. New York: Macmillan.

Hochschild, A. (1983) *The Managed Heart: commercialization of human feeling*. Berkeley, CA: University of California Press.

Holland, J., Ramazanoglu, C., Sharpe, S. and Thomson (1996) 'Reputations: Journeying into Gendered Power Relations' in J. Weeks and J. Holland (eds.) *Sexual Cultures: Communities, Values and Intimacy*. London: Macmillan.

Hollway, W. (1998) 'Gender Difference And The Production of Subjectivity', in S. Jackson and S. Scott (eds.) *Feminism And Sexuality*. Edinburgh: Edinburgh University Press.

Hudson, F. and Ineichson, B. (1991) *Taking It Lying Down: Sexuality and Teenage Motherhood*. London: Macmillan.

Hutt, C. (1972) *Males and Females*. Harmondsworth: Penguin.

Jackson, M. (1994) *The Real Facts of Life: Feminism and the Politics of Sexuality c1850–1940*. London: Taylor & Francis.

Jackson, S. (1998) 'Theorising Gender and Sexuality' in S Jackson and J Jones (eds.) *Contemporary Feminist Theories*. Edinburgh: Edinburgh University Press.

Jackson, S. (1999) *Homosexuality in question*. London: Sage.

Jackson, S. (1982) *Children and Sexuality*. Oxford: Blackwell.

Jackson, S. and Scott, S. (1996) (eds.) *Feminism and Sexuality*. Edinburgh: Edinburgh University Press.

Kinsey, A., Pomeroy, W., Martin, C. and Gebhard, P. (1953) *Sexual Behaviour in the Human Male*. Philadelphia: Saunders.

Kinsey, A., Pomeroy, W., and Martin, C. (1948) *Sexual Behaviour in the Human Female*. Philadelphia: Saunders.

Lacan, J. (1977) *The Four Fundamental Concepts of Psychoanalysis*. London: Hogarth Press.

Layder, D. (1994) *Understanding Social Theory*. London: Sage.

Mac an Ghaill, M. (1996) 'Irish Masculinities and Sexualities in England' in L Adkins and V Merchant (eds.) *Sexualizing the Social: Power and the Organization of Sexuality*. Basingstoke: Macmillan.

Mackinnon, C. (1979) cited in A. Rich (1998) 'Compulsory Heterosexuality and Lesbian Existence' in S. Jackson and S. Scott (1996) (eds.) *Feminism and Sexuality*. Edinburgh: Edinburgh University Press.

Marshall, A. (1996) 'From sexual denigration to self-respect' in Jarrett-MacCauley, D.(ed.) *Reconstructing Womanhood, Reconstructing Feminism*. London: Routledge.

Mason, J. (1996) 'Gender, care and sensibility in family and kin relations', in J. Holland and L. Adkins (eds.) *Sex, Sensibility and the Gendered Body*. London: Macmillan.

Masters, W. and Johnson, V. (1975) *The Pleasure Bond*. Boston: Little Brown and Co.

Masters, W. and Johnson, V. (1970) *Human Sexual Inadequacy*. Boston: Little Brown and Co.

Masters, W. and Johnson, V. (1966) *Human Sexual Response*. Boston: Little Brown and Co.

McFadden, M. (1995) 'Female Sexuality in the Second Decade of Aids'. Queens University, Belfast: Unpublished PhD thesis.

McHoul, A. and Grace, W. (1995) *A Foucault Primer. Discourse, power and the subject*. London: UCL.

McIntosh, M. (1968) 'The homosexual role', *Social Problems*, 16, 2: 182–192.

McNay, L. (1992) *Foucault and Feminism: Power, Gender and the Self.* Cambridge: Polity Press.

Measor, L., Tiffin, C. and Miller, K. (2000) *Young People's Views on Sex Education: Education, Attitudes and Behaviour.* London: Routledge.

Mitchell, J. (1974) *Psychoanalysis and Feminism.* London: Allen Lane.

Morgan, D. (1992) *Discovering Men.* London: Routledge.

O'Farrell, C. (1989) *Foucault: Historian or Philosopher.* London: Macmillan.

Padgug, A. (1979) cited in M. McFadden (1995).

Parker, R., Herdt, G. and Carballo, M. (1999) 'Sexual Culture, HIV Transmission, and AIDS Research' in R. Parker and P. Aggleton (eds.) *Culture, Society and Sexuality.* London: UCL Press.

Patton, C. (1994) *Last Served? Gendering the HIV Pandemic.* London: Taylor and Francis.

Penelope, J. (1992) *Call me lesbian: Lesbian Lives, Lesbian Theory.* Freedom, CA: The Crossing Press.

Phoenix, A. (1991) *Single Mothers?* Cambridge: Polity Press.

Pini, M. (1997) 'Technologies of the Self' in J. Roche and S. Tucker (eds.) *Youth and Society.* London: Sage with OUP.

Plummer, K. (1995) *Telling Sexual Stories: Power, Change and Social Worlds.* London: Routledge.

Plummer, K. (1975) *Sexual Stigma: An Interactionist Account.* London: Routledge and Kegan Paul.

Poster, M. (1984) *Foucault, Marxism and History. Mode of Production versus Mode of Information.* Cambridge: Polity Press.

Ramazanoglu, C. (1993) (ed.) *Up Against Foucault: Exploration of Some Tensions Between Foucault and Feminism.* London: Routledge.

Ramazanoglu, C. (1992) 'On Feminist Methodology: Male Reason Versus Female Empowerment'. *Sociology*, 26, 2:207–212.

Rich, A. (1998) 'Compulsory Heterosexuality and Lesbian Existence' in S. Jackson and S. Scott (1996) (eds.) *Feminism and Sexuality.* Edinburgh: Edinburgh University Press.

Rose, H. (1996) 'Gay Brains, Gay Genes and Feminist Science Theory' in J. Weeks and J. Holland (eds.) *Sexual Cultures: Communities, Values and Intimacy.* London: Macmillan.

Rubin, G. (1989) 'Thinking Sex: Notes for a Radical Theory of the Politics Of Sexuality' in C. Vance (ed.) *Pleasure and Danger.* London: Pandora.

Rubin, G. S. (1999) 'Thinking Sex: Notes for a Radical Theory of the Politics of Sexuality', in R. Parker and P. Aggleton (eds.) *Culture, Society and Sexuality.* London: UCL Press.

Saraga, E. (1998) 'Abnormal, Unnatural and Immoral? The Social Construction of Sexualities' in E. Saraga (ed.) *Embodying the Social: Constructions of Difference.* London: Routledge.

Schwartz, P. and Rutter, V. (1998) *The Gender of Sexuality*. London: Sage.

Segal, L. (1999) 'Sexualities' in K. Woodward (ed.) *Identity and Difference*. London: Sage/The Open University.

Segal, L. (1994) *Straight Sex. The Politics of Pleasure*. London: Virago.

Segal, L. (1990) *Slow motion: changing masculinities, changing men*. London: Virago.

SEU – Social Exclusion Unit (1999) *Teenage Pregnancy*. London: HMSO.

Shakespeare, T., Gillespie-Sells, K. and Davies, D. (eds.) (1996) *The Sexual Politics of Disability: Untold Desires*. London: Cassell.

Simon, W. (1996) *Postmodern Sexualities*. London: Routledge.

Smart, C. (1995) *Law, Crime and Sexuality*. London: Sage.

Smith, D. E. (1988) *The Everyday World As Problematic: A Feminist Sociology*. Milton Keynes: OUP.

Stanley, L. (1995) *Sex surveyed 1949–1994*. London: Taylor & Francis.

Stanley, L. and Wise, S. (1993) *Breaking Out Again: Feminist Ontology and Epistemology*. London: Routledge.

Stoler, L. A. (1995) *Race and the Education of Desire: Foucault's History of Sexuality and the Colonial Order of Things*. Durham, NC: Duke University Press.

Thomas, C. (1999) *Female Forms: Experiencing and Understanding Disability*. Buckingham: OUP.

Thompson, S. (1989) 'Search for tomorrow: or feminism and the reconstruction of teen romance' in A. Giddens (1994b) 'Men, Women and Romantic Love', *in The Polity Reader in Gender Studies*. Oxford: Polity Press in association with Blackwell Publishers.

Thomson, R. and Scott, S. (1991) *Learning About Sex: Young women and the social construction of sexual identity*, WRAP Paper 4. London: Tufnell Press.

Thomson, R. and Scott, S. (1990) *Researching sexuality in the light of AIDS: historical and methodological issues*. London: Tufnell Press.

Trenchard, L. and Warren, H. (1984) *Something To Tell You: The experiences and needs of young lesbians and gay men in London*. London: London Gay Teenage Group, 6–9 Manor Gardens, Holloway Rd, London N7.

Vance, C. (1989) 'Social construction theory: problems in the history of sexuality' in D. Altman (ed.) *Homosexuality, Which Homosexuality?* London: GMP.

Vance, C. (1984) *Pleasure and Danger: Exploring Female Sexuality*. London: Routledge.

Ward, J. V. and McLean, Taylor, J. (1994) 'Sexuality Education for Immigrant and Minority Students: Developing a Culturally Appropriate Curriculum', in J. M. Irvine (ed.) *Sexual Cultures and the Construction of Adolescent Sexualities*. Philadelphia: Temple University Press.

Watney, S. (1991) 'AIDS: The Second Decade: Risk, Research and Modernity' in P. Aggleton, G. Hart, and P. Davies (eds.) *AIDS: Responses, Interventions and Care*. London: Falmer Press.

Watney, S. (1987) *Policing Desire: Pornography, AIDS and the Media*. London: Metheun.

Weeks, J. (1995) *Invented Moralities: Sexual Values In An Age Of Uncertainty*. Cambridge: Polity Press.

Weeks, J. (1989) *Sex, Politics and Society. The regulation of sexuality since 1800* (2nd ed.). Harlow, Essex: Longman.

Weeks, J. (1985) *Sexuality and its discontents*. London: Routledge.

Wellings, K., Field, J., Johnson, A. M. and Wadsworth, J. (1994) *Sexual Behaviour in Britain: The National Survey of Sexual Attitudes and Lifestyles*. London: Penguin.

Whately, M. (1992) 'Commentary: Whose sexuality is it anyway?', in J. Sears (ed.) *Sexuality and the Curriculum: The Politics and Practices of Sexuality Education*. New York: Teachers' College Press.

Wight, D. (1996) 'Beyond the Predatory Male: The Diversity of Young Glaswegian Men's Discourses to Describe Heterosexual Relationships', in L. Adkins and V. Merchant (eds.) *Sexualising the Social: Power and the Organisation of Sexuality*. London: Macmillan.

Wilton, T. (2000) *Sexualities in health and social care*. Buckingham: OUP.

Wilton, T. (1997) *EnGendering AIDS: Deconstructing Sex, Text and Epidemic*. London: Sage.

5. Racial Stereotypes

Michael Pickering

Racial stereotyping cannot be understood without reference to whiteness, the racially unmarked, normative centre from which it stems. Such reference must be central to the way in which racial stereotyping is conceived as a boundary-maintenance practice, a way of designating and reifying cultural 'difference'. This raises the question of cultural racism and its distinction from biological racism. Following discussion of this question, the chapter examines how racial stereotypes operate in their attempts to give a fixed, absolute definition to their objects. These attempts in turn feed into and reinforce racist discourse and social myth. The chapter emphasises the importance of differentiating between categories and stereotypes before going on to consider changes in 'race' and representation over the past twenty years or so. It concludes with a discussion of the relation between racial stereotypes and the subjectivities of those who are their targets. Racial stereotypes deny the capacity of self-determination upon which subjectivity depends.

Cultural racism and the White Norm

In contemporary discourse, 'race' refers to people who are non-white, and denotes cultural 'difference'. 'Race' is used as a way of designating certain categories within our culture, and it does this from an invisible, undesignated position. This is the position of whiteness. As a normative position, whiteness is taken to be a natural fact, existing beyond the bounds of consideration. It is not racially marked *as* white in the way that black is so marked. Newspapers do not routinely refer to someone as a 'white' lecturer or lawyer, whereas the adjective 'black' is commonly appended to descriptions of someone non-white who occupies these professional posts. The adjective racially marks an aberration from the white norm, drawing attention to their skin colour in a way which doesn't generally happen for people who are white. Whiteness is what is standard, regular and tacitly expected as such. That is why it remains racially unmarked. It signifies sameness, not difference.

When a category becomes racially marked, a first step has been taken towards racial stereotyping. It does not of course apply only to black people. Certain white people, such as Jews or the Irish, have been racially marked in ways which call their 'whiteness' into question (Cheyette, 1997: 111; Eliot, 1995; Curtis, 1971; Lebow, 1976; Pickering, 2001: 142–146). The point still holds: white remains the key organising centre against which racial differences are noticed and seen as inhabiting a symbolically peripheral area. In contrast, the white norm-providing centre is hidden from view and not brought into any definitional reckoning. It stands for the standards which are not seen precisely because they are standard. This does not alter the fact that these standards are preferred, but it does make them less obvious as preferences. Of course when we do begin to think about 'being white' we realise that it is just as problematic as 'being black', for both forms of designation cover up multiple diversities, and disguise the intersections of ethnicity with other sources of social identity, such as gender and generation. As labels they say very little about us as individuals, though what they do say will depend very much on situation and context. These are important considerations, and we must be careful about reifying either category as if it refers to something uniform and consensual.

The reason for beginning with the question of whiteness, though, is that it directs our attention to the way 'black' acts as a packaging term, as for instance in relation to sport and music (where it is given positive value) or crime and violence (where the image is wholly negative). You don't find 'white music' or 'white crime' commonly referred to in the media, and if you did they wouldn't carry anything like the same essentialist values as 'black' does. Even those images that seem cast in a positive light often reverberate with the stock racial stereotypes of empire and colonialism when – if not in the lowly role of servant or manual labourer – black people were ideologically positioned and confined as exotic entertainers for white audiences. The restrictive association of blacks with entertainment – and not the serious world of work, in offices and counting-houses – has a lineage running back at least that far. The stereotypical association is at once restrictive and excessive. It is because of this that we simply know, as a natural fact, that blacks are so rhythmical, so in tune with instinct and physical movement. Their physical prowess at sports is likewise simply to be expected: they are considered as natural athletes because they are more body-centred that whites, and historically the corollary of this was that, in contrast to white people, they were deficient in the capacity of reason. Even today, the description of someone as a 'black intellectual' sounds exceptional, a cut above the rest. So beginning with whiteness reminds us of who is designing and applying the labels, it emphasises the generally one-way direction of racial stereotyping, and helps us remember how long it has been the organising centre for representing others.

I have also begun this chapter with another emphasis by saying that 'race' is generally used as a way of designating cultural 'difference'. This requires further discussion, for race is not something that exists in the same way as a table or chair. It is an abstract construction. As such, race is the key term historically associated with a classificatory system for distinguishing between human beings on the basis of biological features and genetic inheritance. Few contemporary racists, though, would explain or justify their beliefs in these terms. They would point to cultural or national differences instead. This has been identified as a new form of racism in Britain, said to have come to the fore in the last twenty years or so. The relative decline of verbal and visual stereotypes based on crude biologistic notions of inferior racial types is one index of its increased prevalence. Cultural racism is predicated not on the fixed typological distinctions of nineteenth century 'scientific' racism but on the notion of the incompatibility of different cultures and the need to defend 'our' national heritage against its adulteration by 'their' foreign ways. The less blatant forms of stereotyping involved in cultural racism have been met critically with a more sophisticated theoretical understanding of what they involve and a move away from earlier moralistic or reductive forms of anti-racism, but it remains unclear how new cultural racism is. On the one hand, the notion of unbridgeable differences between cultures has a much longer history, and racist ideas have often been linked to it, whether this has been in antisemitism, Orientalism or Islamophobia. On the other hand, biological racism and cultural racism both argue for incommensurability and justify exclusionary strategies on that basis. In various ways these two forms of racism are as continuous as they are distinct.

Cultural racism clearly builds on the non-whiteness of those against whom it is directed and does so from an invisibly centred whiteness in order to demand exclusion, exonerate marginality or equate inclusion with cultural assimilation. Monoculturalist values and an emphasis on cultural (as opposed to racial) determinism have attained a higher profile only to the extent that 'race' is now widely discredited as a concept (hence the scare quotes around the term) and so in need of disguise. Yet in the form of racism into which it feeds, cultural 'difference' is still sometimes biologised or quasi-biologised, with distinctions between cultures sliding laterally into phenotypical demarcations, even as biologistic explanations are rarely articulated or required as the basis of racial stereotypes. Heritage is then a camouflage for heredity. That is why British still stands for whiteness. When this unspoken association operates, Britishness is simply a culturalist substitution for whiteness in a way which connects blackness with not belonging. Whiteness remains the privileged sign for what is not part of the equation of colour and culture, and if you are bracketed within that equation you face obstacles in feeling where it is you belong. Your membership of society is somehow flawed and your cultural identity is not part of the mainstream. Stereotyping acts to reinforce this sense of partial belonging and remind you of it constantly. It acts as if anyone's self-description as 'black British' is an oxymoron.

Countering this cannot of course resort to anti-racist arguments dealing only in the errors of biological racism even where this remains implicit in assertions of cultural particularism. The racialisation of cultural difference needs to be opposed by a different language which doesn't equate belonging with cultural homogeneity, for it is this putative sameness among those who culturally stereotype other social groups which is held to constitute the grounds for exclusion. The logic of us/them distinctions can also divide different ethnic minorities off from each other, as for instance in the stereotypical split whereby white working-class boys identify positively with African-Caribbean subcultures 'exhibiting a macho, proletarian style' and discriminate against Asian cultures as 'effeminate' and 'middle class': 'Such boys experience no sense of contradiction in wearing dreadlocks, smoking ganja and going to reggae concerts whilst continuing to assert that "Pakis Stink" ' (Cohen, 1988: 83). These distinctions can then be absorbed by one minority grouping against another. When prejudices and hostilities develop along lines of cultural difference, racist stereotypes are the prerogative of no one ethnic group, but effectively it is the group remaining racially unmarked which retains the greatest power of designation.

Posing the shift to cultural racism in too clear-cut a fashion faces the further problem that it is in some ways a culturally specific change. At the very least it remains unclear how widespread the change may be. For example, in its submission to the Human Rights Commission in South Africa, the ANC made clear that white South African society continues to operate very considerably with a 'black savage' stereotype. They identify the main components of this stereotype of the black African as being immoral, violent, disrespectful of private property, incapable of refinement through education, and 'driven by hereditary dark, satanic impulses'. These images, which clearly derive from a biological rather than cultural form of racism, inform much news journalism in the country, giving greatest prominence to crime, corruption, government ineptitude, moral decay and economic collapse in coverage of blacks and black politicians and leaders. As their submission put it: 'The racist paradigm dictates that facts seen to be inconsistent with the white stereotype should not be given such weight as would negate this stereotype' (ANC, 2000: 21). The result of the paradigm is a continuation of the structuring of South African society around the racist prescription of white superiority and black inferiority, with images of black incompetence, venality and violence given greatest emphasis and salience.

Between Hypervisibility and Oblivion

Usually we think that those who have been socially and culturally margin-alised are rendered less visible than those at the centres of social life. Yet just the opposite can also be true, as the ANC submission attests. Those in Britain who remain largely ignorant about what life is actually like in black communities nevertheless have a very vivid sense of certain images about black people which are derived from the reiterated stereotypical representations associated with the term, whether these are mugger, drug dealer, illegal immigrant or welfare scrounger. Social margins are highly visible by being represented as not belonging to the normalised mainstream.

This is what happens with racial stereotypes as markers of symbolic marginality. Such stereotypes make their objects hypervisible. They make the narrow association of certain groups with certain characteristics stand in the glare of a derogated notoriety. Stereotypes 'fix' these characteristics so as impart to them an unquestioned obviousness. The cultural abbreviation of the stereotype is then allied with a perceptual exaggeration of its visibility. As Patricia Williams has put it in relation to black people in the United States:

How, or whether, blacks are seen depends upon a dynamic of display that ricochets between hypervisibility and oblivion'. While 'the real lives of real blacks unfold outside the view of many whites, the fantasy of black life as a theatrical enterprise is an almost obsessive indulgence (Williams, 1997: 15).

These obsessive indulgences have a long history, which can be traced back to the days of slavery in the United States and the Caribbean, and to the period of European colonialism and imperialism. They became obsessive because they spoke to enduring but difficult feelings of both fear and desire, attraction and disavowal. Black racial stereotypes attempted to overcome and at the same time accommodate these feelings through their attempts at representational fixity, the fixity of their opposed binary extremes. These have included such things as civilised/primitive, culture/nature, mind/body, reason/instinct, intellect/emotion, restraint/abandon distinctions set off against each other as polar opposites. As such they have been evaluatively mapped onto white/black groups, with an underlying distinction of racial superiority and inferiority running centrally through them.

During the nineteenth century, the racialised inferiority of black people was based on notions of their inherent laziness, their childlike character and their closeness to nature. For this reason they were both derided and feared, yet at the same time they gave vicarious access to imagined forms of feeling, pleasure and the cessation of physical restraint that made them the object of overt sentimentality and fun, and a more covertly indulged envy and desire. Along with other modes of cultural representation of black people, these contrary attitudes fuelled the appeal of minstrel show entertainment – a theatrical enterprise based on fantasies of black life – in ways which strongly prefigured later white views of black music, dance and comedy (Pickering, 1997: 181–201; Pickering, 1999; Pickering, 2000). For many whites throughout the twentieth century, from ragtime to rap – and in its blackface impersonations, from Al Jolson to Ali G – black music, dance and comedy continued to act as a source of indulgence, in a range from cultural obsession to occasional pleasure.

Blackface minstrels involved white people (usually men) dressing up and impersonating black people, and it was just one – albeit highly significant – cultural form among many which helped to develop the black racial stereotypes of the modern period, such as the happy-go-lucky 'darky' and the black dandy. These two examples point to a paradoxical feature of stereotyping. As hypervisible symbolic abbreviations of an ethnic category, stereotypes narrow certain categories down to a putative essence which fixes and defines them in absolute terms. This essential meaning is imposed from outside by those who command the process of stereotyping, which operates through an 'us'/'them' dichotomy calculated to guarantee 'our' superiority against 'their' inferiority. The paradoxical feature to which I am referring then acts to undermine and betray this guarantee. Racial stereotypes often take conflicting forms. If we take two further examples among Victorian stereotypes of black men, it is clear that the Uncle Tom caricature of Christian forbearance was opposed to the shiftless, thieving, good-for-nothing, violent 'coon' popularly represented as his young counterpart. While similarly reductive, such images could not both give one singular definition to the black male as an essentialised racial category of person. A generational difference might be observed, but this could only gloss the conflict between a preferred idealisation of racial submissiveness and a projected fantasy of racial deviance. These conflicting figures could be used in opposed ways in the anti-slavery debate, but both in their different ways were white constructions, and both spoke to certain white anxieties about the black man as a threat to good order on the one hand, and on the other as such an exemplar of good order that white Christians were in danger of being out-Christianised by those allegedly inferior to them in the racist rationale.

This may now seem something of a muddle, as indeed it was, but the force of racial ideology at the time meant that it could cogently combine these differences in such a way that they seemed to constitute a seamlessly uniform ensemble despite the ambivalences of meaning and response that were displayed. While this force cannot be underestimated, we should always note the capacity of racism to accommodate different and at times quite contradictory elements. Its cogency depends on this capacity, and for this reason racism is 'a scavenger ideology' whose power derives from 'its ability to pick out and utilise ideas and values from other sets of ideas and beliefs in specific socio-historical contexts' (Solomos and Back, 1996: 213). Racism is ideologically parasitic on other ideas, values and beliefs for the purposes of maintaining existing structures of power and exploitation.

This is true of positive and negative stereotypes alike. Both act in the interests of those who do the stereotyping and remain demeaning to those who are its targets. The stereotypical Other is a one-sided construction which helps to maintain symbolic boundaries between 'us' and other social or ethnic categories in the interests of 'our' own sense of identity, security and legitimacy. It represents cultural 'difference' in terms which diverge from what is taken to be central, safe, normal and conventional. Stereotyping is a way of warding off any threat of disruption to 'us' as the 'same together' through the generation of an essentialised Otherness that can then be dealt with from the point of view of this 'same together'. It is a collective process of judgement which feeds upon and reinforces powerful social and national myths.

Just as the stereotype is conceptually compatible with that of the Other, so it is analytically cognate with myths and myth-making, for stereotypes and myths both aim '...to obscure the ceaseless making of the world by fixating it into an object, to embalm the world so that it can be possessed for ever, to inject into reality some purifying essence which will stop its transformation' (Bronfen, 1992: 213). Like myths, stereotypes deny a central premise in hermeneutics that our ways of seeing, thinking, speaking and acting are historically conditioned and located (Pickering, 1997b). In acting against this premise, stereotypes attempt to fix our own identities, our own sense of ourselves in and over time.

Myths and stereotypes do not appear over night. They often have a long historical lineage. They exist as a popular archive of images and representations from which racialised knowledge of the Other can be extracted. Much of the work done on stereotyping, in both psychology and media studies, is concerned only with contemporary representations, and so can tell us very little about this lineage or how the archive can be activated around the imperatives of social and national myths. I have sought elsewhere to redress this historical amnesia by attending carefully to the deeply rooted development of some of the most entrenched stereotypes culturally in circulation in the West (Pickering, 2001). It is because they are deeply rooted in the sedimented layers set down by past cultural practices and representations, and in past responses to social and cultural change, that they have become entrenched as powerful social myths. Without trying to understand how this has happened in particular cases, whether this in relation to the Middle East, Africa or anywhere else, the argument that stereotyping is unavoidable will only grow stronger.

Categorising and Stereotyping

This takes us to another point in the discussion. Stereotyping is a focus of critical analysis in media and cultural studies as well as in other fields concerned with the politics of representation. The underlying assumption is that stereotypes are damaging, regardless of whether they are taken as positive or negative, and the purpose of their critical analysis is to expose how and why this is so in the hope that it will lead to the diminution and avoidance of such representations in the media and in popular culture more broadly. The problem is that as a concept the stereotype is often confused with other concepts, such as those relating to a category, type or typification. These other concepts refer to the ways in which we move mentally between a particular concrete case and a generalised form, such as for instance in the way we both distinguish and link the tree outside our house and trees as a generic object which we find wherever we go. Cognitively, categories act as a means of making distinctions and connections and are in this way central to the ways in which meanings rely on schemes of classification between one thing and another. We need categories or typfications in order to get along in the world, to organise how we view it and to negotiate our way through our everyday social encounters and interactions. Recognising their importance, though, should not allow us to overestimate their value or distract us from the ways in which they can be imaginatively used, recharged and made to change over time.

Stereotypes are different from other forms of generalised representation because they are never used to refer to the particular person, in any link back from category to individual. They exist in order to deny that sort of connection and are used instead to classify someone only in terms of the symbolic abbreviations associated with their group or category. The particularity of any one person is eclipsed when a stereotype is used to describe or designate them. Now of course we cannot refer to, never mind know, everyone's particularity or individuality in the same way, and this is where broad categories are necessary, as for instance when we refer to mothers, athletes or bankers as labels for very large groups of people. We are then faced with a critical choice. Having established their roles within these broad connections, we can either proceed to discuss how particular people relate to their membership of these categories, which is to start distinguishing them in terms of their individualities, or we can go the other way and relate them only to the restrictive traits associated with a general label in such a way that they are seen in no other terms. This is what happens when we refer to people stereotypically. For example, if we take the categories used earlier, the stereotypes start to kick in once we add certain qualifying adjectives, such as single mother, black athlete or Jewish banker. These epithets act stereotypically because they have been used respectively as forms of negative moral evaluation, of the ideologically channelled confinement of social achievement, and of the racialised deformation of talent and skill. These demeaning designations work so as to cut off any way of working back to particularities, playing with them imaginatively, and recognising their mutability.

Stereotypes have been distinguished from categories before, though sometimes this has acted in a rhetorically self-serving way to demarcate 'us' as rational, normal people who use categories flexibly from 'them' as irrational, ill-educated folk who use stereotypes rigidly. In fact, the distinction was there right from the start, when the stereotype was first formulated as a concept by the American political columnist and writer, Walter Lippmann. In viewing stereotypes as inadequate and endorsing the interests of those who use them, Lippmann contrasted stereotyping with 'individualised understanding' (Lippmann, 1914). Unfortunately, having spelt out the dangers of stereotyping, he then confused the issue by stating that they were necessary ways of processing information amidst the helter-skelter life of modern societies. He thus conflated stereotypes and categories in precisely the way I have been trying to separate them. This has had its own damaging effects throughout the whole subsequent development of the concept of the stereotype (Pickering, 2001).

The point of critiquing the various regimes of racialised representation is to help people see others differently, to go beyond unthinking prejudice and the ideological strategies of 'othering the Other'. The critique is based on the conviction that stereotyping is a habit of thought, and that however entrenched, it is not immutable. Yet if we view stereotyping as an integral feature of rational categorisation this negates the whole point of critique, rendering it off-limits. The psychology of stereotyping can then be used to justify the politics of stereotypical representation, as for example in the statement that the '...major function of attaching labels to different racial and ethnic groups is to impose order on a chaotic environment' (Stephan and Rosenfeld, 1982: 95). This not only equates racism with the need to create some sense of order in our lives, so rendering racist stereotyping as unavailable for serious criticism. It also attaches labels of the racialised Other to notions of chaos and social convulsion in ways which are readily familiar, as for instance in the equation of certain ethnic groups and civil disorder in the tabloid press. For critical interrogations of media and popular culture, this line of thinking is insupportable. It shows clearly the dangers of concentrating exclusively on cognitive processes or 'deep structures' of psychic development at the expense of the ideological and political dimensions involved in stereotyping. Focusing on such processes and structures outside of particular social and historical processes is far too narrow. Our representations, like our deeds, cannot be justified by them.

So we need to avoid conflating stereotypes with categories. Although they are not the be-all and end-all of human perception and thinking, categories are characteristic of a far broader form of organising information and experience. Categorisation can work in productive tension with the conflicting mental strategy of particularisation, whereas stereotyping operates as a strategy of ideologically separating 'us' from 'them' and imparting to 'them' a fixed, absolute definition. When we understand someone as an individual, we recognise them as a particular person over and above their membership of any social group or category, and this is so even when we value them as being eminently representative of a specific group or category. In contrast, when we use a stereotype, we chain a person to a stunted abbreviation for a group or category in a way that denies or diminishes their individuality and agency. With racial stereotypes, an individual is only recognisable in terms of a symbolic abbreviation that is always less-than-normal and less-than-individual. For this reason, a racial stereotype is self-forsaken. It stifles self-determination, and it does so as a double alienation.

Which Way to Go?

The double alienation operates by denying you the ability to participate validly in meaning making, and in stripping you of social agency, it leaves you defenceless against being othered in the stereotypical representation. This representation diminishes you to a reversed image of those who stereotype you, for a stereotype is always biased towards something those who stereotype wants to lose or gain in themselves. As Edward Said puts it in relation to Orientalist stereotypes, their 'logic' is not so much governed by empirical realities as '...by a battery of desires, repressions, investments, and projections' (Said, 1985: 8). Which way do you then go? You can either internalise the stereotype and become who you are alleged to be in the eyes of those who stereotype you, so accepting your inferiority or idealisation as it is set forth in the racial marker of the stereotype, or you can challenge this by struggling for recognition as being different to your representation in the stereotype.

Internalisation of a racial stereotype means conforming to the image given of you in the stereotype, so accepting, at least ostensibly, the inferiority this entails or the restricted group characteristics that are involved. The racial mark of the stereotype not only identifies you by the colour of your skin, but also gets inside your skin, inside your body, and takes it over, makes it perform in accordance with the racialised imperatives of the dominant culture. You may then remember, inside yourself, that this is not really 'the real you', that your sense of yourself involves far more, and strives for far more. Somehow you have to struggle to reach this and so unloosen the tight attitudinal knot of representation and judgement associated with your racial stereotype. Somehow you have to resolve the split between you and the masquerade of your stereotype in order to become one with yourself, to be a subject who is not perpetually struggling against the oppressive 'objecthood' of the white racial phantasm.

It is, once again, a battle against the snug centredness of whiteness. The categories of 'black' and 'white' define each other, but this relational process has historically been realised in terms of the unstated, unimplicated white standard. As the anti-colonial writer and activist Franz Fanon argued:

> ... it is the racist who creates his inferior', and he does so through the exnomination of whiteness as a source of social identity: 'race lives "over there" on the other side of the tracks, in black bodies and inner-city neighbourhoods, in a dark netherworld where whites are not involved (Fanon, 1986: 93).

In these conditions, the power of the stereotype confines you to struggle against the naturalised terms it has established. The extent to which these terms remain entrenched is clear from the reactions that have occurred when they have been challenged. As the process of racialisation of non-white ethnicities has come under greater critical scrutiny, as affirmative action has become an accepted social policy and the issues surrounding multiculturalism have become more widely debated, so the paranoid idea has grown that whiteness is no longer the signifier of privilege, that the privileges of being white are being undermined. The older sense of national identities as culturally unitary and homogeneous has also proved more and more difficult to sustain. White backlash reacts against these developments and attempts to restore previous structures of domination, exclusion and denial. It does this through further essentialising whiteness, making white racial identity more visible, and through cultural bleaching, countering anxieties and insecurities produced by social and global change by advancing '...discourses which seek to purge culture of its syncretic forms' (Gabriel, 1998: 9). A recent example of backlash response was the negative media coverage of the Runnymede Trust report, *The Future of Multi-Ethnic Britain*, in late 2000, with the most hostile coverage being given in *The Daily Mail*, that hallowed organ of Middle England (Runneymede Trust, 2000) This seemed of a piece with the general tendency, over the past twenty years, to address issues affecting minority ethnic groups through a racial optic, so extending media reinforcement of a white normative centre.

Yet against this, as Ian Law has recently shown, there does seem to have been a degree of shift, since the 1980s, in media coverage of racism and ethnic minority issues, with less overt hostility to anti-racism and a diminution of the 'race-relations' frame in British news coverage (the major exception being Northern Ireland, where evidence for these trends is not forthcoming) (Law, 2002). One example of this has been the change from relative indifference to sensitive concern in news coverage of the Stephen Lawrence case, and the ensuing acknowledgement of the problem of institutional racism in which, unsurprisingly, stereotyping is a central component (McPherson, 1999; Malik, 2002: 10–11). Such changes have resulted in a reduction of racial stereotyping in news representations, though it is clear that a resilient core of negative coverage of ethnic minorities continues to be built around a number of well-tried themes, particularly through the linkage of 'race' with violence, crime and danger, and the selective identification of certain ethnic minority groups as a welfare burden prone to fraud and deception. Racial hostility also remains the keynote in reporting migration issues. The hysteria over 'asylum seekers' whipped up by the tabloid press shows that the strength of white backlash culture should not be underestimated. This raises the question as to whether what Law calls the 'great anti-racist show' *is* simply a show, masking abiding white-centrism in news organisations as well as broader forms of institutional racism. Law examines further examples of racialised representations in news coverage of 'race and rape', in the reporting of issues concerning immigrants and asylum-seekers, and in the reification of racial categories, with black people being twice as likely to be described in spurious racial terms than white people. The mistaken idea that 'race' is real is continually reinforced.

Race is, and always has been, an ideological construct, and as such it is part of the common sense way in which many people make sense of the world in which they live. The media have often contributed to this by creating the meanings and images which the term carries and building it around a white-defined problem. Stuart Hall pointed this out over twenty years ago in noting the power of representation of the 'absent' imperial 'white eye' in making 'race' make sense. He claimed that the '…"white eye" is always outside the frame – but seeing and positioning everything within it' (Hall, 1981: 38–39). To say that the idea of 'race' as real is mistaken is not to say that it does not have real effects – quite the opposite; but once you begin to realise that the grammar of racialised difference is one constructed by whites in a long lineage running from Sambo to starving victims (objects of fun to objects of pity), then you at least have a measure of how the lines of unequal relation have been drawn. While we should remember that 'the specific contents of racial stereotyping and the ethnic boundaries it draws are not necessarily fixed or consistent' (Anthias and Yuval-Davis, 1993: 137), once racially marked, claiming your self-worth and striving for self-creation must operate within the dominant/subordinate relations of the racist culture. Your struggle for identity is confined to recognition by those who have denied your identity. The desire to be properly recognised is itself a product of the stereotypical regime in which you have been constructed as inferior or representative of some idealised way of being which is considered lacking in mainstream white culture, at least by certain disaffected groups. In attempting to assert your identity against the representation of you in the stereotype, you begin from the basis of your restriction to a group-signifier not of your own making. The desire to be recognised as you are rather than as you are represented in a racial stereotype is created by the experience of being stereotyped in the first place. The conferral of recognition that is being sought still remains the bequest of the sovereign subject responsible for making you either socially invisible or hypervisible as a stereotypical object. You remain dependent on this subject for a sense of your integrity and self-worth. This is why the African-American writer 'bell hooks' says that central to '…claiming our right to subjectivity is the insistence that we must determine how we will be and not rely on colonising responses to determine our legitimacy' (hooks, 1990: 21).

Subjectivity depends upon this capacity of self-determination. Racial stereotyping dismisses your claim to subjectivity and the sense of an internal life as an individual, as someone able to participate in making meanings and values, since it tells you how you will be and foists alien meanings and values upon you. De-individualisation creates the need to develop your individuality and have it recognised, yet paradoxically the appeal is to those most likely to deny you this precisely because the denial is the result of their racialised imperatives. Indeed, then '…I will quite simply try to make myself white… I will compel the white man to acknowledge that I am human' (Fanon, 1986: 98). The paradox lies in the way that resistance to this denial in the stereotype affirms the power of those responsible for it.

Fanon struggled with the effects of this paradox of racism throughout his writings. The very title of his most famous book, *Black Skin, White Masks*, is indicative of the problem. There is no easy solution to it but we should at least be clear of the limits to the politics of recognition. De-racialisation is a necessary step in such politics as they strive for new forms of representation in place of the self-dislocating effects of demeaning stereotypes. They nevertheless carry the 'culturalist' dangers of reifying group identities, treating such stereotypes as socially ungrounded harms, and displacing the politics of redistribution. Cultural participation is damaged by the unequal distribution of goods, resources and opportunities just as much as by the gross misrecognition of racial stereotyping. Moreover, misrecognition in itself:

> …is not simply to be thought of, looked down upon or devalued
> in others' attitudes, beliefs or representations. It is rather to be
> denied the status of a full partner in social interaction, as a

consequence of institutionalised patterns of cultural value that constitute one as comparatively unworthy of respect or esteem (Fraser, 2000: 113, 114).

Any model of social relations which seeks to overcome this degradation of status requires some conception of what Fanon called 'a world of reciprocal recognitions' (Fanon, 1972: 155). If human relations are seen as essentially based on conflict, aggression and exclusion, how can mutual recognition of each other's active subjectivity and identity ever ensue? The neo-Hegelian model of social interaction that underlies the politics of recognition certainly has explanatory power in terms of conflict and aggression, but the danger lies in its normalisation and general extension into thinking with difference, as if identity is only tenable by abjecting the other as Other, who has in the first place been constructed as a threat and a danger by the repressive strategies of stereotypical representation. Identity and difference are then locked in their self-contained fixities. This leaves us in an impasse that disables any conception of how ethically responsible, compassionate relations are possible (Hegel, 1977: 111–119; Pickering, 2001: 61–78). This is where theories of recognition and notions of identity based on recognition are stuck, for in relations of domination and marginality the power of conferring recognition remains with the privileged, and when orders of domination themselves create the need for recognition, this is always going to be conferred in the terms of existing hierarchies and structures of power. Deficiency or lack is then forever the shortcoming of those marginalised and oppressed, and social justice the mark of these being overcome in the name of what is already familiar, thus precluding any real engagement with difference. Sameness is ensured, difference misrecognised.

Conclusion

Problems of recognition and misrecognition cannot be based analytically on the unequal relations of contrast and deficiency that are the very ground of the stereotyping relationship itself, but must work towards alternative ways of conceiving the dialogical character of subjectivity without at the same time losing sight of conflict and power. To be othered is to be objectified, and to be objectified is a denial of your subjectivity. Subjectivity exists by virtue of the ability to address and be addressed, speak and respond. As a social practice, this is what racial stereotyping denies, and for this reason its critique needs to start from the perspective of those whose identity is racially 'othered', and stop opposing difference and identity. Such an attempt can only ever be partial, but that only makes attentively listening to difference more important, since it is the only valid basis of communication and communion with others. This is all we can do, but it is what we must do, urgently and with care, if we are to refuse racial stereotypes and work towards a world where no other is any longer the Other.

Bibliography

ANC, 'Stereotypes Steer the News', *Rhodes Journalism Review*, August 2000.
Anthias, F. and Yuval-Davis, N. (1993) *Racialised Boundaries*, London and New York: Routledge.
Bronfen, E. (1992) *Over Her Dead Body: Death, Femininity and the Aesthetic*, Manchester: Manchester University Press.
Cheyette, B. 'White Skins, Black Masks: Jews and Jewishness in the Writings of George Eliot and Frantz Fanon' in Pearson, K. A., Parry, B. and Squires, J. eds. (1997) *Cultural Readings of Imperialism*, London: Lawrence and Wishart.
Cohen, P. 'The Perversions of Inheritance: Studies in the Making of Multi-Racist Britain' in Cohen, P. and Bains, H. S. (1988) *Multi-Racist Britain*, London and Basingstoke: Macmillan.
Curtis, L. (1986) *Nothing But the Same Old Story: The Roots of Anti-Irish Racism*, London: Information on Ireland.
Curtis, L. P. (1971) *Apes and Angels: The Irishman in Victorian Caricature*, Washington: Smithsonian Institution Press.
Fanon, F. (1986) *Black Skin, White Masks*, London: Pluto Press.
Fraser, N. (1997) *Justice Interruptus*, London and New York: Routledge.
Fraser, N. 'Rethinking Recognition', *New Left Review*, 3, 2000, pp. 107–20.
Gabriel, (1998) *Whitewash: Racialised Politics and the Media*, London and New York: Routledge.
Hall, S. 'The Whites of Their Eyes: Racist Ideologies and the Media' in Bridges, G. and Brunt, R. eds. (1981) *Silver Linings*, London: Lawrence & Wishart.
Hegel, G. W. F. (1967) (orig. pub. 1807) *The Phenomenology of Mind*, New York: Harper & Row.
hooks, b. (1990) *Yearning: Race, Gender, and Cultural Politics*, Boston: South End Press.
Law, I. (2002) *Race in the News*, Basingstoke and New York: Palgrave (formerly Macmillan).
Lebow, R.N. *White Britain and Black Ireland: The Influence of Stereotypes on Colonial Policy*, Philadelphia: Institute for the Study of Human Issues, 1976.
Macpherson, Sir W. (1999) *The Stephen Lawrence Inquiry*, London: Stationary Office.
Malik, S. *Representing Black Britain: Black and Asian Images on Television*, London, Thousand Oaks, New Delhi: Sage, 2002.

Pickering, M. (1997) 'John Bull in Blackface', *Popular Music*, Volume 16, no 2, May 1997: 181–201.

Pickering, M. (1997b) *History, Experience and Cultural Studies*, Basingstoke and London: Macmillan, 1997.

Pickering, M. (1999) *'A Happy Instinct for Sentiment: A Profile of Harry Hunter'*, Cahiers du Victoriens et Edouardiens, 50, October, 1999.

Pickering, M. (2000), *'Eugene Stratton and Early Ragtime in Britain'*, Black Music Research Journal, Fall 2000.

Pickering, M. (2001) *Stereotyping: The Politics of Representation*, Basingstoke and New York: Palgrave (formerly Macmillan).

Runnymede Trust (2000) *The Future of Multi-Ethnic Britain: The Parekh Report*, London: Profile Book.

Said, E., (1985) *Orientalism*, Harmondsworth: Penguin (orig. pub. 1978).

Solomos, J. and Back, L. (1996) *Racism and Society*, Basingstoke and London, Macmillan.

Stephan, W. G. and Rosenfeld, D. (1982) 'Racial and Ethnic Stereotypes' in Miller, A.G. ed., *In the Eye of the Beholder: Contemporary Issues in Stereotyping*, New York: Praeger.

Williams, P. (1997) *Seeing a Colour-Blind Future: The Paradox of Race*, London: Virago.

6. Mixed Race

David Parker

This chapter explores the social identities of 'mixed race'. It argues for a more sober account of the distinctive experiences of this rapidly growing constituency. It argues for greater attention to be paid to the particular local histories of 'mixed race' arising from various global entanglements. It addresses some of the issues involved in recent population Censuses in Britain and the United States. Through an analysis of interview material, fictional representations, internet sites it calls for 'mixed race' people to be given the opportunity to articulate their complex identities in their own terms. Neither 'mixed race' nor racism will disappear quickly.

In 1991 I was an 'Other – other', by 2001 I was 'mixed'. In between times I hadn't changed, but the checkboxes on Britain's Population Census form had. At last I was no longer relegated to the bottom of the page, invited to fill in the blank space beneath 'Any other', never being quite sure what that lead to. As the racialised demography of Britain becomes more complicated, so thousands of people have made this journey towards administrative recognition. Yet virtually nothing is known about whether individuals' sense of themselves has also changed in the last two decades. Does the onset of bureaucratic neatness and politeness speak to a profound and important new 'mixed race' identity, or is it merely a governmental convenience, for a group with little public voice and even less in common with each other? Are persons of mixed descent pioneers of hybrid, multiple forms of identity defined by contingent, flexible identifications irreducible to single points of origin and thus characteristic of the new identities of the coming century? In short, are 'mixed race' identities the defining social identities of the future?

The popular discourse of 'mixed race'

On both sides of the Atlantic people of 'mixed race' have recently been recruited to paint optimistic portraits of a peaceful multicultural future which they embody. The questioning of fixed racial boundaries which their very existence implies turns 'mixed race' people into exemplary figures of postmodern, post-racial, postethnic fluidity:

> A critical mass of acknowledged mixed-race people heightens
> the credibility of an ideal according to which individuals decide

how tightly or loosely they wish to affiliate with one or more communities of descent. These Americans help move the society in a postethnic direction (Hollinger, 1995: 165)

In Britain also optimistic voices hail the emergence of a new 'mixed race'. Popular discussions in newspapers, radio and television programmes push 'mixed race' people to the fore as living proof of the harmonious intermingling of cultures and peoples. For example, in the aftermath of the attack on the World Trade Centre one newspaper letter writer saw 'mixed race' marriages as the solution to religious and racial conflict:

It is clear from recent tragic events that the source of humanity's suffering comes from the racial divisions between us all (...) Perhaps tax relief could be introduced for couples of mixed race, or else some sort of media relations exercise by the Government to encourage dating beyond one's own ethnic group (...) Soon we would all have nephews and nieces from the other side. A generation after that and many of us would be of mingled blood. The advantage is obvious (Metro newspaper, October 9th 2001: 11)

Such celebration of 'mixed race' should not be unambiguously welcomed and requires further interrogation. Besides often betraying a sly, furtive fascination at what is framed as a simultaneous racial and sexual transgression, there are several things lacking in this popular discourse of 'mixed race'. They lack such things as:

- a sense of historical perspective and the comparative dimension this entails
- demographic data
- testimony from 'mixed race' people themselves
- a theoretical analysis of what 'mixed race' actually means
- an appreciation of the political implications of 'mixed race' identities

I will try to address these deficiencies in what follows.

Global 'mixed race': local histories

Though the name and associated political consciousness might be novel, there is nothing new about racial mixture. In fact 'mixed race' people have been the phenotypical signature of migration, conquest, imperial and military domination through the ages.

Britain's imperial adventures have brought black, Asian, Chinese and Middle Eastern seafarers and traders to these islands for at least five centuries. Conversely British explorers, merchants, soldiers and administrators have traversed the empire. Similar patterns characterised the Spanish, Dutch and Portuguese imperial histories. The terms of the interracial encounters with the respective local populations in the metropole and colonies were usually far from equal. In each case interracial relationships generated a visible 'mixed race' population, often with an embattled and ambiguous social location, at times harshly treated and derided. On other occasions 'mixed race' people were exoticised and sexualised, especially the young women. The English traveller Peter Mundy was beguiled by the 'mixed race' children of a Portuguese magistrate whom he saw on a visit to the settlement of Macao off Southern China in 1637:

> There were att thatt tyme in the house three or four very pretty children, daughters to the said Senor Antonio and his kindred that except in England, I thincke not in the world to be overmatched For their pretty Feature and Complexion, their habitt or Dressing beecomming them as well, adorned with pretious Jewells and Costly apparrell, their uppermost garments being little Kimaones, or Japan coates, which graced them allsoe (Bitterli, 1989: 145–146).

An important theme in colonially driven globalisation and modernisation involved the creation, representation and administration of 'mixed race' in both thought and deed, discourse and practice. As interracial relationships proliferated so too did the attempts to restrict them, at times encourage them, and govern the consequential 'mixed race' constituency (Stoler, 1995).

The increasing presence of mixed-race/colored/mestizo populations (and of miscegenation in all its disruptive configurations) worked to undermine the authority and coherence of colonial and hinterland regimes (Winant, 2001: p. 115). However, new consolidations of power underpinned colonial and post-colonial regimes with variable effects on the 'mixed race' populations (Gist and Dworkin, 1972). In some territories the 'mixed race' group became a distinct community and social force, with politicised identities poised somewhat precariously in-between white and indigenous groups; most notably the 'coloureds' in South Africa (Marx, 1998). In India the distinct Anglo-Indian community, after occupying strategically important posts in transport and health services, largely dispersed throughout the Commonwealth after independence in 1947. Those that remain; English-speaking, Christian, at times ridiculed, face an uncertain future amid a nation keen to erase them from memory (Roychowdhury, 2000). America's post-war military interventions in South East Asia have seen the growth of a 'mixed race' population descended from US servicemen in Vietnam, the Amerasians, many of whom faced severe deprivation (Valverde, 1992).

By contrast in Central and South America those who are 'mixed' predominate with often incalculably fine grained pigmentocracies crucial to the operation of social hierarchies in Brazil for example (Marx, A 1998). In Latin America the question of mestizaje (a Spanish term for racial mixture)

109

has been formative and contentious for nation building projects (Bonnett, 2000). More recently 'borderland' and 'hybrid' writers, often from mixed Anglo-Latino backgrounds, have reclaimed their diverse heritages to signal the emergence of a new creative identity, validating the restlessness and fluidity so often held in contempt in the past (Anzaldua, 1987). In the Caribbean the related term metissage, but more often creolisation, has been invoked by historians and writers anxious to acknowledge and validate the flowing together of different cultural streams on those islands against those cultural theories seeking single-rooted origins distilled into pure identities (Glissant, 1989). 'Mixed race' individuals and families have also begun to be researched in Australia (Luke and Luke, 1998).

Two important lessons can be drawn from this brief summary of interracial history. Firstly, there is no single 'mixed race' experience. The social and political conditions shaping the terms of the wider relationship between population groups in each locality will always influence the interpersonal dynamics. This is true however much we might wish to reduce partnership choices to factors of love and romance alone; or to celebrate racial mixture through concepts and metaphors such as 'hybridity' without due regard to sensitive historical legacies.

Secondly, a sizeable part of the self-defined monoracial population is in fact of 'mixed' descent, much closer to racialised frontiers than it might realise (Stephens, 1999). One striking example is the somewhat unlikely figure of British Conservative Party leader Iain Duncan Smith. In the nineteenth century his great grandfather became British vice-consul of Fuzhou, China, having married a Japanese woman in Beijing. One political commentator was inspired to describe Duncan Smith as '...clearly a rum customer, and no mistake; quite apart from a semi-Oriental appearance deriving from a Japanese great grandmother'. (Alan Watkins in Independent on Sunday, 23rd December 2001). A shadow history of Western modernity could be told through further exploration of the interracial contacts which animated its development. Such a history would be a salutary reminder not to draw solely on concepts, histories and political dynamics drawn exclusively from the United States. North America's specific history of deep-seated segregation, racial polarisation between black and white and the persistence of anti mixed marriage laws (until 1967 in some states) should not provide the only terms for exploring these issues. As Werner Sollors has recently argued:

> Far from appearing exclusively in the United States, interracial themes have been present in writing from antiquity and the middle ages to the Renaissance and the present, with a pronounced increase since the late eighteenth century. (Sollors, 1997: 8)

From Heliodorus's Aethiopica in the 4th century A.D. via Shakespeare's Othello to Nella Larsen's novel Passing, Western writing has recurrently worried away at the issues raised by interracial relationships and 'mixed race' lives. Western philosophy and science also played a formative role in the emergence and consolidation of modern racial categories in no small measure through voicing disquiet at the alleged impurifying and counter-evolutionary consequences of racial mixing (Nietsczhe, 1997: 149). Social science of the early twentieth century made the psychological and social adjustment of 'mixed race' people in the urban metropolis an important theme (Park, R. 1931). In the interwar period, young 'mixed race' children in Britain's seaports were photographed, measured and tested as part of a Eugenics Society study of "Race-Crossing" (Barkan, 1992; Fleming, 1927; Fletcher, 1930; Parker, 2001).

Tracing such discourses is more than an academic exercise. However anachronistic these historical representations seem to us now, they still influence the contemporary analysis of 'mixed race'. The potent combination of sexual and racial transgression implied by 'mixed race', its furtive exoticisation, the virulent hatred at racial impurity and defilement; all these contradictory sentiments and impulses shape the representation of mixed relationships and the figuring of the 'mixed race' body in cultural representations. For example as recently as 1955 in the USA the Virginia supreme court upheld the state's law prohibiting interracial marriage in order to 'preserve the racial integrity of its citizens', avert 'the corruption of blood', 'the obliteration of racial pride' and prevent the growth of 'a mongrel breed of citizens' (Sollors, 1997). Such sentiments persist even today. In December 2001 the Leeds United footballer Lee Bowyer was reported to have ended a relationship with a part-Asian woman with the words, 'We can't do this any more. If we have a baby there could be a throwback and it might be born brown'. ('Yob Bowyer jilted me for being 1/4 Asian', *Sunday People*, December 16th 2001).

The treatment of racial mixture is one significant barometer of how a society deals with racism. It also forms part of the process whereby racialised categories are defined, defended and contested, particularly when it comes to counting the population.

Demography

Successive generations of social statisticians and bureaucrats have grappled with the issue of how to define 'mixed race' people for the purposes of Census enumeration and sociological accuracy. The changing categories used, the lengths gone to in capturing racial diversity, offer a revealing series of ten yearly snapshots into the developing racialised consciousness of the territories in question. Furthermore, the extent to which a social category receives official sanction can itself both reflect and shape everyday processes of identity formation.

David Goldberg's extraordinary analysis of the changing racialised categories used in the United States population Census demonstrates how arbitrary these designations can be (Goldberg, 1997). Over the last two hundred years someone with one white and one black parent would have been designated as coloured, mulatto, negro, black depending on when they were born. In 1890 black people of mixed ancestry were fractionalised into halves (mulattos) quarters (quadroons) and eighths (octoroons) before being collapsed back again into black. Similar fractionalisation was applied to native Americans in 1950, '…listed according to degree of Indian blood: full blood; half to full; quarter to half; less than one quarter', measured like fuel gauges (Goldberg, 1997: 42).

Great Britain's history of racialised naming in Census data is more recent. Prior to 1991 only country of birth gave a clue to a person's ethnic origins. This was obviously an imperfect indicator given the number of white soldiers, sailors and administrators who had started families overseas; and the number of British-born children of non-white migrants from those territories and elsewhere. The 1991 population Census was the first to directly probe respondents' ethnic origins. It partially recorded 'mixed race' via the provision of 'Black other' and 'any other ethnic group please write below' options. It estimated the number of people of mixed descent at 230,000, less than 0.5% of the total population.

Further analysis by Charlie Owen (Owen, 2001) has disaggregated this figure into:

- Black/White   54,569
- Asian/White   61,874
- Other Mixed   112,061

The high figure of 'Other Mixed' includes many who are in fact of black/white origin, as the coding rules placed all those who wrote in 'half caste' or 'mixed race' in the 'Other Mixed' category. These figures must be treated with extreme caution for as Owen points out the Census enumerators had a welter of written responses to code, with coding rules as sensitive as this: 'English West Indian' was coded as Black, but 'English-West Indian' was taken to imply 'mixed race'. Such coding decisions might well make the 1991 figure an underestimate of those with 'mixed race' backgrounds.

The 2001 Census modified the option boxes available to respondents replying to 'What is your ethnic group'?, with the addition of a 'mixed' option, significantly the first option listed on the form after 'white'. The 'mixed' category was further subdivided into:

- White and Black Caribbean

- White and Black African
- White and Asian
- Any other mixed background. Please describe.

The invitation to self-identify, together with the prompt of an explicit 'mixed' category is likely to increase the numbers identified as 'mixed race', even before taking into account the children of the mixed marriages and partnerships likely to have occurred in the last decade.

Pending the publication of the 2001 Census data for Great Britain in 2002/3, the closest population estimates available come from the quarterly Labour Force Survey. A recent article reports some significant findings, suggesting a rapid growth in the population that identifies as 'mixed', and clarifying the British 'mixed race' population's distinctive demographic profile (Scott, Pearce, and Goldblatt, 2001 in Population Trends, Autumn No. 105, pp. 6–15). The manner in which the responses to the survey question on ethnic origin are assigned to different categories does not conform exactly to the previous 1991 Census, so the two data sets are not directly comparable. The Labour Force Survey codes those who respond 'Black British' as 'Black Other non mixed'. Those who explicitly identify as 'mixed' are coded as 'Black-mixed' or 'Other-mixed'. Averaging the results across the years 1997–1999 for Great Britain gives the following results:

- 'Black-mixed'   183,000
- 'Other-mixed'   235,000
- Total   418,000

(Source: Scott, Pearce and Goldblatt, 2001)

Since 1992–1994 those two 'mixed' groups had grown by 49% and 28% respectively. Although taken together they account for only one in ten of the minority ethnic population, they accounted for over one-fifth of its growth in the 1990s.

Perhaps the most striking feature of Britain's 'mixed race' population is its youthful age profile compared to both other minorities and the white population.

Percentage of each category under the age of 15

- 'Black-mixed'   58%
- 'Other-mixed'   52%
- Population as a whole 19%

(Source: Scott, Pearce and Goldblatt, 2001).

In addition the mixed population is overwhelmingly British born; 89% of the 'Black-mixed' and 75% of the 'Other-mixed' population were born in the UK, as against only 25% of Britain's Chinese population. Thus, rather than being born overseas and arriving in Britain when young '...the majority of the people classified as mixed were children of unions between UK residents of different ethnic origins' (ibid: 13).

113

'Mixed race' children under 15 were less likely than the average for both the white and minority ethnic group population to be living with both natural parents, particularly so where one of the parents was black. Percentages of under 15 year olds living with both natural parents were:

- White   73%
- All minority ethnic groups   69%
- 'Other-mixed'   63%
- 'Black-mixed'   41%

(ibid)

These data do not provide detail on the patterns of interracial marriage and partnership. Analysis of the Policy Studies Institute's Fourth National Ethnic Minorities survey (conducted in 1992–1994) indicates important variations between different minority groups.

- For British-born Caribbeans, approximately half the men and a third of women had a white partner; among Indians and African Asians one in five men and one in ten women had a white partner; very few Pakistani and Bangladeshi people had white partners.

- Two thirds of the Caribbean and South Asian people who had entered 'mixed race' partnerships were male, for Chinese mixed relationships two thirds of those with white partners were women. For two in five children with a Caribbean mother or father, the other parent was white; for one in six children with a Chinese mother or father the other parent was white, whereas this was the case for only 1% of children with a Pakistani or Bangladeshi mother or father (Modood, T. et al, 1997).

In summary, Britain's 'mixed race' population is growing rapidly, with children of Black/white, Indian/white and Chinese/white backgrounds predominating. It is a very youthful and overwhelmingly British born group.

The United States population Census of 2000 provides instructive comparative data. Although there was no 'mixed race' or 'multiracial' category, respondents could check all racial categories that applied. The results began to be released in spring 2001 by the United States Census Bureau. Overall 6.8 million respondents identified as belonging to more than one race – 2.4% of the population. The tabulation even went so far as to enumerate the precise numbers who had opted to check two, three, four, five and six categories. The vast majority who checked more than one racial category checked just two (93%). The largest sub-categories being white and some other race (32%) which would include many of Hispanic origin; White, American Indian and Alaska Native (16%) White and Asian (13%) and White and Black or African American (12%) (United States Census Bureau, 2001).

As with the British demographic profile, youthfulness and urban concentration are hallmarks of the United States mixed descent population.

The proportion of Americans under 18 identified as 'multiracial' was 4.2%, against only 1.9% of all adults being multiracial (Washington Post March 13th 2001, Page A01). California is the state with the most multiracial residents, 1.6 million or 4.7% of its population. Eight of the top ten multiracial cities in the United States are in California (*Washington Post*, March 30th 2001 Page A03).

At the time of writing, data from the United States 2000 Census on interracial marriage and partnerships are not available. However the annual United States Current Population Survey has recorded a significant increase in the number of 'mixed race' marriages from 994,000 in 1991 to 1.464 million in 2000, 'mixed race' marriages as a proportion of the total growing from 1.9 to 2.6%. The most recent data in the United States, albeit with different configurations and definitions of 'race', match the British experience of rapid growth, youthfulness and a rising proportion of interracial marriages.

Analytical implications

The analytical significance of 'mixed race' for sociological analysis of racialised identities and racism has, until recently, been largely overlooked, particularly in British texts on 'race' and ethnicity. The issue of 'mixed race' provides a strategically important vantage point for exploring the frameworks currently in play for theorising racialisation at the start of the twenty first century. There are three ways in which 'mixed race' has been conceived: as a stable social identity in its own right; re-expressed as 'multiracial'; and a temporary pre-figuration of a post-racial future.

In Britain the term 'mixed race' is now widely recognised as the identity of self-designation by people with mixed ancestry (Tizard, and Phoenix, 1993). Older and more derogatory terms such as 'coloured', 'half caste' and 'half-breed' although still in circulation have been displaced. For all the difficulties of invoking a concept 'race' which it then places under erasure, the notion of 'mixed race', by drawing attention to the permeability between so-called races, may have a role in weakening the hold of racialised forms of thought and action in the years ahead.

The second perspective displaces 'mixed race' with the designation 'multiracial'. Primarily associated with the United States, it secured administrative recognition in the population Census of 2000 which offered an exhaustive set of racial options for respondents: six basic categories and 57 possible combinations of two, three, four, five or six 'races'. There is an implacable assertion that White, Black, American Indian, Asian, Native Hawaiian are 'races' with clearly identifiable boundaries, consequently any one individual may derive from any combination of these backgrounds. 'Multiracial' is preferred to 'mixed race' on the grounds that it captures the multiple ancestries of a growing proportion of the North American population.

Such taxonomic rigour is both a strength and a weakness. The precise enumeration of ancestry highlights the intertwining of complex histories and breaks beyond a simplistic racial dualism of black and white. However, without further qualification the assertion of a multiracial identity multiplies the allegiances to an unquestioned notion of 'race', and can pay little attention to the variable salience of the different components of ancestry, implying an equal weighting between them. It may compound at least as much as it contests the allocation of social significance to defining racial categories. To be 'multiracial' today one has to confidently identify monoracial branches of one's past, projecting homogeneity backwards in time, implying evolutionary progression to today's complexity, valorising the latter over an allegedly simpler past. Claiming to be multiracial can also become a form of vanity: competing for the longest list of diverse antecedents, a symbolic ethnicity with little regard for today's harsh inequalities.

Thirdly, the most idealistic advocates of 'mixed race' see it as a temporary identity position to be occupied strategically en route to a world beyond 'race'. In this post-racial framework, colour should not matter. We are all individuals, the marking of difference by racial categories is outmoded, a residue of imperialism, something for wise libertarians to 'move beyond', something which 'mixed race' people have an edge over others in both recognising and experiencing for themselves:

> Mixed-race people are performing a historic role at the present moment: they are reanimating a traditional American emphasis on the freedom of individual affiliation. (Holdinger, 1995:166)

Among the most eloquent and consistent exponents of post-racial libertarianism is Charles Byrd, editor of the Internet journal Interracial Voice. He argues that:

> In my experience people who consider themselves of "mixed race" inevitably question not only the wisdom of racial identification but also the very scientific and biological foundation of 'race' itself (…) Individuals of mixed race backgrounds quickly begin searching for a higher spiritual truth, something that allows them to make sense of the madness behind lumping human beings into separate and distinct racial groupings. (Byrd, 2001 "Transcending race consciousness", *San Francisco Chronicle*, 25th July, page A19).

Here Byrd aspires to a transcendent, disembodied form of existence. Laudable in intent, it ignores the deep-seated ambiguity of embodiment central to contemporary 'mixed race' experiences. Looking 'different' can be the bane of 'mixed race' life. The social constructions of norms of physical appearance still decisively influence identity formation. In the light of the continuing salience of this and other forms of racialisation, the declaration of post-racialism seems premature (see eg. Eze 2001 and Goldberg, D. 2002).

It has been argued that post-racial viewpoints are too naive and stand in the way of attempts to monitor and remedy racialised forms of disadvantage. As Winant puts it:

> ...racial hierarchy lives on, it correlates very well with worldwide and national systems of stratification and inequality, it corresponds to glaring disparities in labor conditions and reflects differential access to democratic and communicative instrumentalities and life chances. My view is that the race concept is anything but obsolete and that its significance is not declining. We are not 'beyond race'. (Winant, 2001:2)

Winant has a point, but it does not clinch the argument. He recognises that (Omi, and Winant, 1994) the formation of racialised categories and patterns of disadvantage is ever-changing. Part of the prevailing dynamic involves an emerging generation who do not feel the existing handful of major racial identities captures the subtlety and variety of their experiences and the complex realities of their backgrounds, families, everyday lives and futures. Surely one can recognise the continuing force of racial inequality alongside paying heed to new fluidities and flexibilities in racial identification when they emerge? It is only by engaging more extensively with the experiences of 'mixed race' people that we can appreciate the emerging multiple identity formations that may require a longer-term rethinking of the modalities of racialisation.

What's it like to be you?

No-one has ever quite asked me that question, or "What are you?", but hairdressers, dentists, schoolmates have occasionally been curious about my ambiguous appearance. Only one brick and rare verbal insults have been thrown in my direction, with one childhood head wound to reflect upon painfully. Several North American collections of social science commentary have begun to document the common experiences along these lines many 'mixed race' people face, particularly when growing up (Root, ed.; 1992, Root, ed., 1996; Camper, 1994). Britain is notable for very few systematic collections of evidence from persons of mixed descent (Tizard, and Phoenix, 1987). Here I will summarise the findings of others, and some of my own interviews with 'mixed race' people over the last few years.

Jayne Ifekwunigwe's interviews with 'mixed race' women in Britain tap into the distinct patterns of long-established Black/'mixed race' populations in seaports such as Liverpool, Bristol and Cardiff (Ifekwunigwe, 1999). The main concerns of the interviewees lie in building a relationship with black identities and communities; distinct gendered and sexualised patterns of identification, the stresses, strains and complex joy of forming families which disrupt convention.

Some of my own work has recorded the testimony of the early twentieth century generation of Anglo-Chinese people in Britain's seaports, the children of Chinese seafarers and white women. Those who had grown up in the close-knit atmosphere of Liverpool's Chinatown stressed their role as multicultural pioneers:

> We had the best of both worlds, you had your Chinese and now you've got your English part of you. You can mix equally with the both (…) It's getting easier to live in England now, as it's becoming more multicultural, but I think as children we paved the way, we had to pave the way.
>
> Lin (Aged 60: born in Liverpool, Chinese father, British mother)

Talking to the current generation of 'mixed race' people with East Asian backgrounds, I found that 'mixed' identity is not simply about racialised duality or multiplicity, but is part of a wider formation of contingent identity across all affiliations:

> I don't feel my identity is fixed. I do feel it's moving and expanding and my racial identity is also very much to do with my identity as a woman and also my sexual identity…my political identity. I can't separate them, they're all mixed, my mind is open to learning and questioning myself and finding my own solutions within that.
>
> Michelle (Aged 26: English father, Chinese mother)

This open formation of identity could crystallise in different ways. For some it involves a general disposition towards individualist non-alignment:

> I don't think I could ever really identify with anybody now; I feel as if I've gone over the edge! I don't particularly want to, it's certainly nice to, but I feel as if I've grown up by myself, even though I'm part of a family unit I feel as if I don't belong to that family, I might be alien.
>
> I've considered that idea sometimes (…) I like the idea of being comfortable with non identity as an identity, you don't have to be anything.
>
> Lee (Aged 28: Chinese father, English mother)

For others being 'mixed race' matched the social conditions of choice, fluidity and pluralism associated with postmodernism:

> You grow up knowing in your bones, in your heart, that no one's sense of values and ideas are universal and are final. The British/West sense of values is not universal, the Chinese is not

> universal, because you embody them both, all the contradictions, all the compatibilities you have it all...and...people say it's unusual, but I've known nothing else, don't tell me that's unusual, to me this is normality. People from one culture they are linked to, that's unusual for me...It sets you up to be a bona fide postmodernist! What better grounding could you have?
>
> Liam (Aged 30: Irish father, Chinese mother)

Another respondent stated:

> I've got a choice that lots of people haven't got between elements of culture – I guess we've all got that choice – but I feel I've got more permission or I'm allowed to give myself permission if you like. The permission to choose my affiliations, I don't feel pinned down, I can appreciate many cultures and their different elements.
>
> Simon (Aged 30: Singaporean father, English mother)

The timing of one's parents' marriage, the class and cultural milieus of upbringing undoubtedly influence forms of identification. Ka Yan grew up in Hong Kong, with an affluent background and had an international education. She speculated on the source of her self-professed liberal cosmopolitanism:

> You've got to think about whether the fact that people like our parents got married at a time when society was only just beginning to accept the idea (the 1960s)...perhaps people HAVE to be more liberal about certain things. So maybe you could make a generalisation that because Eurasians come from societies which are more liberal and at the forefront of that more liberal thinking, and the fact that their parents marrying was going against trends, maybe that "going against trendness" influences the kids, which in turn influences their other views.
>
> Ka Yan (Aged 26: Chinese father, English mother)

In the absence of extensive intergenerational research these remarks can only be tentative indicators of 'mixed race' identity. More systematic exploration of how other social relations and identities interact with being 'mixed race' is required. One thing is clear, the current generations of 'mixed race' people cannot be represented as living identity crises and deserve the chance to explore and express their identities in their own terms, not as adjuncts to the political projects of others. In the words of one commentator there is now '... a critical mass of young adults who are of mixed origins and who do not see themselves as carrying either burdens or solutions for the entire society'. (Alibhai Brown, 2001: 5)

Artistic representations

As a supplement to research data there has been a boom in fictional and autobiographical publishing with the lives of 'mixed race' people and families centre-stage. What was once decried (ambiguity and uncertain social position) is now a source of insight and cultural validity. A 'mixed race' character in a story by Claude McKay in the 1930s stated that white people '...hate us more than they do the blacks. For they're never sure about us, they can't place us' (McKay, 1972 (1932): 95–96). Today the 'mixed race' person is hailed as the exemplar of hybridity, a condition to which we all should aspire because we are all being propelled there by globalisation, like it or not.

In the realm of fiction, three recent novels have had 'mixed race' heroines and heroes (Mo, 1999; Smith, 2000; Senna, 1999). For these characters there is no one point of origin from which all else flows. Selfhood is an ongoing journey picking up and discarding cultural fragments, a contingent improvisation in the present, not an unconditional affirmation of the past. For each of the novels' main figures their ambiguous status is signified by their bodies. Physical incongruity and a lack of fit with preconceived images lead to comic, poignant and telling attempts at corporeal transformation, which neither fail nor succeed completely. When Irie Jones, the heroine of White Teeth, tries to straighten her hair a disastrous application of ammonia and a reparative transplant leads her to recognise that 'Sometimes you want to be different. And sometimes you'd give the hair on your head to be the same as everybody else' (Smith, 2000: 245–246).

Zadie Smith's characters make localities such as Willesden in North London the meeting point for diverse migrant trajectories, whose different time frames complicate both family histories and collective identities, making Britain a country '...which is new to us and old to us all at the same time' (ibid: 155). Settings like the school playground lead multicultural societies to a recognition that

> ...this has been the century of strangers (...) of the great immigrant experiment (...) Children with first and last names on a direct collision course. Names that secrete within them mass exodus, cramped boats and planes, cold arrivals, medical checks. (ibid: 281)

In these works the stance adopted towards 'mixed race' existence is an emphatic embrace of uncertainty and indecision. By the close of the novels a calm and realistic 'coming to terms' with the meaning of being 'mixed' is apparent. In Senna's Caucasia Birdie Lee notices another 'mixed race' girl looking 'black like me' in the back of a departing school bus. She restrains the urge to wave and claim a commonality that may not exist (Senna, 1999: 413). At the end of Mo's novel Renegade the black/Filipino hero Rey Castro has learnt to laugh at the Filipinos who gawp at his black body. He returns to the aspirational metaphor which opened the book of trying to concoct a 'sundae confection' of all the 'bests of' he knows, but recognises the folly of attempting to mix the best elements of all cultures into one person. In fact the best and the worst always go together (Mo, 1999: 478).

The lives narrated in these works of fiction explore tendencies becoming more prevalent with each generation and those '...who live this condition are no longer (in their consciousness) pathetic victims: they are laden with exemplariness' (Glissant quoted in Dash, 1995: 97). Works such as this and many others speak to the new experiences of migrants and their descendants, prefiguring new formations of identity which have yet to be fully thematised.

Visual art may provide another subtle medium for registering these complexities. One example is the British-based artist Lubaina Himid's painting My Parents/Their Children (1986). On either side of the middle of the canvas stand the white father and black grandmother of the artist, around them the words:

> My grandfather never met my grandmother
> the sea
> the sand and the time
> kept them apart
> their children/my parents

Out of these diverse histories 'mixed race' people are made and make themselves.

'Mixed race' and adoption policies

The importance of appreciating the complexity of 'mixed race' identity is highlighted sharply by shifts in government and social service agencies policies towards transracial adoption. In the 1970s in the United States and Britain black social work professionals began to express disquiet at the practice of transracial adoption – a concern focused on the predominant pattern of these adoptions, a black or 'mixed race' child (usually with one black and one white biological parent) being adopted by a white family. 'Mixed race' young people have always been disproportionately represented in the care system and thus acutely influenced by policies in this sphere. An emotive debate with profound political and personal consequences ensued with attention focused on whether these children could be appropriately raised in a white family. Could white parents and adoptive siblings provide sufficient knowledge about how to cope with racism? Would 'mixed race' children develop strong senses of identity giving their black origin full weight? Was transracial adoption encouraging the disavowal of black heritage and condemning 'mixed race' children in particular to a future of maladjustment, and in the extreme, alienation and self-hatred?

Critics of transracial adoption called for a policy of same race placement – ensuring that adoptive families were of the same racial background as the child, and that 'mixed race' children should be placed with black, not white families (Small, 1986). Social service departments throughout Britain and the United States and social work training began to adopt this policy from the 1980s onwards, and it is still the approach favoured by childcare specialists.

In Britain, opposition took two forms. Populist interventions, often by newspapers opposed to so-called political correctness, would highlight cases where children were denied a 'loving home' due to parents being deemed insufficiently conscious of race-based issues (*Sunday Times*, 18 July 1999). In these cases, the fact that 'mixed race' children are disproportionately present in long term residential care for several years awaiting 'matching' families is highlighted. In 2000 17% of those British children awaiting adoption were 'mixed race' (The Times, 19 February 2000). There is an implicit resentment at 'politically correct' social service professionals for elevating 'race' above other factors.

Partly in response to such cases Britain's Labour Government, in reframing adoption policy, has tried to reduce the emphasis on racial matching. A Department of Health Circular instruction sent to all social service departments in 1998 stated '... it is unacceptable for a child to be denied loving adoptive parents solely on the grounds that the child and adopters do not share the same racial or cultural background' (Department of Health Circular LAC, 1998: 20). A White Paper 'Adoption, A New Approach' prefigured legislation which passed through Parliament in autumn 2001 to reduce all obstacles to adoption, including those based on 'race'. In practice, social service departments with high minority ethnic populations follow a broadly same race placement policy, but are now asked not to consider racial difference between adoptive children and parents as the only obstacle to an adoption where same race solutions are not available.

The second dimension to the debate is more analytical and explores the assumptions about 'mixed race' identity formation embedded in policy prescriptions. Those in favour of same race placement argue that a positive identity for a 'mixed race' person can only be generated by explicit recognition of black identity, a recognition that can only be secured through upbringing in black families and contact with black communities. The most strident critic of same race placement has been Paul Gilroy (1987). He regards the theory of culture and identity underpinning same race placement as reductive and simplistic. Black identity, like any identity, is complex, heterogeneous and multifaceted. There is no guarantee that black parents can embody and nurture it any better than others. Furthermore identity development is not simply a question of 'race' and matching the skin tones of one's carers. Those whose biological parents are from different racial backgrounds cannot fail to be uneasy at the implied criticism of 'mixed race' families embedded in the policy prescription of same race placement: it seems to be legislating to keep identities fixed, in both physical and cultural terms, with the unspoken accusation that all 'mixed race' couples and peoples are 'sell-outs', keen to disavow their minority heritage and assimilate as rapidly as possible.

In the last few years the sharpness of the debates about adoption practice has subsided (Kirton, 2000). Professionals acknowledge that 'race' is only one factor in determining successful adoptions; social class, place of residence, the knowledge of prospective parents about racism must be weighed in the balance. All agree that more adoptive parents from minority communities must be sought to widen the pool of potential homes for 'mixed race' children in care. The very existence of a widely recognised constituency of 'mixed race' people and families in itself has helped soften the dilemmas, without eliminating them completely.

'Mixed race' identities and resources on-line

The beginnings of a 'mixed race' political movement have been remarked upon by several analysts (Nakashima, 1996 in Root (ed); Spencer, 1997) particularly with reference to the United States where debates over population Census categories in the run up to 2000 brought organisations representing 'mixed race' families and individuals to the fore. The development of the Internet has facilitated the promotion of institutions and electronic resources for a group whose widespread geographical dispersal can hamper the forms of community-building associated with other minority groups. There are three types of on-line presence: voluntary organisations; formal discursive intervention points; more expressive artistic web sites.

Voluntary organisations on-line

In the United States the most prominent organisations pressing the public case for the recognition of 'mixed race' experiences have been the Association of Multiethnic Americans (Association of Multiethnic Americans) and Project RACE (Reclassify All Children Equally). Project RACE aims to institute a 'multiracial' option on all forms collecting racial data in the United States.

Among the key organisations in Britain are People in Harmony, established in 1972, whose aim is to 'promote the positive experience of interracial life in Britain' and Intermix which offers 'friendship, support, information and advice' to 'mixed race' individuals and families.

Many of these organisations offer on-line educational resources and information about the history of 'mixed race' and the lives of prominent people of 'mixed race', past and present.

Commentary and discussion sites

There are numerous discussion and viewpoint sites with varying degrees of formality and depth. Across these sites, there is no single 'mixed race' experience, correspondents move between the 'mixed race', multiracial or post-racial formations of identity I described earlier. Among the most important commentary sites are:

- Interracial Voice. Edited in the United States by Charles Byrd, the dominant stance of the pieces adopts a strongly post-racial viewpoint. Racial categorisation is viewed as regrettably regressive, and there is a spiritual undertow to the calls for individuals to transcend racial divisions.
- The Multiracial Activist. This site is 'a libertarian oriented activist journal' based in the United States. It advocates the abolition of all forms of official racial classification and asserts the right of individuals not merely to self-identify as they wish racially, but to choose no racial identity and eschew the concept of 'race' completely.

Personal and creative web sites

There are more and more Internet sites posted by 'mixed race' individuals, often creative artists expressing various forms of dissident racial sensibility. One example is the special on-line issue of the Canadian literary magazine Absinthe called 'HypheNation: a mixed race issue'. Sabu's on-line mixture of art, poetry and commentary is signposted by an eloquent summary of the ethos often underlying such interventions: '.. while humankind continues to naively imagine itself separate, immovable stones, the so-called 'mixed race' through nothing more than (albeit) often tested, sometimes painful, love of our families, shall remain the binding cement'.

Conclusion

Changing social practices and social attitudes are mutually reinforcing in most areas of human life, particularly so in respect of 'mixed race'. The widespread criticism of the former Conservative MP John Townend's animus at the so-called 'mongrelisation' of Britain during the 2001 General Election campaign indicates that the ground has shifted. Increasingly it is those who are opposed to mixed relationships who have to answer for their views, not the other way round. Amidst the dispute Britain's most popular tabloid newspaper ran an article and editorial roundly condemning the implied criticism of 'mixed race' children ("How dare you call my boy a mongrel", *The Sun* May 2nd 2001) – something inconceivable a decade earlier.

Despite signs of progress, problems and difficulties still remain, and our understanding of them is limited. Residues of old conceptions of 'mixed race' identity as inherently problematic resurface periodically. For example the singer Mariah Carey recently stated

> My sensitive point is that I'm a person of mixed race and therefore I've always felt like an outsider (...) What does that make these children that are very ambiguous-looking? Who are we? And are we acceptable human beings? That's an intense thing. (*The Times*, 6th August 2001)

The interview, published just after her hospitalisation allegedly for mental exhaustion, was headlined 'The breaking of Mariah Carey'.

Conversely, 'mixed race' people are often portrayed as having 'the best of both worlds', and 'mixed race' relationships as proof of how love conquers all. Such romanticisation can obscure harsh realities. Couples in mixed relationships (particularly in mainly white areas) continue to face deep-seated resentment, verbal abuse and physical attack. The most notable example of harassment in Britain being an Asian-white couple subjected to over 2,000 attacks in the 1990s (*Guardian*, 13th April 2000). The intersection of gender, class and racialised inequalities can also place particular pressure on the growing numbers of white single mothers with 'mixed race' children.

Finally, analysts of racialisation must approach 'mixed race' with a recognition of the diversification of diversity. 'Race' and racial mixture involves far more than placing 'mixed race' halfway between Black and White on a one-dimensional colour spectrum. The most dramatic indicator of this diversification of diversity has been the demand for recognition voiced by mixed-race Americans whose affirmation of their own difference has complicated the argument over what kinds of sameness and what kinds of difference matter (Hollinger, 1995).

'Mixed race' people are a complex three-way mirror. To minority communities defensive about the degree to which they have already assimilated and who see 'mixed race' people as evidence of betrayal and racial 'traitorhood'. To a white majority fearful of the visible evidence of demographic change and mixture which 'mixed race' people embody. To liberals who see 'mixed race' children as signs of peaceful integration and living prefaces to a harmonious multicultural future.

Appreciating this strategic importance, 'mixed race' identities are among several forces deconstructing the existing pattern of social categorisation. This does not destroy or undermine all forms of belonging, rather it implies the creation of new, less certain, affiliations, identities and understandings to be explored sensitively rather than asserted baldly. 'Mixed race' people dramatise and focus issues of identification and self-naming faced by all, but the answers they are tentatively forging should not carry the hopes or fears of the whole world. 'Mixed race' and racism have co-existed for centuries already, both will persist for some time to come, albeit in new forms.

Bibliography

Alibhai Brown, Y. (2001) *Mixed Feelings: The Complex Lives of Mixed-Race Britons*, London: Women's Press.

Anzaldua, G. (1987) *Borderlands/LaFrontera: The New Mestiza*, San Francisco: Aunt Lute Books.

Barkan, E. (1992) *The Retreat of Scientific Racism*. Cambridge: Cambridge University Press.

Berthoud, R. (2000) *Family Formation in Multicultural Britain: Three Patterns of Diversity*, University of Essex: Institute of Social and Economic Research www.iser.ac.uk/pubs/workpaps/pdf/2000-34.pdf

Bitterli, U. (1989) *Cultures in Conflict: Encounters Between European and Non-European Cultures, 1492–1800*, Stanford: Stanford University Press.

Bonnett, A. (2000) *Anti-Racism*, London: Routledge.

Byrd, C. (2001) 'Transcending race consciousness', *San Francisco Chronicle*, 25th July, page A19.

Camper, C. (1994) *Miscegenation Blues*, Toronto: Sister Vision.

Dash, M. (1995) *Edouard Glissant*, Cambridge: Cambridge University Press.

Eze, E. (2001) *Achieving our Humanity: The Idea of the Postracial Future*, New York: Routledge.

Fleming, R. (1927). 'Anthropological Studies of Children'. In *Eugenics Review*. 294–301.

Fletcher, M. E. (1930) *Report of an Investigation into The Colour Problem in Liverpool and Other Ports*. Liverpool: Liverpool Association for the Welfare of Half Caste Children.

Gilroy, P. (1987) *There ain't No Black in the Union Jack*, London: Hutchinson.

Gist, N. and Dworkin, A. (1972) *The Blending of Races: Marginality and Identity in World Perspective*, New York: John Wiley.

Glissant, E. (1989) *Caribbean Discourse*, Charlottesville: University Press of Virginia.

Goldberg, D. (1997) *Racial Subjects*, New York and London: Routledge.

Goldberg, D. (2002) *The Racial State*, Malden and Oxford: Blackwell Guardian, 13th April 2000.

Hollinger, D. (1995) *Postethnic America*, New York: Basic Books.

Ifekwunigwe, J. (1999) *Scattered Belongings*, London: Routledge.

Kirton, D. (2000) *Race, Ethnicity and Adoption*, Buckingham: Open University Press.

Luke, C. and Luke, A. (1998) 'Interracial Families: Difference within Difference' in *Ethnic and Racial Studies*, 21 (4) pp. 728–754.

Marx, A. (1998) *Making Race and Nation*, Cambridge: Cambridge University Press.

McKay, C. (1972) {1932} *Gingertown*, Freeport: Books for Libraries Press.

Metro newspaper, October 9th 2001: 11.

Mo, T. (1999) *Renegade*, London: Paddleless Press.

Modood, T. et al (1997) *Ethnic Minorities in Britain*, London: Policy Studies Institute.

Nakashima, C. (1996) 'Voices from the Movement: Approaches to Multiraciality' in Root, M. ed. (1996) *The Multiracial Experience*. Thousand Oaks: Sage.

Nietsczhe, F. (1997) {1881} *Daybreak*, Cambridge: Cambridge University Press.

Omi, M. and Winant, H. (1994) *Racial Formation in the United States*, New York: Routledge.

Owen, C. (2001) "Mixed Race in Official Statistics" in Parker, D. and Song, M. eds. *Rethinking 'Mixed Race'*, London: Pluto Press.

Park, R. (1931). 'Mentality of racial hybrids', in *American Journal of Sociology*. 36, 534–551.

Parker, D. (2001) " 'We Paved the Way': Exemplary Spaces and 'Mixed Race' in Britain" in T. Kay Williams and C. Nakashima eds. *The Sum of Our Parts*, Philadelphia: Temple University Press.

Parker, D. and Song, M. eds (2001) *Rethinking 'Mixed Race'*, London: Pluto Press.

Root, M. ed. (1992) *Racially Mixed People in America*, Newbury Park: Sage.

Root, M. ed. (1996) *The Multiracial Experience*, Thousand Oaks: Sage.

Roychowdhury, L. (2000) *The Jadu House: Intimate Histories of Anglo-India*, London: Doubleday.

Scott, A.; Pearce, D. and Goldblatt, P. (2001) 'The sizes and characteristics of the minority ethnic populations of Great Britain – latest estimates' in *Population Trends*, Autumn No. 105, pp. 6–15.

Senna, D. (1999) *Caucasia*, New York: Riverhead Books.

Small, J. (1986) "Transracial Placements: Conflicts and Contradictions" in A. Cheetham and J. Small eds. *Social Work with Black Children and Their Families*, London: Batsford.

Smith, Z. (2000) *White Teeth*, London: Hamish Hamilton.

Sollors, W. (1997) *Neither Black nor White Yet Both: Thematic Explorations of Interracial Literature*, New York: Oxford University Press.

Spencer, J. (1997) *The New Colored People*, New York: New York University Press.

Spickard, P. (2001) 'The Subject is Mixed Race: The Boom in Biracial Biography' in Parker, D. and Song, M. eds (2001) *Rethinking 'Mixed Race'*, London: Pluto Press.

Stephens, G. (1999) *On Racial Frontiers*, Cambridge: Cambridge University Press.

Stoler, A. (1995) *Race and the Education of Desire*, Durham and London: Duke University Press.

Stonequist, F. (1937) *The Marginal Man*, New York: Russell and Russell Sun *The* May 2nd 2001.

Sunday People 'Yob Bowyer jilted me for being 1/4 Asian', December 16th 2001.

Sunday Times 18 July 1999.

Times *The*, 6th August 2001, 19 February 2000.

Tizard, B. and Phoenix, A. (1993) *Black, White or Mixed Race?* London: Routledge (revised edition 2002).

United States Census Bureau (2001) *Overview of Race and Hispanic Origin, Census 2000* Brief, March 2001 available at: www.census.gov/prod/2001pubs/c2kbr01 - 1.pdf.

Valverde, C. (1992) 'From Dust to Gold: The Vietnamese Amerasian Experience' in M. Root Ed. *Racially Mixed People in America*, Newbury Park: Sage.

Watkins, A. in Independent on Sunday, 23rd December 2001.

Wilson, A. (1987) *Mixed Race Children*, London: Unwin Hyman.

Winant, H. (2001) *The World is a Ghetto: Race and Democracy Since World War II*, New York: Basic Books.

Washington Post March 13th 2001, Page A01, March 30th 2001 Page A03.

Intermix (www.intermix.org.uk).

Interracial Voice (www.webcom.com/intvoice).

The Multiracial Activist (www.multiracial.com).

absinthe (www.acs.ucalgary.ca/~amathur/hyphenation.html).

Culture of 1 (www.1love.com).

Association of Multiethnic Americans (www.ameasite.org).

Project RACE (www.projectrace.com).

People in Harmony (www.pih.org.uk).

7. English character and identity

Kevin Myers

Judging by recent publishing across a range of genres and disciplines both the people of England and their characteristics are very much in vogue. For writers of fiction and autobiography, commentators on politics and popular culture and academics from a range of disciplinary backgrounds, the English appear to be a subject of considerable and continuing fascination (See Barnes, 1998; Scruton, 2000; Duffy, 2001; Shah, 2000; Gikandi, 1996; Davey, 1999). Yet the outcome of all this discussion and debate is not an emerging consensus on the identity and characteristics of the English but rather more studies, more confusion and, occasionally, rancorous argument. Just what is Englishness?

Given that this question has not only many potential answers but also a wide variety of ways in which it might be explored, it is important to set some parameters for what follows. First of all, this chapter is concerned only with what has been variously referred to as national consciousness, sentiment or identity. It has nothing, or at least very little, to say on the origins and development of nationalism as a political doctrine since these are topics more than adequately covered elsewhere (A good place to start is the collection of essays in G. Balakrishnan (ed.) 1996, 'Mapping the Nation'). Second, an increasingly common method for defining Englishness is to conduct opinion polls and surveys that ask people about the 'character of the nation'. Typically, the responses reveal a bewildering range of activities or images associated with Englishness and a series of contradictory and vague statements about the values that define it. Indeed, the sheer variety of responses indicates not only how elusive an essential Englishness is, but how inevitably flawed are those attempts to define it in absolute terms. So instead of providing a descriptive and necessarily selective list of the values of the English or of the activities commonly associated with Englishness, this chapter tries to explain how and why certain values, qualities or characteristics come to be thought of as uniquely English.

Given the confusion surrounding these English qualities the task is not an easy one. Indeed, according to a recent poll, the English were so confident about their national identity they couldn't be bothered to define it (*Daily Telegraph*, 22 April 2000). As will become clear below, there are good reasons to dispute this statement but it does point to something of a paradox. Englishness appears to be at the same time everywhere and nowhere, much

129

discussed but little understood, a keenly felt identity capable of stimulating great passion but one that escapes clear definition and is sometimes associated with racism, xenophobia and violence. Nevertheless, in the midst of all this uncertainty there is one factor that is consistently and widely understood to both make and define Englishness; history.

History is widely recognised as the most important component of Englishness. In academic circles it has become proverbial to note the link between a sense of history and national identity, and more popular accounts of the English seem to concur. A recent MORI report argued, for example, that most people believed that Britishness was better and different to other nationalities because of it 'unique culture and heritage' (MORI poll digest, 21 March 2000. Though the relationship between Britishness and Englishness is both complex and debatable, for the sake of clarity the terms are used interchangeably here (Davies, 1999). Similarly, a recent Gallup poll found that '...one important factor underlying the English people's collective sense of self is undoubtedly the fact that England has existed as a united nation for a thousand years' (*Daily Telegraph,* 22 April 2000). It is this perceived relationship between history and Englishness, between the past and national identities lived in the present, that is the specific focus of this chapter.

History, sometimes conflated with heritage or common customs or national traditions, is almost universally accepted as *the* fundamental ingredient in all national identities (Wright, 1985). And all those interested in the future of Englishness, both those who wish to 'save it' and those who would celebrate its demise, necessarily rely on history for the force of their argument. This is because it is now widely accepted (though still far from unproblematic) that all investigations into forms of identity, all attempts to define who 'we' are, necessarily involve some reflection on where we have come from. In order to understand and assess such claims to identity it is therefore necessary to engage in debates about not just what happened in the past, but, more importantly, about how the past comes to be produced and applied in the present.

This chapter is in three parts. Parts one and two outline and contrast two ways of studying history and understanding its relationship with national identity. On one hand there is a long tradition of narrative and nationalist histories that claim to reveal the real essence of the English (or the German or French or Irish) character. On the other hand, there is now a large body of academic work that sees national identities as works of imagination, the product of specific ways of writing, picturing and thinking about Englishness. The third part of this paper then proceeds to analyse what kind of historical understanding underpins contemporary constructions of national identity and briefly analyses the effects of this for people living in England today.

The English story: narrative

According to the philosopher and critic Roger Scruton the English were a decent and gentle, orderly and respectful, pragmatic and private people. Their ideals were those of the gentleman, 'of fair play and of the stiff upper lip in times of trouble', and though their character was reserved and moderate, they remained committed to the principles of justice and fair play. Such principles served England well as it 'conducted the greatest experiment in constitutional government that the world has ever known' and their culture 'produced the world's greatest poet', the world's 'most flexible and comprehensive language' and the world's most 'just and impartial system of law' (Scruton, 2000). England did experience occasional conflicts but these were always mediated by the essential gentleness of the English and by their deep attachment to their land and their home. Put simply, English characteristics made England a uniquely happy, moral and stable society.

In terms of historical veracity there is, to put it mildly, much that is open to debate. Even leaving aside some of the dubious claims for greatness, Scruton's account of the English is a history of isolation (home is a vaguely expressed but central concept), continuity (national identity is fixed and stable) and uniformity (the English have identifiable characteristics that immigrants simply threaten). The British Empire makes only fleeting appearances and, it is claimed, had no lasting impact on the identity of a people absolutely immersed in the ideology and culture of imperial expansion. It is also a history almost devoid of any kind of conflict. Whilst class differences are briefly recognised, for example, these are explained away in peculiarly mystical terms. For the English 'class was not an economic but a 'spiritual fact' and a 'mysterious social process' that was at once absurd but also amusing. Sometimes it provoked resentment but the class system, and the variety of social institutions and customs that developed alongside it, was 'part of the enchantment that lay over England' and was 'by and large acceptable, even to the losers' (Scruton, 2001: 11, 64, 149). In fact, there is an abundance of evidence that demonstrates how class is primarily economic and that the changing ways in which economic life was organised in the 18th and 19th centuries led to systematic inequalities in terms of ownership, wealth, health and opportunity. These inequalities were a prominent cause of revolts, attempted revolutions and more peaceful political campaigns for change. Yet Scruton barely recognises either these campaigns, or the millions of people who took part in them, and in choosing to ignore or marginalise these people and these events he suggests some of the problems associated with these popular histories of national identity.

The most popular accounts of national character or identity work by constructing simple historical narratives that purport to explain the origins, development and impact of Englishness (It should be noted that there are both conservative and radical versions of the national past. See Samuel, 1981: xv–xxxiii). These narratives are broad in scope, often tracing the development of national character over a number of centuries, and proceeding chronologically, all consist of detailed historical sketches designed to illustrate the essential continuity in national history and the fixed nature of national identity. In these texts the past leads inexorably to the present. Beginning with some highly personalised and intuitive observations on the state of Englishness in the present, these authors then routinely turn to history and collect a set of facts that supposedly explain the contentious situation they have already observed. In other words, in these accounts the past is reduced to a simple prelude to the present and what is a very particular and often exclusionary version of national character or identity becomes the *inevitable* product of centuries of slow, organic and unconscious growth (Scruton, 1990: 58–59). In order to understand why, it is necessary to make some brief remarks on both the form and theory of these narrative histories.

The development of history as a recognised academic discipline occurred in the 19th century at the very same time that modern nation states began to emerge in Northern Europe. The timing is something more than a coincidence. The professional historians of the 19th century in some senses helped to make national identity because they organised their work around a basic theme of historically transmitted common identities. Indeed, perhaps the greatest legacy of these narrative historians is the common sense idea that history makes people, gives them identities and explains who they are. Arthur Bryant eloquently expressed the point back in 1940:

> The key to a nation's future is in her past. A nation that loses it has no future. For men's deepest desires – the instrument by which a continuing society moulds its destiny – spring from their own inherited experience. We cannot recreate the past, but we cannot escape it. It is our blood and bone. To understand the temperament of a people, a statesman has first to know its history. (A. Bryant, 1940: 1)

Here the assertion of English identity (or temperament) is the combined effect of a simplistic narrative form that allows the historian to imagine continuity over centuries, and a belief in the ubiquity of national character. These kinds of histories were central to the processes whereby a national consciousness, or sense of Englishness, was produced in the 19th and 20th centuries. As Roy Foster notes, 'narrative has been used as an actual component of nation building' and there are, moreover, indications that it is coming back into fashion as a way of 'uniting the nation' in uncertain times (R. Foster in G. Cubitt (ed.) 1998: 38).

It will become clear in the second part of this chapter that narrative histories claim much of their authority from their adherence to the 'facts'. The important facts and the key events, it is frequently claimed, will give people a healthy respect for the national past and give them a narrative in which to live their lives. Problematically, however, those who preach the importance of the facts tend to obscure the processes of selection and organisation that are central to any work of history. They treat the nation as a natural object of study and write about the 'national interest' as though it were an obvious, unproblematic and enduring historical reality (See Zinn, 1999: 7–11) Yet these are important and usually unargued for conceptual choices that have significant consequences for the histories that are produced. Not least amongst these is the tendency to laud individuals who allegedly embody the nation's past or to hinge the whole course of history on the vague concept of national 'character' or 'destiny'. The problem is that whilst the narrative form may make for good stories, it is far less convincing in explaining why things happen. As John Tosh puts it, the '...analytical complexity [of history] means that narrative is unlikely to be the best vehicle for historical explanation' (Tosh, 1991: 117). So whilst narrative imposes a particular unity and coherence on the past, the 'cost of telling stories to make the journey of the past easier', as Simon Schama recently put it, is a heavy one (Schama, 2000: 17).

Contingency and conflict are rooted out in favour of a national history unfolding like a costume drama before the eyes of the people (Samuel, 1989: 9–17). The reader (or viewer) is cast in the role of passive spectator, absorbing simplicities about national history that endows with them an identity, a sense of security and providing lessons for the future. The implications of this form of history writing are explained in more detail below. For the moment it is important to realise that if the form of this argument is problematic, so too is its implicit epistemology.

Underpinning the grand narratives of nation is a theory of knowledge (or epistemology) that holds to the view that all knowledge is derived from observation, experience or, particularly in history, the collection of facts. They proceed on the assumption that '...out there, in the documents, lay the facts waiting to be discovered by historians' (Evans, 1997: 20). In other words, the documents hold the truth of the past within them and it is the task of the historian to collect, verify and report them. Whilst the process of discovering the facts may present practical challenges – finding the sources, reading them accurately, relating them to other relevant documents – in principle it is unproblematic. With rigorous training, patient archival research and learned scholarship, accurate and objective historical accounts are possible. Indeed, not only are these accounts possible, it is one of the duties of historians to care for the national memory and to provide reliable historical accounts for the nation (Burke (ed) 1997: 43–59).

This description of Scruton's *England: an elegy* (2001) has attempted to briefly identify the defining characteristics of a particular genre of writing about English history and identity. It is genre that is avowedly empirical, proud of its adherence to the narrative tradition in history writing and, above all, committed to the historical reality that is revealed by the discovery of the 'facts'. Though this argument is pursued in more detail below, it is also important to note in passing that this empirical method is extremely influential in terms of political debate and the formation of social policy. Wearing its theory lightly and claiming the authority revealed by the 'facts', these stories of national identity are easily put to work in everyday life and remain potent as a source of political mobilisation (Dodd, 1995).

As has already been suggested, however, it does not follow that those who repeatedly proclaim their respect for the facts are necessarily the most neutral or objective. Actually, as the third section of this chapter will endeavour to show, the reverse is probably the case. Even, or perhaps especially, those historians and pundits who insist on the sanctity of 'facts', and often give the impression they are defending standards of objectivity and neutrality in historical research, are tied, more or less directly, to particular political positions (Collini, 1999: 99–100). For the moment, however, attention now switches to different ways of examining the relationship between Englishness and history.

The English story: imagination

The kind of popular and empirical accounts of national identity exemplified by Roger Scruton's work can be contrasted with a number of works that have different, and arguably more critical, theoretical and methodological starting points (Hobsbawm, and Ranger, 1983). A very rough sketch of these positions might encompass three basic but significant points.

First, and to put it bluntly, the facts never speak for themselves. In writing the history of the English, or indeed any other history, all historians must both establish the facts (or some of them at least) and then select, arrange and order them into a coherent historical account. The process inevitably requires the analysis and organisation of material and it demands that the historian make a series of judgements about events, situations and people. In this sense, the facts cannot speak for themselves but require the active mediation of the historian.

Second, the mediating role played by historian is a demonstrably inventive process. It requires historians to invent or employ organising concepts, theories and devices and it is these that give the facts their meaning. Even if empirical historians tend to deny the significance of these practical necessities and dispute the charge that it has important consequences for the possibility of objectivity, it is now widely accepted in academic circles that their work is not a neutral report on an unchangeable past. Instead historians help negotiate the meaning of the past and, in doing so, transmit ways to make sense of the present.

Third, and to elaborate a little on the previous point, history is not – and cannot be – a neutral subject (Jordanova, 2000: xiv). The creation of historical knowledge and the negotiations about the meaning of the past are activities that are both conducted, and have affects, in the present. So history is not just about what happened in the past but also about how it comes to be remembered and reproduced in the present. In this sense history and historiography is about how historical knowledge is organised and produced and how it helps (or imposes) on people and communities particular understandings of their place in the world.

Taken together these theoretical and methodological questions imply a rather different starting point for historical investigations of national identity. Instead of accepting national identity as a real empirical phenomenon and then narrating an Englishness that organically and naturally develops through time, scholars have recently approached nationality as a cultural product that is an active and on-going work of imagination that does, however, have real material effects. It is important to be clear about this. Englishness, like any other national identity is continually made and remade – as Hobsbawm puts it, it is the 'result of exercises in social engineering' – that can be identified, examined and critically assessed (Hobsawm and Ranger, 1983: 13). According to this explanatory model national identity is imagined rather than real, learnt rather than inherited. This means, as Kevin Davey has recently argued, 'there is no singular, univocal, national essence or identity, old or new, simply waiting to be uncovered' (Davey, 1999: 7). What can be achieved are discovering the processes of invention and reinvention, identifying changing constructions of national identity, forms of distribution and critically analysing their affects in particular times and places.

Recognising that national identity might be an artificial invention of some past historical actors is not to dismiss its influence over individuals and societies. Only in the crudest forms of classical Marxism is national identity still seen as a form of 'false consciousness' and only the most arrogant of researchers would dismiss the intensity of feeling and emotion now associated with the nation. Yet particular constructions of Englishness 'make sense' or connect with people not because they are biologically inherited or instinctive, but precisely because they have become naturalised or 'common sense' ways of thinking about the world. And for those writers who share these theoretical positions, historical analysis can potentially illuminate just why a particular version of Englishness may come to dominate. A brief example will serve to illustrate.

Hugh Cunningham is only one of the many historians who have pointed to radical constructions of national identity that legitimated protests against the state in the 19th and 20th centuries (Cunningham, 1988; Hill, 1954). It can be argued that the radicalism bound up with this version of Englishness slowly declined, however, because in capitalist societies the social distribution of knowledge is skewed. To put it another way, the ways in which the world is understood is not natural but the result of knowledge that is produced by, and distributed through, particular agencies and institutions. And those institutions most obviously bound up with the production and distribution of knowledge (schools and the media for example) are usually owned or controlled by those with a vested interest in the continued existence of a particular set of social relations. Indeed, the decline of radical patriotism might be attributed to the development and control of the modern nation state.

The development of compulsory systems of state schooling and the regulation of both the print and broadcast media in the 19th and 20th centuries provided the mechanisms by which particular versions of national identity became dominant. The versions of Britishness or Englishness that dominated these institutions were based firmly on the twin myths of English racial superiority and cultural homogeneity with devastating consequences for so-called alien peoples. Schooling systematically sought to inculcate a new set of patriotic values that emphasised militarism, loyalty to monarchy and state and a sense of national superiority that was based either on a crude racism or a unique and exclusionary definition of culture (Mackenzie, 1984; Grosvenor, 1999). Similarly, the media helped project a decent, moderate and private Englishness that, particularly in the 1930s, was used to emphasise the essential cohesion of England (Lunn in Jenkins & Sofos (eds) 1996: 83–100). As a result of all this, the radical patriotism of the earlier period was comprehensively challenged – if not completely obliterated – by versions of national identity that, though changing, always stressed the unique qualities of the English and always demanded the loyalty of the subject to the nation.

It should already be clear from the foregoing discussion that this method of investigating national identity does not look to a reified history for definitive answers to questions about 'who we are'. It does not attempt to identify obligations of inheritance on the basis of a selectively constructed past but seeks instead to critically understand how concrete historical processes shape current understandings of the world and our place in it. In this view the way that people describe their Englishness today is not the result of some mystical inheritance but the outcome of particular ways of representing Englishness in the dominant cultural institutions of the period.

This way of conceptualising the relationship between history and national identity has the advantage of emphasising human agency. It allows not only for a critical evaluation of the effects of particular kinds of Englishness but also gives space to the idea that new forms of national identity can be imagined, produced and applied. It is these issues about the production and distribution of particular types of national identity that are discussed in the final part of this paper. More specifically, it is to a necessarily brief analysis of the politics of history in contemporary society that attention now turns.

Learning about the English

When Margaret Thatcher, and the Conservative Party that she led, came to power in 1979 it was already clear that she had a firmly established view of national history (Thatcher, 1977: 29). Her story of post-war Britain was one of decline. The foundation of the welfare state had encouraged dependency, nationalised industries promoted inefficiency and a liberal consensus attempted to excuse the problems caused by immigration, the collapse of standards in education and the alleged growth of sexual deviancy. The self-appointed task of the Conservative Party in the 1980s and 1990s was the restoration of a sense of national vigour, decency and purpose. Central to the whole political philosophy of the New Right and the Thatcher project was a specific sense of national identity that, Phillip Dodd has argued, depended '.. .upon a sustained process of purification and exclusion. In her British story enemies were here, there and everywhere' (Dodd, 1995: 26–27).

Insofar as Thatcherism constituted a coherent political philosophy, it was based on nostalgia for old times and old values. The Second World War and the year 1940, for example, offered evidence of the British ability to act decisively, independently and with decency (Smith, 2000: 125–8). Victorian values, once a term conjuring images of cruelty, squalor and want became associated with hardy self-reliance and respectability. Reading Thatcher's memoirs it is tempting to think that this was essentially a personal nostalgia translated into a political programme. Yet it is important to recognise that her story of the national past had significant academic support. Robert Phillips argues, for example, that the New Right was an 'important ideological grouping' that consisted of 'an eclectic and varied group of intellectuals, writers and academics' (Phillips, 2000: 14). Similarly, writing in the early 1990s Frank Furedi identified '…an intellectual programme designed to elaborate a coherent national identity for Britain. It has the support of leading Conservative politicians and involves the active participation of the establishment intelligentsia (Furedi, 1992: 4). This intellectual programme found its most concrete expression in a series of educational reforms introduced by successive Conservative governments in the 1980s and 1990s.

Amongst the most important of these extensive reforms were new provisions for controlling both what is taught in schools (through the introduction of the National Curriculum) and how it is taught (through new regulations covering the training and practice of teachers) (Education Group II, 1990). Whilst these reforms crucially affected the delivery of every curriculum subject, it was history that stimulated some of the most extensive debate.

New Right proposals for history repeatedly stressed the importance of teaching the 'facts' of the past or of learning history 'for its own sake' (Phillips, 1998). According to this powerful group, there existed a series of 'inalienable facts' and a core knowledge that was the birthright of every pupil. Specific content, clear chronology and a proper respect for the important facts of the past was the mantra of the New Right and it developed as a reaction to of those forms of teaching, developing throughout the 1960s and 1970s, that valued historical skills as highly as historical knowledge. It was opposed to focusing in depth on particular events in history and using them as a method for practising skills in critical reasoning, but wanted a renewed emphasis on 'narrative', 'chronology' and the 'past itself' (Kedourie, 1988: 10). Though the grouping was not given to extensive methodological discussion, it was always quite clear that they defended a simple kind of empiricism. Establishing the facts, evaluating their significance and deciding on their meaning was unproblematic precisely because the advocates of traditional history, the champions of the facts, had a very particular view on what historical knowledge was for.

The New right ideological grouping were especially interested in history because they saw it as a valuable tool for transmitting a particular kind of national identity. Taught properly, schools' history would inculcate a sense of patriotism in young people. It would give them a proper pride in the history, values and institutions of the nation and its unifying theme was, as then Minister for Education Kenneth Baker put it, to be 'how a free and democratic society has developed over the centuries' (Samuel, 1998: 198). The Englishness suggested by this history was defined by the wisdom and vision of great leaders and was most clearly articulated in a set of parliamentary institutions whose historical development mirrored the increasing freedoms enjoyed by the people. And though the people were frequently referred to by their unique virtues of tolerance and decency, in some of the proposed schemes of work they were barely to make an appearance at all, save for receiving the vote and making necessary sacrifices for the sake of the nation. Discussing proposals for a new history curriculum in 1987, Kenneth Baker argued pupils needed to have:

> ...a well developed sense of the national past. They need to have some feeling for the flow of events that have led to where we are, how our present political and social fabric and attitudes have

> their roots in the English Reformation, the Reform Bills, the Tolpuddle martyrs and the Suffragette Movement, and how our national security, our place in the world, was shaped by Waterloo and El Alamein. The selection is crucial. (cited by Grosvenor, 2000, Arthur & Phillips (eds) p. 152).

The final reference to selection is an important recognition that the facts of the past do not, however, reveal themselves neutrally. Instead, they must be chosen according to some more or less explicitly formulated criteria. These criteria are hinted at when Baker says that the purpose of studying history is to understand how present political and social arrangements have 'roots deep in the past'. This suggests that the revamping of the history curriculum was designed precisely to reveal (or construct) these roots, and, as Prime Minister Thatcher put it, help make children conscious of the nation's 'greatness and unique qualities'. Indeed, it became almost proverbial in the 1980s and 1990s to claim that unless people were connected with 'national roots' then society would somehow disintegrate. In order to understand just how ignorance of a particular kind of history allegedly leads directly to social implosion it is necessary to return to theories of nationhood and national identity.

According to conservative thinkers like Roger Scruton a nation is constituted by its common past. Nations and national identities consist of a set of common roots and shared historical experiences and it is these that lead to a set of shared values or a common culture that allow cohesive societies to develop. For those who hold to this view an ignorance of the national past is not just an absence of knowledge, but also a void of identity and, ultimately, the demise of a whole culture. The reason why history matters so greatly to so many contemporaries is precisely because it has been endowed with this quite phenomenal power to define whole cultures and to maintain national identities. As Roger Scruton, puts it '... the consciousness of common descent ...creates the obligation of inheritance: we must receive from our forefathers what we also pass to our children' (Scruton, 1990: 58–59).

It should already be clear that the argument has moved some distance from a simple belief in the importance and objectivity of historical facts. Selected facts are being put to work in the present, identifying 'obligations of inheritance' and legitimising or rendering 'natural' conduct and identities that have been deliberately constructed. The problem with all this, as many commentators have argued, is that the way that Englishness continues to be imagined is both no longer relevant and deliberately harmful to the England of the 21st century. The story of the Island race – decent, tolerant and homogeneously white – that still informs so much political discourse, social memory and cultural production can help explain in a rational and reasoned manner so many of the social attitudes that are usually ascribed to habit or instinct. Suspicion of the European Union, hostility towards immigrants and

139

asylum seekers, racism (intended or otherwise) in schools, the health service and the police force can all be partly explained by the existence of so-called common sense attitudes towards national identity (see Grosvenor and Meyers, 1999; Macpherson, 1999). Yet despite all the obvious problems of contemporary constructions of Englishness it remains obstinately in place. Indeed, the popular reaction to The Runnymede Trust's recommendations on national identity indicates the forces ranged against those seeking a more equitable version of the national past.

In 2000 The Runnymede Trust – a body established to monitor racism in Britain -issued a report on *The Future of Multi-Ethnic Britain*. The report explores ways in which a multi-ethnic community might successfully develop in Britain and, as part of this, included a section on the problems associated with the term British (Report of the Commission on the Future of Multi-Ethnic Britain, 2000: 2–26). It argued that the idea of Britishness is usually imagined as white and therefore had a largely unspoken but nonetheless systematic racial connotation. Arguing for a more inclusive, flexible and cosmopolitan national identity, it called for a new national story that would better represent the needs of the contemporary nation. Responding to these calls, an editorial in *The Daily Telegraph* thought that it an 'outrageous lie that the history, identity and character of the British people is racist' and compared the Runnymede Trust report with that of the Macpherson Report whose 'bigoted conclusions' were another example of the 'bullying of the anti-racists' (Daily Telegraph, Editorial and letters, 13 October, 2000). Similarly, *The Sun* reported on the 'Curse of the British Bashers' and then, in an indignant editorial, also misrepresented its content:

> It says British history needs to be 'revised, rethought or jettisoned' in case it offends anyone. Rewriting History is what Stalin and the Soviet politburo did (The Sun 'Curse of the Britain Bashers' and Editorial, 11 October, 2000).

All this says much about the context in which attempts to build a society free from racism takes place. British history is seen as something written, complete and stable and attempts to challenge the widely assumed homogeneity of British history fervently resisted. Rational attempts to explore the power of the past over contemporary society are lambasted (its authors were 'worthy idiots', its conclusions 'extreme and tendentious') and practical recommendations aimed at promoting social cohesion dismissed as 'political correctness' or 'sub-Marxist gibberish' (*Daily Telegraph*, Editorial, 10 October, 2000). Ironically, of course, these outraged reactions impose their own form of censorship. Attempting to understand how popular accounts of the past contribute to present inequalities becomes impossible if national history is treated as a sacred story rather than an invented tradition. What results is a singular and exclusionary 'Island Story'; increasingly outdated but clung to by politicians and commentators who want to save it from the 'politically correct', the 'anti-racists', the 'Europeans' or whoever the particular enemy maybe.

Conclusion

History is always based on selection. Everybody makes their selection of history differently, based on their values and what they think is important. If it is accepted that a multicultural and inclusive society is a desirable end, then it is imperative that the telling of the national past reflects that. A static and immutable sense of national identity and culture, the singular 'island story', must give way to a more flexible, plural and accurate version of the English past. Yet it also important to be clear about what this new kind of national history is expected to deliver. History should not be deliberately sought out as the oracle with answers to contemporary 'problems of identity' and nor should it be endowed with the power to define people (as English or Irish, as part of a radical movement or ethnic identity). The real power of history lays not in telling people who they are, but how they have come to be. That distinction is an important one. If history is granted the power to determine our identities, argues Furedi, 'then human action becomes subject to the constraint of the past' (F. Furedi, 1992: 268). We are passively what history reveals us to be. Alternatively if history is used as a tool for understanding, as a method for rationally explaining attitudes, forms of behaviour and social organisation that appear instinctive then it becomes a method for developing a critical consciousness. Such a consciousness seeks not a fixed identity but gains an understanding of both how conceptions of the past help organise contemporary societies and how these are open to contestation, struggle, and ultimately, change. As Christopher Hill once put it '...we ourselves are shaped by the past; but from our vantage point in the present we are continually reshaping the past which shapes us' (cited in B. Schwarz, 1982: 95).

Bibliography

Balakrishnan G. (ed) (1996) *Mapping the Nation*, Verso, London.
Barnes, J. (1998) *England, England*, Picador, London.
Bryant A. (1940) *English Saga, 1840–1940*, Eyre & Spottiswoode, London.
Burke P. (1997) 'History as social memory' in P. Burke (ed) *Varieties of Cultural History* London: Polity Press.
Collini S. (1999) *English pasts: essays in history and culture*, Oxford University Press, Oxford.
Commission's Eurobarometer http://europa.eu.int/comm/public_opinion/.

Cunningham, H. (1988) 'The language of patriotism' in R. Samuel (ed) *Patriotism*, pp. 57–89.

Daily Telegraph 'Will there always be an England?', 22 April 2000.

Daily Telegraph, Editorial, 10 October 2000.

Daily Telegraph, Editorial and letters, 13 October 2000.

Davey K. (1999) *English imaginaries: six studies in Anglo-British modernity*, Lawrence & Wishart, London.

Davies N. (1999) *The Isles: a history*, Macmillan, London.

Dodd P. (1995) The Battle over Britain, Demos, London.

Duffy M. (2001) *England: the making of the myth*, Fourth Estate, London.

Education Group II (1990) Department of Cultural Studies, University of Birmingham, *Education Limited: schooling, training and the New Right in England since 1979*. Unwin Hyman, London.

Evans R. J. (1997) *In defence of history*, Granta, London.

Foster, R. (1998) 'Storylines: narratives and nationality in 19th century Ireland' in G. Cubitt (ed) *Imagining Nations*, Manchester University Press, Manchester.

Furedi, F. (1992) *Mythical past, elusive future: history and society in an anxious age*, Pluto Press, London.

Gikandi S. (1996) *Maps of Englishness: writing identity in the culture of colonialism*, Columbia University Press, New York.

Grosvenor I.D. and Myers K. (1999) '*Engaging with History after Macpherson*', The Curriculum Journal 12.

Grosvenor, I.D. (1999) *"There's no place like home": education and the making of national identity*,' History of Education: Society Bulletin, Maney Publishing.

Grosvenor, I.D. (2000) "History for the Nation": multiculturalism and the teaching of history' in Arthur and Phillips (eds) Issues in history teaching, Routledge.

Guardian, : '*Secret government report finds racism flourishing in the NHS*', 25 June 2001

Hill, C. (1954) 'Norman Yoke' in J. Saville (ed), *Democracy and the labour movement*, Lawrence & Wishart, London.

Hobsbawm E. J. and T. Ranger (eds) (1983) *The Invention of Tradition*, Cambridge University Press.

Jordanova, L. (2000) *History in Practice*, Edward Arnold, London.

Kedourie, H. (1988) *The errors and evils of the new history*, Centre for Policy Studies, London.

Lowenthal, D. (1998) *The Heritage Crusade and the Spoils of History*, Cambridge University Press, Cambridge.

Lunn, K. (1996) 'Reconsidering Britishness: the construction and significance of national identity in 20th century Britain' in Jenkins B. and Sofos A. (eds) *National and identity in contemporary Europe*, Routledge, London.

Mackenzie J. M. (1984) *Propaganda and Empire: the manipulation of British public opinion 1888–1960*, Manchester University Press, Manchester.

Macpherson, W. (1999) *The Stephen Lawrence Inquiry. Report of a Committee of Inquiry*, The Stationery Office, London.

MORI poll digest (21 March 2000) 'What is Britishness?'.

National Centre for Social Research, British Social Attitudes (2000) 17th Report: *Focusing on Diversity*, (edited by R. Jowell) Sage, London.

Phillips R. (2000) 'Government policies, the State and the teaching of history' in J. Arthur and R. Phillips (eds) *Issues in history teaching*, Routledge, London.

Phillips R. (1988) *History teaching, nationhood and the state: a study in educational politics*, Cassell.

Report of the Commission on the Future of Multi-Ethnic Britain, (2000) *The Future of Multi-Ethnic Britain: the Parekh Report*, Profile Books.

Samuel R. (1981) 'People's history' in R. Samuel (ed.), *People's history and socialist theory*, Routledge & Kegan Paul, London.

Samuel R. (1989) 'Continuous national history' in R. Samuel (ed.), *Patriotism: the making and unmaking of British national identity*, volume I: history and politics, Routledge, London.

Samuel, R. (1998) *Island stories: unravelling Britain*. Theatres of memory volume II, Verso, London.

Schama S. (2000) *A History of Britain: at the edge of the world?*, BBC, London.

Scruton R. (1990) 'In Defence of the Nation' in J.C.D. Clark, (ed) *Ideas and Politics in Modern Britain*, Basingstoke: Macmillan.

Scruton, R. (1 April 2000) *'Don't let Blair ruin it'*, The Spectator.

Scruton, R. (2001) *England: an elegy*, Pimlico edition, London.

Shah I. (2000) *The Englishman's Handbook*, Octagon, London.

Schwarz, B. (1982) The people in history: the Communist Party Historians' Group, 1946–56' in Centre for Contemporary Cultural Studies, *Making histories: studies in history-writing and politics*, Hutchinson, London.

Smith, M (2000) *Britain and 1940: history, myth and popular memory*, Routledge, London.

Sun, (11 October, 2000) *'Curse of the Britain Bashers'* and Editorial.

Thatcher M. (1977) *Let our children grow: selected speeches 1975–77*, Centre for Policy Studies, London.

Tosh, J. (1991) *The Pursuit of History: Aims, Methods & New Directions in the Study of Modern History*, 2nd edition, Longman Group.

Wright P. (1985) *On living in an old country: the national past in contemporary Britain*, Verso, London.
Zinn H. (1999) *A people's history of the United States, 1492 – present*, Harper Collins, New York.

8. European Identity

Timothy Baycroft

> Today there is a European nationality, just as at the time of
> Aeschylus, Sophocles and Euripides there was a Greek nationality.
> Victor Hugo (1843)

While Hugo was specifically referring to the 'nationality' of the educated, enlightened elite of artists and writers, his words evoke the multiple links between geography, culture and nationality which surround the enigma of European identity. Enigma because of the variables associated with each of the terms, and the numerous difficulties involved with any comprehensive analysis of identity across Europe. The term Europe itself can at the very least be used in two different ways: to describe the continent in general, although the eastern boundary has always been open to question, or alternatively to refer more specifically to the territory which has developed the institutional structure known as the European Union. In addition to a territory, be it simply geographic or political, 'European' may refer to any number of historic or cultural characteristics, which leave both of the key delineators of identity – self and other – fuzzy around the edges at best (see Pagden & Pocock, 2002: 33–54, 55–71). Even after establishing which Europe is being discussed, problems of chronology and measurement of the extent of a European identity remain manifold. One difficulty of such measurement, certainly from the second half of the twentieth century onwards, is the role of political bias. Under certain circumstances having a European identity may become conflated with being in favour of a greater degree of economic and political institutional integration. Debate surrounding the existence of a European administrative and political structure always forms the background of any discussion of European identity, and often the asking of the question itself presupposes a certain degree of political bias towards 'Europe'.

Like other sorts of political identity linked to geographical territories, European identity in all of its various forms is subject to a duality of simultaneous complementarity and opposition with other forms of identity. It can at the same time be seen as one from among a series of overlapping territorial identities, identifying simultaneously with neighbourhood, town, region and country, each forming one layer. Alternatively, each territorial identity can be seen in opposition with another place at the same level (belonging to one village, not another, or one region not another) (see Sahlins, 1989: 110–113). At this basic level, European identity can fit into the model as a simple addition to the various national, regional or local identities within the continent on the one hand, or as an opposition to other continental identities such as North American or African on the other. A further complication arises when, unlike many regional and national identities which straightforwardly overlap, European identity is seen to conflict with a national identity. Because of the potential threat to national sovereignty which many see in increased European institutional integration, a greater sense of Europeanness may directly imply a weakening of individual national identities. Hence in some contexts European identity can be seen to fit the model of 'nested' identities characteristic to political-territorial identities, peacefully coexisting with national and regional identities, and thought to oppose only other continental identities, but in other contexts it can be felt as a direct threat or challenge to national identities. In this way to be Spanish or Italian may at one moment be perfectly compatible with being European, and at the next moment to claim a European identity may be felt as undermining Spanish or Italian national strength.

In order to cover the numerous shades of identity which can come under the heading of 'European', this chapter will begin with the post-Second World War economic and political construction and the sorts of identity which are associated with the institutions of the European Union. It will then turn to other perspectives on Europe, and ways to be European, which include the incorporation of areas not within the EU, particularly Eastern Europe, the process of globalisation and its impact upon European identity, the influence of decolonisation on the way Europe and Europeans view themselves, and the way in which other non-EU organisations have contributed to a sense of being European.

European Construction and Identity

The history of the complex institutional structure known at the start of the twenty-first century as the European Union seems at first to have little to do with European identity. It involves a myriad of agreements, treaties, organisations and acronyms which were created, adapted, merged, and often altered beyond recognition from one decade to the next. The end product is so large and wide-ranging that the number of histories of European construction presenting the entire post-war period as a long march to unification has increased dramatically in recent years. The European Union is not, however, a constitutional regime, based around defining principles in the same manner as a democratic constitutional nation, but a vast compromise, the result of countless individual negotiations, often quite dissociated from the larger picture (e.g. see Dinan, 1999; Blair, 1999). It would be a misrepresentation to suggest that it was clear from the outset what the end product would be, and while principles may have influenced discussions, the determining factor in the direction and structure of the resulting institutions was always the interests of the individual states involved in the negotiations. While the resulting Union exhibits characteristics of both an 'international regime' and a 'domestic regime', with models of neither completely appropriate for purposes of detailed analysis, popular identity does not appear significant from either perspective (See Marks, 1997 in Klausen, and Tilly (eds.), pp. 23–43). The entire process was goal-oriented and policy driven, and therefore not a question of appealing to popular support or a mass feeling of European identity to achieve integration, much less a European State. No preexisting identity lay at the foundation of the union, but rather the twin goals of peace and prosperity, sought on the part of each state via co-operation in well-defined areas at specific times.[1] Many of the early leaders did hope eventually to unify the hearts and minds of Europeans, but even the most prominent promoters of European integration such as Jean Monnet, the first High Commissioner of the Coal and Steel Community (precursor to the EU), sought to mobilise support around concrete projects rather than theoretical or principled beliefs, given the likelihood of success (see Marks, ibid: 30; Passerini, 1998 in Pagden: 199–208).

While certainly not at the origin of economic and political integration, one can question the degree of European identity which has grown out of the institutional construction. One might expect that insofar as European construction was political, a sense of solidarity common among political communities would develop. After national unification in 1861, Massimo D'Azeglio famously said 'We have made Italy, now we must make Italians': did the construction of Europe lead to the creation of Europeans? (in Baycroft, 1998: 34). In so many words it was certainly never the overt and publicised goal of the European leaders, as it had been for the nation-builders of the previous century, given that they stood in a different relationship to the population and had realised that consensus was only likely around individual pragmatic policies.

The nineteenth and twentieth centuries in Europe were primarily a time of the continuous strengthening of national identities. Nineteenth-century nation builders had set up national primary school systems which taught national history and languages, propagated national symbolism for public consumption, solidified national economic infrastructures and overtly

---

[1] This is also true of national identities which did not often exist before their corresponding state, and only come into being afterwards, often as a result of deliberate initiatives from the national leadership. See below.

encouraged increased national sentiment through military service. National sentiment in much of Europe was dramatically increased further through participation in two world wars for which the population and national economies had been extensively mobilised and emotionally integrated into the war efforts (see e.g. Weber, 1979; Hobsbawm & Ranger (eds.), 1983). Participation in national politics also served to create a sense of national cohesion and identity, as did the growth of parallel organisations along national lines. In the second half of the twentieth century, higher levels of publicly monitored (if not run) education, increased state intervention in daily life via the welfare state, technological developments in communication and changing lifestyles due to economic prosperity all contributed to the further enhancement of national identities, which benefited from what Michael Billig has termed 'Banal nationalism'. He claims that national identity has at its root 'the embodied habits of social life,' in which the national element becomes ever present, and each day's activities filled with small, unconsciously accepted reminders of the nation (Billig, 1995: 8). In this way the shape and colour of post boxes, lettering on car number plates, bureaucratic procedures and vocabulary developed to describe diplomas, jobs, laws or customs, serve everywhere as subtle and subconscious reminders of the nation. The scope and number of such national reminders was multiplied by the expanding material culture of the twentieth century and through the mass media of radio, television, the cinema and newspapers, each of which used national vocabulary and content repeatedly in unspectacular ways.[2]

Over the years since the Second World War, as national identities were strengthened and culture became increasingly national, European institutions were unable to encourage the development of a similar style of European identity partly because they lacked the means of the nation states, and partly because they had to keep a reassuring profile in the issue of conflict of loyalties between 'Europe' and its component nations. There was also some hesitation to seek a simple transfer of loyalty to the level of Europe, as one of the goals of the Union was peace, and nationalism was seen as a root cause of war and conflict. Paradoxically then, national identities represented for Europe a model of the process of identity building, yet were that which needed to be overcome. In terms of means, in spite of the general consensus in favour of democracy among the countries forming the EU, the European institutions themselves were not democratic, and therefore lacked a democratic call upon the population (see Scully, 2000 in M. Green, Cowles & M. Smith (eds.), pp. 228–45). Nor did the material advantages of the welfare state acquired via the payment of taxes or the security of national defence

---

[2] Further examples include national sports leagues and national weather reports which mean that those living in a border area will regularly hear about the weather of their own country hundreds of kilometres away, but not be told about the area only a few kilometres away across the border.

secured through compulsory military service take their origins in the EU. With neither democratic legitimacy nor the traditional state-citizen exchange of rights for duties, even inferred, the various institutions of the EU and its predecessors were not, therefore, in the best position to act as natural poles of attraction for community spirit, solidarity or even consciousness among the wider population. The EU was not set up as a larger 'civic' nation, and its institutions limited in their capacity to mould identity. The school systems remained national in orientation, and the symbols and vocabulary spread both overtly and subconsciously by the mass media meant that no kind of 'banal Europeanness' was created or built up in the second half of the twentieth century.

The strength of established national cultures as a basis for identity leads to the question of what cultural characteristics could be used to form the basis of a European identity which resembles national identities. This is a question which has been asked for several centuries by such members of the European intellectual elite as Victor Hugo, quoted at the beginning of the chapter, who identified a cosmopolitan culture of art, literature, music, philosophy and science as the common heritage of a European culture which began with the ancient Greeks. While such an inclusive and flexible definition is necessary to correspond to the reality of European cultural diversity, it does not, however, follow the same pattern as national cultural identities, which are by definition exclusive and as particular as possible, and were created and developed around myths of cultural or ethnic homogeneity (see Gellner, 1983; 1Hobsbawm, 1990; Smith, A.D., 1998). A team of researchers led by René Girault, seeking to identify characteristics truly common across European society came up with six: family structures, employment patterns, the division into social classes, the welfare state, urbanisation, and consumption pattern (Girault, 1994: 28–35). While useful as analytical descriptions to differentiate European society from others, none of these characteristics are likely as foundations of popular identity. Outside of the cosmopolitan literary and artistic high culture described above, a further tradition extending back to the nineteenth century sought to define 'individualism' as a typically European ideology upon which 'European character' was founded (See Herzfeld, 1998 in Pagden (ed.), p. 170). Although as an image, individualism figured less prominently during the phase of integration, it in some ways draws upon the tradition of Europe of nations, using an overarching unity primarily to defend the interests of individual nations (see e.g. Chebel d'Appollonia in Pagden, 2002: 171–90). Sport is one area which can highlight the difficulties of defining a truly European cultural identity along the model of nations, being as much an area of re-asserted national rivalries as a meeting point of a common culture. Even common territory, ostensibly the simplest and most straightforward of symbols, becomes complicated, for as a 'geographic expression' Europe's eastern borders are fuzzy at best. Thus for the most part the apparently objective criteria commonly used by nation-builders to define nations – shared ethnicity, language, religion, history, culture in its popular forms – were awkward to apply to Europe given the powerful presence of national cultural and ethnic identities and their supporting institutional structures, which are fundamentally opposed to the development of a cosmopolitan culture as a unifying cultural myth (see Smith, A.D., 1995: 55–76). Anthony Smith suggests that a middle ground could be found, a 'family of cultures' which is not a simple acceptance of diversity in all of its forms, but which draws upon the many shared, overlapping traditions and heritage which can be found across Europe, even though no one of which is shared by all Europeans (ibid: 67–74).

Such a homogeneous European culture which could serve as a basis for identity remained elusive in part because the institutions of the EU did not have the kind of manipulative control of cultural development which national governments have had. The political will and institutional backing to actively galvanise historical or cultural criteria into a myth of European unity was continually lacking, held in check throughout the twentieth century by the strength of national identities and national cultural myths (for attempts to define and identify 'European' culture, see Deschamps, 2002: 85–95). Part of the very appeal of the sort of cosmopolitan 'high' cultural identity favoured by those such as Hugo was its dissimilarity with national ones, encouraged in part by the hope that a European identity would grow at the expense of nationalist identities which it was felt had caused so much trouble.

If unifying European cultural myths upon which an identity could be formed are difficult to find, common collective memory may be less so, especially with regards to the twentieth century wars. In her exploration of European nationalism, Ariane Chebel d'Appollonia argues that in spite of the incredible division which they brought to European society, '... the interpretation of the wars by the Europeanists ... has been a supremely unifying factor.' (Chebel d'Appollonia in Pagden, 2002: 179) She argues that in spite of different individual experiences and memories of the war across national, gender or class lines, the collective belief that the wars were all bad, that everyone suffered (if not to an equal degree) and that the primary lesson to be drawn is that in the future unity is necessary to prevent their repetition is a single historical myth around which European identity could potentially crystallise. Such a unity of interpretation and single collective memory will be even more possible once individual living memories have disappeared, and more closely resembles the nation-state model than the cosmopolitan cultural myth. Other possibilities for common collective memories can be drawn from more remote history and could include periods of political unity such as the Roman or Carolingian Empires, other continent-spanning conflicts such as the Protestant Reformation or the Napoleonic wars, and cultural or artistic movements such as the renaissance.

Within the EU, it is the presence of a European political culture which most resembles the potential foundation of a nation-like identity, but only insofar as the population could be implicated and aware of the political issues at a European level. Such an increased profile would have required higher levels of democracy and more potentially controversial issues resolved within the European institutions rather than national ones, as well as the presence of higher profile political leaders at the European level. It would also have required the surmounting of the challenge of the neo-nationalist parties which present a clear, alternative vision of European construction as an 'ethnic federation' which can be used expressly to strengthen individual national identities and at the same time buttress the united groups against others from outside of Europe, and drawing upon the historic Europe of nations model (see Peled and Spektorowski (eds.), 2000: 132–3). At the sub-conscious level, the single currency more resembles a nation-like common characteristic which is a genuine part of daily life and can be identified, potentially forming at least the 'banal-style' common culture discussed earlier. The more general common economy which lies at the origin of European construction and is the most integrated sphere of activity within the EU, while it may also help to create a common culture of consumption, is an unlikely candidate as a basis for conscious identity, given the low levels of awareness of detailed economic issues and patterns among the population.

Lacking a solid foundation through citizenship or a single cultural myth of homogeneity, but possessing the potential for shared historical collective memories and the beginnings of a common political culture, European identity bears some resemblance to national identities. Using a slightly different measure, the EU had not yet become a fully-fledged 'imagined community' by the end of the twentieth century, whereby individuals could perceive themselves as a part of a Europe whose shared characteristics they could identify (see Anderson, 1991). Nevertheless, a sense of European identity had begun to develop, and while the specific criteria may be less clear cut than for nations, measuring its extent and growth is not completely impossible.

One way to capture the evolution of European identity is through an analysis of perceptions of boundaries between the component states by inhabitants, and their place in border societies as real or imagined barriers. Historically, inter-European boundaries were open and flexible, with workers, traders and travellers crossing at will. Although in some areas borders were fixed as divisions in the minds of the locals, in others they had less significance in terms of fixing identities (see Sahlins, 1989; Baycroft,

1999: 417–38). It was only in the late nineteenth and early twentieth centuries that borders began to be tightened, and movement of goods and people restricted in a serious way. Partly due to industrialisation and the nature of the goods traded, and partly due to increased efficiency of administration which meant that work and travel permits could be required (see Strikwerda, 1997 in Klausen & Tilly: 51–70). During the twentieth century, the movement of both population and goods became more strictly regulated and with the advent of the welfare states economies and markets, including labour markets, became increasingly national, and the borders real limits. These developments, coming after the mass mobilisation of the two World Wars and coupled with the phenomenon of *banal nationalism* described above, meant that the borders were more present in the minds of Europeans. Similarly, the development of mass culture within these national structures meant that borders came to represent cultural realities and divisions such as they had never done before (e.g. see Baycroft, 1999). In the first decade after the European Union removed the restrictions on the mobility of goods, people and capital in 1992, inter-European migration levels between the member states did not go up significantly, and remained far lower than they had been at any point during the nineteenth century. The economic and legal barriers of the twentieth century had created real cultural barriers which prevented large-scale migration and which remained a part of the landscape of identity. Thus paradoxically the borders had never been more firm in the minds of individuals as a component of their identity, nor had they ever corresponded with such clear and decisive cultural differences as at the moment when the EU removed their status as barriers.

To measure the extent to which such a European identity actually grew among the European population, as with measuring any kind of identity accurately, is difficult at best. The possibility to find a question formula which will test for the presence of European identity, while at the same time reflecting its place relative to other identities and not leading the respondent towards a particular answer is limited. It is likewise difficult to get around the ambiguity of the term Europe, not knowing whether an identification is with the continent as a whole, or more specifically with the institutions of the EU. In the final quarter of the twentieth century, numerous studies of opinion across Europe have investigated the level of European identity among the population, with mixed results. Even where the same organisation has carried out surveys over several decades, altered question formats make it difficult to draw conclusions about change over time (see Green, 2000, in Cowles & Smith (eds.), pp. 292–322; Eurobarometer). The types of surveys range from asking individuals to rank a series of identities as they apply to themselves and then checking to see how many put European in the top few, to asking about whether individuals think of themselves as European often, sometimes or never. Another manner is to ask whether 'European' and 'national' identities were held to be compatible or contradictory across different countries. In 1988, the results showed that across the countries of the (then) EEC, over half thought that they were complimentary, with less than a quarter thinking of them as contradictory (see Girault, 1994: 188). Differences emerged between countries however, with Great Britain the only country with more respondents thinking of the two as contradictory than complementary (39 against 36 per cent, with the rest not knowing or not answering), although Germany had a much lower response of belief in complementary than the other continental countries (43 per cent against well over 50). Such measures of European identity, with respect to other politico-territorial identities, have also been made comparing Europe not only with nations, but also with regions. The results of a 1998 survey comparing sacrifices that individuals were willing to make in terms of standard of living, higher taxes or participation in military activities for their region, nation and Europe respectively showed repeatedly that Europe scored ahead of the regions on every count, and occasionally ahead of nations (see Green, 2000: 316–18).

Such surveys have begun to allow for a quantitative measurement of 'European identity', but the results are sufficiently limited that in overall terms one cannot conclude much more than that there was such an identity among the population of the countries of the European Community and Union in the last quarter of the twentieth century, but one could not yet write a history of identity in statistical terms. David Michael Green's analysis of the data from these surveys is particularly useful, along with supplementary qualitative evidence, to test a series of widely accepted hypotheses and preconceptions regarding the presence, extent and nature of European identity within the EU. He shows, for example, that the belief that smaller countries will have higher levels of European identity is not supported by the evidence of opinion, nor is the belief that the side a country fought on in the Second World War (axis having greater tendency to identify themselves as Europeans) influences the level of European identity. He also found no evidence that excluded national minorities sought refuge in a stronger European identity, nor that the longer a country was a member of the EC/EU the higher the degree of European identity among the population (indeed he found the opposite). The trends which he did find supported by the statistical and qualitative data are that individuals and nations with higher levels of education, cosmopolitanism and greater wealth will tend to have a greater sense of European identity, as will those who perceive that they will benefit directly from increased integration (see Green, 2000: 302–3).

Empirical evidence for the presence of a European identity must be taken with a pinch of salt, as the majority of the sponsors of such surveys have a vested interest in promoting EU institutions. The most comprehensive survey data are collected by Eurobarometer, which is run by the European Commission. One must also question whether feeling European means supporting greater European institutional integration. Up to this point the 'Europe' being discussed is the EU and its political-institutional structure, which is hardly the whole picture. A sense of Europeanness or European identity can also be found in the non-EU countries within the continent of Europe, other processes besides economic, political and institutional construction have influenced identity formation in the twentieth century, and other organisations besides those connected directly with the EU have a European level, and it is to these questions which we will now turn.

Europe outside of the European Union

When confronted with criticism for his European policies because of his position with respect to the European Economic Community, Charles de Gaulle would re-articulate his vision of Europe as running from the Atlantic to the Urals, and that no smaller unit could justifiably be termed Europe (De Gaulle, press conferences of 25 March, 1959 and 4 February, 1965, quoted in Cogan, 1996: 146–8). Yet it is true that much of the European continent is not covered by the institutions of the EU, and that Europe has a purely geographic meaning independent of the political and economic institutional structure which only covers part of it. For many, it is the EU which could not be truly European until its institutions represent the whole of the territory of the continent, while others, with De Gaulle, try to deny the EU status as representing 'Europe' without qualification. The question of identity in the rest of Europe, which with a couple of exceptions means Eastern Europe, is in part reduced to the cosmopolitan elite culture of art and letters when the political, economic and institutional dimensions are removed.

When considering the eastward expansion of the EU in the post-communist period, when it was at least a theoretical political possibility, the discussion centred primarily around economic issues, with a few political ones thrown in. Consideration of identity and social perception has not entered into the question of 'European expansion', such as it is termed. Most of the countries of Europe not a part of the EU by the early twenty-first century experienced a half a century or more of Communism, and the impact of the communist experience upon identity and perceptions of the continent as a whole have not been widely discussed in public. Unlike 'Europe' in geographical terms which has included an eastern European heritage, the EU is primarily a western construction, and in identity terms this has often been overlooked by 'pro-Europeanists' seeking unifying cultural characteristics from exclusively within the western framework. While from the eastern perspective, a feeling of European identity may also be politically or economically motivated by a desire to join the EU, the western dominated view of Europe can also give rise to alienation. Short of renunciation of the communist past, before a commonly accepted vision of common history or culture is possible, a way of integrating the east and its twentieth-century heritage will need to be found. While this chapter focuses primarily on the western viewpoint, it is important to note that it is by no means the only perspective to understand European identity.

Decolonisation and Globalisation

The changing global environment in the twentieth century had a large impact on the way in which Europe and Europeans thought of and defined themselves. During the nineteenth century European nations, through colonisation, controlled the vast majority of the globe and as often as not when the world was referred to, writers or politicians actually meant Europe. In terms of the power structure, the two could be conflated, and no continental identity opposed the coloniser to the colonised. This perception was reflected in the vocabulary in current use, when 'world affairs' meant 'European affairs', 'universalist' ideologies referred to specifically European values and debates, and politically organised 'Internationals' were primarily, if not exclusively, centred upon Europe (See Milza, in Girault (ed.), pp. 61–2). Europe was the world in the mind of Europeans, and thus consciousness of the continent was necessarily limited.

The early twentieth century saw little modification to the nineteenth-century pattern, but the discourse of self-determination, when applied to the colonies on a large scale in the wake of the Second World War, led to a sea change in the relationship between the European nations and their former colonies. The process of decolonisation brought out and re-emphasised the differences between them, the 'European' colonisers and the rest of the world. Within the newly established United Nations, European countries became one group among many, and the series of multi-lateral debates and discussions which took place within that and other international forums increased awareness of the world as a whole, and the place of Europe became more distinctly outlined. Increasing consciousness of the indigenous cultures of former colonies and the manifold differences with European traditions helped to cement the similarities across Europe in the minds of Europeans. One can exaggerate the profundity of such a consciousness in European society, but its presence by the end of the twentieth century could be found in scholarly works, popular literature and newspapers (see Chakrabarty, 2000).

Awareness of the place of the continent within a larger global context was further heightened by the Cold War. Europe, divided between east and west, grew increasingly conscious of its place between the superpowers, and the relationships of the respective blocks towards the United States and the Soviet Union. This was not only a new place in the scheme of things, but for the first time it was forces outside of Europe which governed its primary position in the global environment. The transformation from the centre of global power to the focal point for a conflict which took its origins outside or beyond the boundaries of the continent, from primary mover to subject of external pressure, brought with it heightened consciousness of the continent as a source of identity. It may be that a European collective memory of the Cold War can serve as a unifying historical myth even across the east-west divide. In a similar way to the memories of the World Wars discussed earlier, different individual or national recollections can be subsumed in a general interpretation of 'innocent' Europe caught between the Soviet and American superpowers. Such a view could of course include eastern Europe, also caught in the middle, even if the western viewpoint on 'victory' is likely to predominate. Thus decolonisation and the Cold War both help to bring an 'other' more sharply into focus, against which a European self could emerge.

The process of globalisation, taken to mean the interconnectedness of the global economy such as it developed in the second half of the twentieth century, has also had an impact upon identity formation in Europe with respect to perceived 'others'. Previously, when trading within a colonial empire, economic activity could be conceived of as domestic, in the same way that Europe thought of itself as the world and the rest subordinate. Nothing is new about high volumes of world trade and the large scale movement of goods, people and capital from one place to another, it is awareness of the process which has increased, alongside of world-wide recognition of brand-named consumer goods. Although the position could be taken that such items form a kind of 'banal' global culture, they do not represent a sub-conscious reinforcement of a defined global entity. Nor did the processes of globalisation and international co-operation lead, by the end of the twentieth century, to a convergence of policies or structures across the world which could in turn serve as a basis for global identity (see Fioretos, 2001: 242). It is rather the vocabulary of globalisation which suggested change and outward connections and which by reinforcing a sense of that which is outside, also served to stimulate a sense of outside threat and thereby to re-emphasise a perception of self within the world. This does not necessarily mean the European self, however, but just as likely the national self (see Smith, 1997: 213–216; Clark, 1997). When asking the question of who Europe's 'others' might be, against which a specifically European identity might emerge, Smith suggests that in addition to the Cold-War protagonists, the 'disaggregated Third World' was a possible candidate to oppose a 'uniting' Europe (Smith, 1992: 75–6). The global 'other' against which such identity might be defined was of course a variety of others, representing an entire range of degrees or types of difference according to the circumstances, and which did have a bearing upon continental identity, in that other Europeans appear 'less foreign' within a global context (see Lawrence, Baycroft, and Grohmann, 2001: 51–71). The 1973 *Declaration on European Identity,* while it did attempt to define unifying cultural traits, devoted a great deal of space to defining a hierarchy of relations with the rest of the world (see Passerini, 2001: 194–5). Within such a global hierarchy of others, even if national identities were also strengthened, the process of globalisation in the second half of the twentieth century nevertheless did contribute to as sense of continental affinity, and the development of a European identity of difference, even if vaguely defined.

European Associations

The nineteenth and twentieth centuries saw the proliferation of organisations, societies, or interest groups which were not the direct creation of any state, several of which had an international dimension covering much of Europe. Examples include trade unions, charities, religious groups, ecologists, hobbyists, amateur artistic or athletic associations and youth groups such as the boy scouts. Although only ever a secondary objective at best, such bodies were in a position to encourage the mutual identification of individuals across the continent, and create a sense of common bonds which could lead to European identity. There is little evidence, however, to suggest that such organisations did in fact contribute to the development of a European identity, at least not on a large scale. This can be explained in part by cultural and linguistic differences, and in part by the fact that even international solidarity and understanding, pursued with the goal of ensuring future peace between Europeans or simply the attainment of specific objectives using co-operation to strengthen claims, is not the same thing as mutual identification and the perception of Europe as one large community of belonging.

The relatively limited effect of such organisations upon the formation of European identity is furthermore linked to the way in which they have been bound within nations as the framework in which decisions, actions and thought processes are couched. Turning first of all to trade unions as an example will help to clarify the point. These unions were originally conceived in a large part as elements within a single international movement which aimed at creating international solidarity and action in order to bring about large-scale change not restricted to individual countries. With economic, regulatory and legal structures increasingly differentiated from one country to another, combined with the effects of the world wars, the national branches of such organisations became divided, and formulated more limited and resoundingly national aims. Paradoxically perhaps, what began as a theoretically international movement, gained its greatest successes in the twentieth century after abandoning internationalism and working within national contexts, and national and international strength became. Even within the institutional framework of the EU, internal and external barriers to trade union solidarity remained powerful influences up to the end of the twentieth century (see Ebbinhaus & Visser, 1997; Klausen and Tilly (eds.), pp. 195–221). Further evidence of the importance of national political, economic and legal frameworks determining the parameters for organisations' activities and mental horizons can be found examining women's groups across Europe. Chiara Saraceno concludes that the mobilisation of women's organisations at the European level has only taken place 'amid contradictions and misgivings' and that they are stronger at a national level (Saraceno, 1997 in Klausen and Tilly (eds.), p. 250).

The implications for individual interest groups reflects more general patterns for the successful application of ideas, theories and political programmes within nineteenth and twentieth century Europe. Liberal economic theory was originally universalist in orientation, but was realised within nation-state structures. The same could be said for socialism, which succeeded once it had more or less abandoned its internationalist aspirations in favour of working within individual national frameworks (see Strikwerda, 1998). Carl Strikwerda has outlined a clear chronology for the process, identifying 1914 as the turning point. With popular mobilisation, the war and the subsequent statist organisation of society, the nineteenth-century legacy of transnational co-operation, interdependency and freedom of movement was destroyed. along with the universalist theories which lay behind them were swept away (ibid). There has been some debate about the lessons to be drawn from this process – some arguing that the nineteenth-century legacy of openness and internationalism is evidence that it is still possible, while others argue that its destruction in the early twentieth century is evidence that it can never work (see Klausen and Tilly (eds.), 1997). Once more general theoretical movements and the organisational structures which supported them became firmly oriented and anchored within national contexts, the international dimensions did not altogether disappear, but become weakened to the point that they did not become sources for the development of European identity or consciousness during the twentieth century.

Conclusion

European identity presents several problems for objective analysis. Statistically growing in the second half of the twentieth century,

Europeanness is nevertheless difficult to measure and can only be understood as one among a hierarchy of identities for those who possess it, and almost invariably not the primary one. Partly arising from the inherent difficulties of defining Europe and its boundaries, defining European identity precisely is further complicated by the occasional confusion which arises between having such an identity and being politically in favour of a greater degree of European integration within the European Union. In form, it exhibits some of the characteristics of national identities, usually in a watered down version – common memories, cultural myths, political cultures, a sense of others outside – but differs in the nature of the vested political interests and objectives of those seeking to promote its growth and does not include a common need for defence against outside threats or a democratic-style state-citizen exchange of rights for loyalty. Partly derived from internal cohesion and preoccupation with integration along a model similar to that of national identities, European identity has also developed as a result of the changing global environment in the twentieth century, as Europe's place within the world has evolved within the contexts of the Cold War, decolonisation and globalisation. Often clearly limited to a western model of European society understood as referring to the EU, such visions of European identity exclude Eastern Europe, which a full consideration of European identity needs to take on board. As an imagined community, Europe exists weakly at several levels among hierarchies of identities, varying according to circumstances, but clearly increasing among the population during the twentieth century.

Bibliography

Anderson, B. (1991) *Imagined Communities*. 2nd edn., Verso, London.
Baycroft, T. (1999) 'Changing Identities in the Franco-Belgian Borderland in the Nineteenth and Twentieth Centuries', *French History* 13, No. 4, pp. 417–38.
Baycroft, T. (1998) *Nationalism in Europe 1789–1945*. CUP, Cambridge.
Ben-Ami, S., Y. Peled and A. Spektorowski (eds.) (2000) *Ethnic Challenges to the Modern Nation State*. Macmillan, Basingstoke.
Billig, M. (1995) *Banal Nationalism*. Sage Publications, London.
Blair, A. (1999) *The European Union since 1945*. Longman, London.
Chakrabarty, D. (2000) *Provincializing Europe: Postcolonial Thought and Historical Difference*. Princeton University Press, Princeton.
Clark, I. (1997) *Globalisation and Fragmentation: International relations in the Twentieth Century*. OUP, Oxford.
Deschamps, E. (2002) '*L'Européenn* (1929–1940): a Cultural Review at the Heart of the Debate on European Identity,' *European Review of History/Revue européenne d'Histoire* 9, 1, pp. 85–95.

Dinan, D. (1999) *Ever Closer Union: An Introduction to European Integration.* 2nd Edition. Macmillan, Basingstoke.

Eurobarometer: public opinion in the European Union (Brussels: Commission of the European Communities).

Gavin, B. (2001) *The European Union and Globalisation: Towards Global Democratic Governance.* Edward Elgar, Cheltenham.

Gellner, E. (1983) *Nations and Nationalism.* Basil Blackwell, Oxford.

Girault, R. (ed.) (1994) *Identité et Conscience Européennes au XXe siècle.* Hachette, Paris.

Green, D. M. (2000) 'On Being European: The Character and Consequences of European Identity', in Cowles, M. and Smith, M. (eds.) *The State of the European Union,* Volume 5: *Risks, Reform, Resistance, and Revival.* OUP, Oxford.

Hall P. A. and D. Soskice (eds.) (2001) *Varieties of Capitalism: The Institutional Foundations of Comparative Advantage.* OUP, Oxford.

Hobsbawm, E. J. (1990) *Nations and nationalism since 1780: programme, myth, reality.* CUP, Cambridge.

Hobsbawm, E. and Ranger, T. (eds.) (1983) *The Invention of Tradition.* CUP, Cambridge.

Hugo, Victor, Preface to 'Les Burgraves' in *Oeuvres Complètes.* (Le Club Français du Livre, Paris, 1968) p. 574. (original edition 7 March, 1843).

Klausen J. and L. A. Tilly (eds.) (1997) *European Integration in Social and Historical Perspective: 1850 to the present.* Rowman & Littlefield, Lanham.

Lawrence, P., T. Baycroft and C. Grohmann (2001) "Degrees of Foreignness" and the Construction of Identity in French Border Regions during the inter-war period,' *Contemporary European History* 10, 1 pp. 51–71.

Marks, G. (1997) 'A Third Lens: Comparing European Integration and State Building,' in J. Klausen and L. A. Tilly (eds.) *European Integration in Social and Historical Perspective: 1850 to the present.* Rowman & Littlefield, Lanhampp. 23–43.

Pagden, A. (ed.) (2002) *The Idea of Europe From Antiquity to the European Union.* CUP, Cambridge.

Passerini, L. (2002) From the Ironies of Identity to the Identities of Irony,' in Pagden (ed.), *The Idea of Europe,* pp. 191–208.

Peled, J. and A. Spektorowski (eds.), *Ethnic Challenges to the Modern Nation State.* Macmillan, Basingstoke, 2000, pp. 132–3.

Preece, J. J. (1998) *National Minorities and the European Nation-States System.* OUP, Oxford.

Sahlins, P. (1989) *Boundaries: the making of France and Spain in the Pyrenees.* University of California Press, Berkeley.

Scully, R. (2000) 'Democracy, Legitimacy, and the European Parliament,' in M. Green Cowles & Smith M. (eds.) *The State of the European Union*

Volume 5: *Risks, Reform, Resistance, and Revival*. (OUP, Oxford), pp. 228–45.

Smith, A. D. (1992) 'National identity and the idea of European unity,' *International Affairs* 68, 1 pp. 55–76.

Smith, A. D. (1998) *Nationalism and Modernity*, Routledge.

Strikwerda, C. (1998) 'Reinterpreting the History of European Integration.: Business, Labor, and Social Citizenship in Twentieth-Century Europe.' In *European Integration in Social and Historical Perspective, 1850 to the Present*, ed. Jytte Klausen and Louise Tilly. Lanham, Maryland: Rowman and Littlefield, pp. 51–70.

Weber, E. (1979) *Peasants Into Frenchmen: The Modernisation of Rural France 1870–1914*, Chatto & Windus.

http://www.gesis.org/en/data_service/eurobarometer/standard_eb_trend/indexframe_trend.htm

http://www-polisci.tamu.edu/Robertson/WebResources/eurobarometer_survey_data.htm

9. Paganism

Jenny Blain

Increasingly, anthropologists and social theorists look at identity as fluid, constructed within social relationships and discourses – including discourses of spirituality and religion. Whereas there have been tendencies to look at religion as a cultural 'given' (and to investigate it as a factor of cultural maintenance or cultural expression), today's theorists deal in choices, changes and deliberate, agentic constitution of belief, practice and 'self'. If, as Bauman (1997) indicates, post-modernity is 'about' choice, religion is an area where 'choosers' are evident and spiritualities are chosen, and, often, changed. In an article in *The Times*, January 2001, Mark Chadbourn commented that:

> Around 1,000 people swap every week; "religious traffic" is heading in all directions as traditional barriers between religions crumble…none of the religions quite seem to satisfy. (source of figures: Romain, 2000)

However though it is possible to view those who change as shoppers in a 'spiritual supermarket', a view only of religious affiliation as consumer choice disregards the importance, the centrality, which spiritual practice has in the lives of at least some choosers. Further, some of these spiritual consumers become involved in the invention or development of practices and theologies, particularly where they are part of the fluid groups that constitute emergent religions, notably those of paganisms and the so-called 'new age'. Religion, spirituality, identity and life-style are interwoven so that, as with indigenous religions elsewhere, a division into sacred and secular is neither practical nor appropriate.

This chapter will discuss some ideas relating identity and religion, taking as examples areas from my work on shamanic practices, Paganisms within post-modernity, and people's approaches to 'sacred sites'. I will begin with some examples of pagan concepts of self, land, 'nature' and community, give an example from my work with seidr or northern European shamanistic practice, and conclude with how in the UK 'sacred sites' form identity foci for various pagan groups.

Paganism and Identity

The terms 'Paganism', 'earth-religion', 'nature religion' cover a number of practices and belief systems. These can be traced historically, and are achieving growing levels of acceptance in post-modern Britain, Europe, North America and other areas, as well as growing numbers of adherents (see e.g. Hutton, 1999). Many concepts and images of paganism are familiar as part of non-pagan culture – a glance into any vaguely 'alternative' or 'new-age' shop shows 'Celtic' patterns, tarot cards, images of goddesses and candles decorated with spirals or pentagrams: these are not all, or necessarily, 'pagan' but many pagans will consider them part of their cultural engagements with spirit worlds, deities, and hence accomplish identity in relation to such concepts and images.

The most visible such religion, at least from a scan of bookstore shelves, is Wicca. However the variety of pagan expressions belief includes those who draw on various mythologies and deities – e.g. Greco-Roman, Egyptian, Indian, Sumerian, 'Celtic' or 'Nordic', European 'Goddess' imagery, African or 'Native American' belief systems, indigenous practices from Siberian or circumpolar shamanistic cultures and a whole host more. In this chapter, though, my focus is not on beliefs or even practices so much as on meaning, and how meaning and practice come together in group or individual accomplishment of identity. Discussions of groups, practices and how practitioners describe their spiritualities are increasing within academia, and so I refer interested readers to some of the work of Bowman, Harvey, Hardman, Greenwood, Letcher, Wallis and indeed myself. Less academic accounts are obtainable via a host of websites.

I begin from where people are, with words and experiences: the words of ordinary practitioners in interviews, people's descriptions of how they came to feel 'pagan' and how their paganism became part of their perceptions of self and everyday activities, and my own experiences of ethnographic research in a variety of settings (see Blain, 2002; Blain & Wallis, 2000: 395–411). Concepts of body, mind and spirit form part of informants' discourse and practice. Dimensions which informants identify as important include associations of body and spirit; connecting with the past and with ancestors; earth-awareness and environmentalism; healing of self and others; power and empowerment of women and men. Importantly, these dimensions encompass many areas of their lives. Often they speak of their religion as informing even small actions of their lives, viewed as part of a larger whole. 'I can't litter any more', one young man told me, sounding surprised at this realisation. Conversely, everyday gestures may become political acts.

In investigating discourse and practice, I explore some of the sources of knowledge, example or inspiration referred to by informants, attempting to link these with their everyday lives. Participants' discourse moves from today's authors to older literature such as the Icelandic Sagas and Eddas, to accounts of shamanic practitioners either today or previously, and to interpretations of structures and images from earlier periods back to the neolithic and paleolithic 'goddess' figures. Sources can bear multiple interpretation, and participants' interpretations relate to, and sometimes challenge, their situated awareness of what 'paganism' may be and themselves as pagans. In other published work I examine how practitioners – particularly Heathens or followers of North European paths – move between past and present, drawing on (sometimes contradictory) words, images, and solitary and community ritual practice, in constructing 'truths' and identities for themselves as spiritual beings in a post-modern world. They speak of landscape and 'sacred site', constituting contemporary folklore as they draw on past interpretations of place and spirit (e.g. Blain, 2000, 2002; Blain and Wallis, 2002). Practitioners seek 'holistic', unfragmented lives, but may find contradictions between personal expressions of spirituality and workplace restrictions or family practices and beliefs: their worlds are not seamless, and their quests for empowerment may meet contestation. At times they see themselves as political players, challenging establishment rules or conventional interpretations.[3] Interwoven with 'pagan' discourse are popular and academic concepts, phrases, indexing narratives of being, 'self', belonging: not all are unproblematic, for the speakers or for others who seek to define themselves as 'pagan' and construct their own relations with Earth and her creatures.

Practitioner voices, pagan beginnings

Many pagans, though not all, base their expressions of spirituality around seasonal festivals: eight 'stations of the sun', including solstices and equinoxes interspersed with the four 'Celtic' festivals of Imbolc, Beltane, Lughnasad or Lammas, and Samhain. While these festivals may not necessarily be as 'traditional' as their practitioners consider them (see Hutton, 1996), they are none the less part of today's rediscovered – or invented – 'traditions', and they have a grounding in recent folklore.

Judith runs a small store in a Canadian Maritime town, selling herbs and essential oils, which has become known, she says, as 'the witch's shop'. She described how, for her and her family, seasonal understandings are expressed through celebration and ritual.

> We have our seasonal celebrations. You know the autumn equinox,
> and with the kids we do solstice...special things like on

---

[3] For instance, many people concerning themselves with the campaigns focussed on Stonehenge – 'freeing the stones' or opening the site to celebrants at festivals – are avowedly pagan. See R.J. Wallis, *New Shamans: Ecstasy, Alternative Archaeology and Contemporary Paganism.* London: Routledge, forthcoming 2003, for a substantial discussion of pagans engagements with archaeology. This discussion is continued in our website at http://www.sacredsites.org.uk.

winter solstice, my husband and I would stay up all night, and we get the kids up in the morning to see the sun rise. Little things like that. Autumn equinox, that was when our big Thanksgiving dinner would be, and summer solstice is like the end of school for them. So really by just doing the little seasonal celebrations. Not that they have to be anything big, but sort of taking note. But I think even by noticing them – oh yeah, today's summer solstice sort of thing – we do sort of tune in to (the changing) seasons...you become aware of things, of simple things, like changing tides, and when certain things bloom each year, and weather patterns, and they really connect you to all that.

But pagan attempts to celebrate the cycles of the earth are not necessarily straightforward. Pagan holidays do not always coincide with those of the wider society. Pagans seeking holiday time may be supported or rejected by employers: personnel working shifts, particularly in health care professions and essential services, may find that a wish to take Dec 21st, and work Dec 25th, is very well received. Secretaries, however, have reported being put under pressure to work extra hours around the solstice, in order to clear work before a 'Christmas holiday' period. Spiritual observance and daily work-life intersect in ways that are complex: and these intersections construct practice and equally construct others' understandings of paganisms and what these are about. Workplace discussions of Samhain or Winternights, for instance, may in one workplace appear 'cool and interesting', in another attract proselytising attempts from other religious groups. Some pagans or heathens are more open about their spiritualities than others, and fear of recrimination, attempted 'conversion', dismissal, or simply not being seen as serious citizens, is a contributing factor for those who remain in the closet.

To an outsider, pagans may seem interesting and colourful, set apart by culture and discourse, or by lifestyle choices, depending on how you look at it. However today's pagans and shamanic practitioners live in the urban world of the early 21st century, in environments of plastic and concrete, dealing with today's information technologies and bureaucratic systems. If even the occasions of community celebration become problematic, how is an identity constructed within ongoing relationships of daily life, in the intersections between spirit and structure, nature and technology?

Negotiations of daily living are complex, and paganisms involve their practitioners in adjustments and contradictions. Internet discussions often position pagans in opposition to dominant groups: in North America Christians of various types; or in academia, or within much of Europe, atheists. This can sound like quite a battle. The realities are more complex: members of earth religions work alongside members of other religions, their children attend the same schools, they shop for the same foods, pretty well, in the same groceries, or in the farmer's market which could not exist if it were only supported by pagans. Many aspects of the 'everyday lives' of pagans look and sound very like the 'everyday lives' of non-pagans. Differences, if and where they exist, are in approach, degree, and underlying assumptions which influence action – and the constructions of meaning arising from these – as Judith indicates:

> …we don't do the regular church thing or weekly lessons or anything like that. More like a daily basis with life, we try to fit it in, just relate life to certain beliefs: What you do is what comes back to you, or how you act…We don't really do anything special besides the seasonal things, and you know, our beliefs. I mean, we do say…a blessing over the food. You know, we join hands and do a circle, a thing like that…I made them dream pillows and they take those at the full moon and just sleep with them for three nights…Helping me in the garden with herbs. Learning to respect plants, that they are alive. You know, stuff like that.

In starting with differences between her practices and those she perceives as associated with other religions or spiritualities, she moves to daily or monthly routines, and then to events that link the family with other beings or lives. Helping in the garden leads in this description to the importance of her children learning to respect plants: and approach, part of a wider philosophy of connection of people and earth, as she said:

> That humans aren't just here to conquer the Earth, that we all combine. And of course, we do the recycling, and the composting, the basic sort of ecological things. But I think instilling in them that respect for the Earth, that type of thing.

When asked what her spiritual path meant to her, Judith's reply linked spiritual meaning with daily life:

> because it's such an Earth-based [path], you sort of begin to become in touch with the Earth or in tune with the rhythms, you know, the cycles of the seasons, and of the course the cycles of your body. So it all fits in. So you sort of feel part of the universe, it makes you feel actually connected. That you're not just plunked here on the planet as a separate entity. I think humans sort of see themselves as apart from the world and nature. Not as connected. I think it probably gives you that sense – for me it does, anyways – that sense of connectedness.

These links of connectedness, nature, and daily life are central for many pagans, and I will return to them later.

Spirits and shamanisms

So, the obvious expressions of paganism, even the major festivals are (aside from getting dressed up and having a party with friends) not much different from the 'everyday' in terms of sacredness, sanctity, or ability to touch what earth-religion practitioners hold sacred. Relationships with spirits or deities exist in the everyday: for many pagans, earth is sacred; plants, animals and people are children of earth, and hence sacred likewise. Part of my work on pagan identities involves 'sites' of inscription of meaning, whether these be historical or archaeological (but particularly prehistoric), places of great 'natural beauty', or simply the corner where a tree grows, on a city street, and pagans pick up the litter dropped around; embodied 'selves'; texts from old or new writings that earth-religion practitioners find compelling, interesting or useful; and events such as rituals or festivals. The meanings so inscribed are constructed within the relationships that pagans create, framed by their existing knowledges.

Here it is useful to turn to consider shamanic practices and their focus on communication with spirits or ancestors. A considerable academic literature exists, of course, and indeed practitioners have come across some of this: notably the demarcation and categorisation of shamanism as 'archaic techniques of ecstasy' by Mircea Eliade (1964). Many shamanic practitioners look to accounts of North American or other indigenous cultures for sources of ideas – though more rarely to Siberian shamanisms. 'Core Shamanism' derives from the work of anthropologist Michael Harner, through his attempts in teaching and writing to define a 'core' of shamanic practice that could be independent of culture: a number of 'core shamanists' now find that they are 're-embedding' their practices in mythologies and folklores of the spirits of their local areas. Ideas of shamanic practices within Western European contexts were popularised by Brian Bates' novel, *The Way of Wyrd* and more latterly by a succession of practitioner books on, for instance, 'Celtic Shamanism' by John and Caitlin Matthews and others. Other accounts or types of 'indigenous shamanisms' are being developed, re-developed, re-invented within Druidry and displayed various accounts on Druid websites and in magazines such as *Druid's Voice* or *Tooth and Claw*. (see Lindquist, 1997; Bates, 1983; Matthews, 1991).

'Shamanism' as an abstraction, though, can be viewed as a construction of Western modernity, and before proceeding further I will digress into the history and implications of the term. The derivation of 'shamanism' from the Tungus/Evenki 'sama:n' via Russian and German explorers and the curiosity of a Western public seeking to romanticise while differentiating themselves from a 'primitive' 'other' has been discussed elsewhere (Flaherty, 1992; Wallis, 1999: 41–49; Blain and Wallis, 2000). Some attempted, and competing, definitions have been more persistent that others: that of a 'master of spirits' versus Eliade's 'Archaic techniques of ecstasy' (Shirokogorov, 1935; Jakobsen, 1999). Each of these has relevance – for some places, and some times – and Merkur has pointed out that all definitions of shamanism exclude some people who by other's definitions – including those of practising shamans – are 'shamans' (Merkur, 1992). Rather than definition, we can seek 'shamanisms' in the accounts of both shamans and anthropologists, as processes and relationships by means of which specific people work in specific ways for specific communities, to connect past and present, spirits and people, ancestors and those of today. Within anthropology, Greene discusses South American practitioners' 'appropriations' of what works – a shaman works creatively and inventively, and western medical practice becomes drawn upon by indigenous practitioners, for their own purposes – and Taussig's locating of Colombian shamans within politics and history serves as a reminder that their practices cannot be regarded only as individual 'techniques of ecstasy': they and their practitioners are part of the processes of change, power and resistance, that structure and shape communities, and have their own relationships to state and society (Greene, 1998: 634–658). The locating of practitioners within western structures may be less obvious but still pertains, particularly if we see societies of post-modernity as fluid, wherein boundaries are becoming permeable and identities dynamically constituted. Theories of 'neo-tribalism' suggest fluid and temporary adherence to discursively-derived identities, with a sense of change and impermanence that drive many in Europe and America in quest of roots.

To the outsider, 'paganisms' may appear very similar. Within today's practice there is distinct diversification, in theology and philosophy, in ritual format, in practitioners' relationships with Earth, spirits and deities, and in the extent to which practitioners or groups draw on source material from outside paganisms. For the most part, pagans acknowledge and value diversity, but not all are aware of its extent, and pagans who do not base their practices in Wicca can find it difficult to explain to other pagans that their practices and understandings of 'sacredness' may be very differently constructed. For instance, in Britain, the Pagan Federation presents three 'principles' that members sign agreement to, as a condition of membership, yet which many non-Wiccan pagans (including many heathens and shamanic practitioners) find problematic in their wording and assumptions.

The Northern shamanistic practices I have researched, known as 'seidr', are partly described in the literature of the Sagas and Eddas of Iceland, and indications of practice may be also found in Old English literature, with parallel situations possibly described in Welsh and Irish accounts. Practitioners work from the principle that documents or artefacts from 'the past' hold clues to religious or spiritual practice, and that this practice can be used meaningfully in today's world. This 're-construction' (itself a disputed word) does not mean re-enactment. Today's practitioners point out that they are attempting to reach what they consider the centrally important points of religion – for instance an understanding of how people approached their deities – and work with this to create something that 'works' within today's environment.

These Heathen shamanistic groups therefore draw on material from the Icelandic Eddas and sagas, English healing charms, archaeology and folk-tales from Britain and Scandinavia. They have come across references to seidr, a type of magical practice referred to in the sagas and possibly reflected in some of the Eddic poems,[4] associated with connecting with 'ancestors', deities and spirits (see Larrington, 1996). References in the literature are ambiguous – and so some argued about whether seidr was 'good' magic, as it's usually described as performed against the hero of the sagas; some argued about precise meanings of the term; some became terribly worried by inherent ambiguities of gender and sexuality that appear in some of the descriptions (see Blain & Wallis, 2000; Meulengracht Sorenson, 1983); and some others simply attempted to 'reconstruct' seidr practices, for protection, for healing, and notably for divination, which they called 'oracular seidr'.

Northern shamanism today

The most complete description in the sagas comes from *The Saga of Eirík the Red* (for a translation see Smiley & Kellog, 2000). A farm in Greenland faces famine; a seeress is invited to prophesy, and comes to the farm. Her costume is described in detail, her cloak, her staff, even her eating utensils and the laces on her shoes. A special meal is made for her, and a platform (hjallr) prepared on which she will sit to prophesy. The next day she makes what preparations she needs, sits on the seidhjallr, and a woman sings to call the spirits. The seeress speaks of the end of the hard times, prosperity for the community, and prophesies also for individuals, notably the young woman who sang so beautifully that more spirits attended than ever before enabling clearer vision or more detailed knowledge. Some, both pagans and academics have considered that the seeress would not only 'see' future prosperity, but work actively with the spirits, to create it (Borovsky, 1999: 6–39).

For today's practitioners, of course, some of the details are missing: what song was sung, how the ritual was structured, what 'preparations' the seeress made. So groups have investigated other forms of shamanistic practice to fill in what they could. Some use a drum, others chant, singing their own songs to summon the spirits. Some have set the central 'seeing' within a ritual that

---

[4] *The Poetic Edda* consists of mythological and heroic poems written down in the early Christian period in Iceland from apparently older oral forms.

169

includes calling upon land-spirits, and Óðhinn and Freyja, the deities who are described in the old texts as making seidr. A seeress sits on a raised chair of platform, and sees for the community and the individuals within it.

One notable practitioner, writer Diana Paxson, has described the experience of being a present-day practitioner of seidr within a non-shamanic culture: her own rationalistic world-view wars with her seidr experiences (pers. com.), and in describing the experiences she falls back on the discourses of archetypes, symbols, and the collective unconscious. Other seeresses, possibly with less exposure to psychological explanations, are more direct. Raudhildr, working within Heathen cosmology of the well of wyrd, the Norns and the tree Yggdrasill, dealing with the beings of all the nine worlds, describes her own initiation – by spirits, not by humans – which appears as a classic shamanic experience of death-and-dismemberment.[5] She went, naively she says, to visit the Maurnir – female giants or etins, the oldest ones who live in a cave. They have much wisdom and knowledge from earliest times. She asked, again naively, if they would share with her their wisdom. No, said they, but she could become part of the wisdom – and when she agreed, they ate her, throwing aside the bones. Her bones were lying on the cave floor when Loki – a trickster deity, regarded somewhat suspiciously within Heathenry – appeared, dancing what she described as 'a shaman dance', and calling on the gods to put her back together. Once re-membered, she thanked him to which he replied, 'once, you gave me a drink', that is, by honouring him in a blót, a heathen ritual with an offering of mead. She did not discuss what might have been the outcome had Loki not appeared.

Others report their own experiences: for instance, Bil, a seid-worker in New Mexico, discusses a several illness lasting two years, and recovery in which he came to recognise that his life was no longer his own, but was co-ordinated by a team of 'helper' spirits. He is not an oracular practitioner: his work is chiefly with bringing balance to specific situations involving humans and spirits, and much of his work is with those who are dying. Malcolm, in Scotland, engages with healing. Winifred puts people in touch with deities. Thus, people report specialising in specific areas of practice. Their spirits-helpers differ also: Bil works with animal and plant spirits, and local spirits or deities relating to place. Raudhildr speaks with ancestors, aided by her fylgja or familiar. Thus, people create new shamanisms for today, connecting human and spirit communities – not always the deities of mythology. Spirit communities – wights or spirits of place – therefore become part of the

---

[5] This incident is discussed in Blain, 2002, and Wallis, forthcoming 2003. 'Death and dismemberment' relates to shamanic initiations – by spirits – and is displayed in Eliade's (1964) and other's accounts as part of what makes traditional shamanic calling dangerous and difficult, and as often resisted by those called. In traditional societies, being a shaman is often not a popular vocation.

awareness of western shamanic practitioners, who in turn relate this to similarities with indigenous religions elsewhere.

In the days described by the Icelandic sagas, most had an everyday ongoing relationship with the spirits closest to the people and their daily tasks: those of the land, and ancestors. That Wight[6] who lives in that rock, *there*, is intimately involved with the productivity of this farm. They were neighbours, helpers, friends and colleagues. Occasionally the farm people would approach the high deities, Goddesses and Gods (also conceived of as Elder Kin, more distant relations), just as, says Gundarsson, they would a chieftain – or more often if they were particularly friendly with the deity, as in the case of poets gifted by Ódhinn or Freyja and dealing with them on a daily basis. But the average person, according to Allsherjargodhi Jörmundur Ingi, would greet the High Gods once a year, at the Althing. Important, yes, but not everyday: spirits of rock and stone were local, ancestral, connected, and close. Other beings could be beautiful, tricky, such as the Elves of folklore who are interesting but potentially dangerous to deal with. Some were, and are, closer than others. Sociologist Michael York, approaching a tentative definition of paganism, frames this as:

> ...an affirmation of interactive and polymorphic sacred relationship by individual or community with the tangible, sentient and nonempirical. (York, 2000: 9)

Thus, not only deities but animals and plants, land, water, air become at least in part sacred, in ways that permit relationships between people as pagan practitioners, and other beings or realms of being, who or which are dealt within the course of the everyday just as much as in specialised or ritual contexts.

Culture, nature: dualist categories, totalising concepts?

At times practitioners' discourse reflects a dualism of 'people and nature'. At other times this is more critically examined and at still others there is a range of mediating beings that form part of the construction of both 'people' and 'nature'. Summer, a Canadian 'green-witch' and farmer, identified tensions in her own accounts of 'nature':

> Sometimes I feel extremely connected. Sometimes I feel completely disconnected from myself, from the earth. Sometimes I feel so ignorant and such a, like I stick out incredibly in this beautiful thing called nature...My, my academic self problematizes the notion of nature. What is nature? Does nature include us? Of course it does but how do we talk about this entity

---

[6] A wight is an entity, a being – whether a physical being (human, animal etc.) or a spirit-being.

outside of us without then resigning it to be other than human therefore different from human?

Pagan practitioners speak of nature religions and themselves as connected to nature. Clearly, nature is a constructed concept, and one could examine different constructions of 'nature' in opposition to 'people' and of people as part of 'nature'. What practitioners' discourse indicates to me is rather more complicated. First, that there is a range of positions that practitioners occupy, but second, that practitioners alter their orientation to nature, according to the context of their talk. Their positioning is at times deliberate, reasoned, drawing on what they know to create effect, in the context of the interview or in the realms of teaching or political life: construction of self in community, and communities with respect to each other.

For instance, some explicitly link environment, indigenous spiritualities elsewhere, and political activism. For Anne, another Canadian pagan and activist, both nature and her own practices are experienced as personal and political:

> You read in the Jesuit relations how when (Mi'kmaq chief) Membertou was making the decision about the conversion of the Mi'kmaqs, he went and dug a hole at the base of a tree and sat all day and conversed with the hole in the ground. And of course, the Jesuits wrote this up as another example of stupid, useless, idiotic suspicion. Well, that's a relationship with the Earth that I can't even imagine. However, given that I'm a North American in the 20th century and I can't quite recover that...[yet] I did learn how to feel when I'm drawing energy out of the Earth and into my feet. Or if I'm lying on the ground and doing it. So I can feel it come and go, to some extent. And it's fast. You just get this feeling that it's this huge, huge, huge! reservoir of energy.
>
> Then you get out into the more political realm where the gardening, the camping and the canoeing have to do with connecting...And it's amazing...And then there's the whole business of the environmental movement. Which I'm not connected to very directly, because my more direct connections have been poverty, anti-racism, feminism, anti-heterosexism, that kind of thing. But to my mind, that's all related. Because the relationships between human beings are so integral with our relationship to the Earth....So the whole understanding in political/economic terms of saving the Earth – because it's in desperate straits...I see all of the anti-oppression stuff as having a direct relation.

The political nature of paganism has a more personal dimension: embodiment, which appears continually in pagan publications, yet remains contentious. 'Sacred bodies, sacred sex', are illustrated in some women's publications with both the nubile young woman and the athletic, naked 'crone': and in gender-mixed publications primarily with the first of these (Examples include the magazines *SageWoman, Pagan Dawn* and *Pentacle*). So, while many pagans valorise 'the body' in terms of 'sacred sexuality', a number of women, and men, point to the insertion of images and discourses of the 'perfect body' only as it relates to conventional heterosexuality, into paganisms. Questions of ability and disability are similarly problematic: pagans with disabilities have pointed to problematic assumptions about ways in which they 'should' live and their relationships with earth. The turning of the seasons or the approach of summer may mean something 'different' to someone who is confined to an apartment and who cannot see a tree from her window.

Sexualities are contested within a number of traditions: for instance, Gay Heathen shamanic practitioner Jordsvin says that many areas of the Heathen community need some education in this matter (Blain & Wallis, 2000). Less overtly but possibly more basically, concepts of 'The Goddess and The God' within Wicca and some other 'traditions', whether presented as dualism or duality, may be empowering for many practitioners, yet disempowering for those who do not see their sexualities reflected: and it still happens that gay pagans raising this issue for debate are accused of 'flaunting' their 'difference'. Pagan communities vary enormously in their awareness of complex interrelationships of body, sexuality, and identity. The 'race issue' evident within some paganisms (see Gallagher, 1999: 19–29), provides another example. Specific pagans adopt specific stances within prevalent discourses of 'race', 'ethnicity' and 'identity', and often these may act to obscure complexity and essentialise difference, by removing political and historical process so that (for instance) 'being Celtic' becomes a matter of 'bloodline' (see e.g. Blain, 2001). Paganisms, or religions more generally, have their existence within other contested areas of today's society, and incorporate their discourses. Pagan weavings of 'wyrd'– constructions of life or destiny – are interwoven with many other choices and processes, and these interweavings connect not only people today, but land, spirits, other beings – and ancestors.

Pagans, the Greenwood, and sacred sites: points of connection and contestation

Graham Harvey talks about how the Greenwood enters practitioners' discourse (Harvey, 1997). The Greenwood is not only the actuality of forest, grove or 'where wild things are', but the concept(s) of what this represents for pagans today, the places where they can go physically or spiritually to refresh 'self', to connect with 'nature', and which give points of entry that different practitioners can approach and use, and hence ways in which they can access the realities not only of other pagans but of the other beings within the Greenwood. While Paganisms (as already pointed out) are extremely diverse, increasingly Pagans celebrate the Greenwood not primarily in its creation (as product of an abstract relationship to a transcendent being), but in its existence, continuity of a network of social relationships, dynamic patternings of trees and rocks, plants and those who eat them, predators and prey, *continuation*, the cycle of life. Pollution is not merely an eyesore or a problem of resource management, but a disruption to the relationships and networks of being. Yet most pagans are urban dwellers, users of today's technology, transport mechanisms, mobile phones and the internet. The balance between people and 'nature' is something that pagans debate, and again occupy a range of positions in debating. Not all see themselves as environmentalists, and many recognise that people have modified their environments from early times: carving, painting, mining, removing, building, planting and harvesting. Ideas of protecting earth or assisting nature-spirits vie with the recognition that pagans and shamanic practitioners live in a complex present-day society, and that they need to eat: tension is apparent between discourse and practice, even in the act of driving out to 'the land' to spend time in relationships with trees and 'nature'. For some, though, issues of access to 'sacred sites', and protection of sites, becomes paramount (e.g. see Ancient Sacred Landscapes Network website at http://www.symbolstone.org/archaeology/aslan/index.html).

Here we are dealing with Pagan understandings or landscapes and ancestors–those who have previously lived in the landscape. Often, research literature on sacredness and landscape suggests that a place or site is sacred because people honour it, or treat it as sacred, i.e. landscapes are *cultured*. In such accounts, people have agencies, and meaning is inscribed, by people, in the land (e.g. Carmichael, Hubert, Reeves, Schanche, 1994). Some indigenous and western pagan understandings reverse that understanding. Sites are spoken of as 'sacred', because at these people feel touched by a 'sacredness' or a connection that emerges more strongly than elsewhere, which is embedded *a priori* in the site: a site is a point in the landscape at which people seem more likely to acknowledge that living presence. The stories in the land may be those of how sacredness becomes known, and how people thereby become changed, rather than how people have constructed it. Let us take, first, an example of indigenous perception elsewhere, from an ethnographer's account.

Always changing, this landscape was alive on many levels, natural, historical, personal. The landscape was explicitly shared and socialized. It was also known at a most intimate level, and it was only through shared moments of intense silence of through equally intense burst of poetry...that I came to glimpse the passionate longing that linked each of my instructors to the world around them. My instructors did not seem to separate the stories from the landscape...included in the definition, both as a carrier of traditions (as content), in the forms of resources, life style, and landmarks, and as a medium (as process) through which the Dene ways could be transmitted and created. All my Dene experiences lead me to conclude that the Dene territory is best defined not as 'cultured' but as cultural. From this perspective the land is perceived as a process and as an unfolding story (Guédon, 1994 in Young and Goulet (eds.), p. 47).

The account is that of ethnographer Marie-Françoise Guédon, describing how during her fieldwork in the north of Canada she learned to appreciate how the Déné people lived within, and as part of, landscape. She refers to her own attempts to learn to 'be' Déné, to walk in the landscape and see it as 'alive'. Today's pagans do not have the cultural immersion into stories of landscape and the sacred land, which may be still current among indigenous people elsewhere. Yet many pagans see themselves as in process of learning to be indigenous – re-embedding their practices in the stories of the land, and in relation to place, ancestors, and land-spirits. In our Sacred Sites project we are using the term 'new-indigenes', and indeed pagans can be seen as an example of today's 'neo-tribes' – forming shifting and fluid groups in which identities are authored and re-authored continually, as groups change and memberships drift and fragment (Blain & Wallis, 1996; Letcher, 2001). We are pointing out that elements such as place and landscape – and appreciation of the ways in which pagans interact with site and spirit – need to be understood as contributing to these identities, and equally that understanding pagan interactions with sites requires consideration of practices in spiritual context. Why pagans go to sacred sites – whether well-known ones such as Stonehenge or Avebury, or small remote places such as the circles of the Peak District – is tied in with their perspectives on sites as places where deities can be more easily addressed, or particularly with ideas about interacting with ancestors.

Many Druids like to make ritual at [Avebury and other sacred sites] since there is a strong feeling that they are places where communion with our ancestors may be made more readily than elsewhere...I am drawn to Avebury ...because it is my heartland...the place where I feel most spiritually 'at home'...I am not the only person who has experienced the spirit of the place as a great mother with open arms, welcoming all who come (Druid leader Greywolf in Wallis forthcoming 2003, and Blain and Wallis, 2002 in press).

Increasingly, therefore, pagans are becoming politically involved with issues including conservation, preservation, and with ideas about reburial of excavated human remains. For instance, the Druid Paul Davies writes in *The Druid's Voice* about how some archaeological practices impact on him.

> As far as archaeologists are concerned, there are no cultural implications to stop them from their work. As far as Druids are concerned, guardians and ancestors still reside at ceremonial sites such as Avebury and the West Kennet Long Barrow...When archaeologists desecrate a site through excavation and steal our ancestors and their guardians, they are killing me as well as our heritage. It is a theft. I am left wounded. My identity as a Druid is stolen and damaged beyond repair. My heart cries. We should assert our authority as the physical guardians of esoteric lore. We should reclaim our past. (Davies, 1997: 12–13)

Such statements locate some pagans with respect to place and spirit, and also make claims for community identity: though groups may change even from day to day, a sense of discursive continuity is emerging as members relate to concepts and their framing. Not only are land, and spirits of place, 'Dísir' and ancestors said to call various pagans, to inspire them, to cause personal transformation, but this is understood in context within pagan groups. While pagans draw on multiple academic and popular discourses to 'explain' their experiences, they are increasingly finding ways to frame experiences as 'authentic', ignore the charges of 'irrationality' raised by non-pagan site curators and others. Pagan researchers too, interpreting between communities of paganisms and academia, are finding ways to 'queer' the discourses and frameworks of research, in order to present apparent 'irrationalities' as challenges for scholarship (Wallis, 2000: 252–262).

Conclusion

Discourse and narrative analysis attempts to examine how people speak of their daily lives in order to understand how they use social discourses and processes in creating their understanding of these lives. In my work concerning paganisms and shamanisms, I am attempting an integrative understanding of people's constructions of meaning and identity within practices and discourses that they identify as central to their being. In doing this, I acknowledge my own location within the web of meanings: as a heathen shamanistic practitioner, with links to practice, places and people on two continents, who in my everyday work of research is privileged to talk with numerous others about those relations and concepts that to me seem to matter.

This paper stems from my location and understanding, but is not, I believe, limited to my own situated knowledges. George Marcus points out that the challenge of postmodernism's critique of ethnography is leading to a re-emergence of comparison, not in the older sense of direct (controlled) comparing of points or categories, but as juxtaposition which emerges from

> ...putting questions to an emergent object of study whose contours, sites, and relationships are not known beforehand, but are themselves a contribution of making an account which has different, complexly connected, real-world sites of investigation. (Marcus, 1998: 186)

Paganisms or earth-religions today are multiply situated, and I have the multiple task of maintaining and preserving the 'voices' and narrative of diverse participants, wherever they are, while juxtaposing their accounts to provide a multivocal display of partial meanings that reflects an approach, an orientation that is constructed within the interviews and the events that I observe. Most of my work on what appears to be the 'extraordinary', shamanic practices which appear exotic to the 'outsider's' gaze, strange, different, entrancing even to many pagans, and which as I've said elsewhere (e.g. Blain & Wallis, 2000) transform the participant in many ways. But the extraordinary is a development of everyday practice, shamanisms (as opposed to the western abstraction of 'shamanism' as 'primordial' religion) are culturally rooted, embodied in and by their practitioners, emergent from relationships and practices of daily life, and changing with socio/economic/cultural/political relations (Blain & Wallis, April 2001). 'Ordinary' and 'extraordinary', therefore, inform and transform each other.

Within paganisms, identities are constituted within sets of social relationships surrounding each practitioner. Here we can see that selves are situated, and locations interactive. Today's pagan identities are developed in the context of everyday, as well as extraordinary, relationships, and that everyday activities arise from possibly-contested community and individual understandings of potential, resources, capabilities and relationships. The everyday, the personal, is indeed political. Practices however developed have to make sense in the daily lives of their practitioners, and concepts of body, spirit, Greenwood, 'nature' site and sacredness are constituted and linked by the simplest of actions.

These everyday lives are contested and political: processes of gender, 'race', sexuality are situated and constituted in daily practice, within the institutional practices and mediated discourses of post-modernity. The mere label, 'Paganism', is not a guide to political practice: nor is it a guarantee of environmental 'friendliness'. Inspection of sacred sites, for instance, can show remarkable collections of ritual litter, candles and wax, joss-sticks, offerings of (now soggy) bread and (now rotting) fruit, crystals, coins, pentacles and clay figurines, flowers sometimes picked from the wild hedgerows around. Pagan theorising of practice sometimes stops short of examining the effects of their practices on other human or non-human frequenters of sites – and the

177

impulse to make an offering, to show a physical trace of their respect, is a strong one. Other pagans will warn about damage to sites, offence to earth spirits, difficulties for animals encountering the material: one person's votive offering is another's eyesore. But pagans, of whatever persuasion, are likely to see themselves, and other people, as linked with earth or the beings of earth;[7] their concepts of 'self' include relationships they construct with the 'imaginal' that they describe as 'empowering' or affirming – whatever these are, however they are phrased.

Contestations abound in this area, as in others. Paganism is not a unified movement: no college decrees discourse and practice, no leader issues dictates. People create their ways of being pagan, from observation, example, insertion into practices, reading and other resources; and from their experiences and understandings of themselves in relation to Earth, spirits, ancestors and other people and beings – performing ritual with friends and finding friends through their paganism, meditating at sites and examining the experiences they meet there, communicating those experiences and creating those fluid groupings of 'new-indigenes'. Anthropologist Clifford Geertz has said, of any or all religions, that:

> …in what we are pleased to call the real world, 'meaning', 'identity', 'power', and 'experience' are hopelessly entangled, mutually implicative, and 'religion' can no more be founded upon or reduced to the last, that is, 'experience' than it can to any of the others. It is not in solitude that faith is made. (Geertz, 2000: 184)

Today's paganism exists within overlapping contexts of sacred and spiritual; politicised, as with the 'reburial issue' and environmental campaigns, yet personal as each pagan creates her/his own ways of being pagan, and increasingly within communicative processes of publishing and the internet. In this chapter – which has barely sketched the surface of an area that many will find strange, even bizarre – I have attempted to indicate some of the complexities involved in understanding paganisms and identity, some of the concepts that pagans share or dispute, and some of the implications for studies of identity that may be highlighted by considering this area of people who 'choose' spirituality and finds that the connections it brings involve almost all parts of their lives. As David Green (2002) has pointed out, paganisms and their interpretation challenge theories of religion within contexts of late modernity and post-modernity. Indeed it seems to me that the

---

[7] This is not as simple as saying they are 'earth-religions'. While many pagans do consider themselves part of an 'earth-religion' or 'nature-religion', some strongly deny this, pointing rather to the importance of magical practices (addressed by D.A. Green, The Season of the Witch? Pagan Magic in Psycho-Social Context. Ph.D. Thesis, University of the West of England, 2002) or to the importance of specific relationships with individual beings rather than with a generalised (Goddess) of Earth. Again, paganisms are not all the same, and the phrase 'earth-religion' is not clear.

continued interplay between self and spirit, between community authoring and individual quest, poses challenges for social theory as well as for the societies that must deal with the emergence of the new-indigenes.

Bibliography

ASLaN Ancient Sacred Landscapes Network website, available online at http://www.symbolstone.org/archaeology/aslan/index.html
Bates, B. (1983) *The Way of Wyrd*. London: Arrow.
Bauman, Z. (1997) *Postmodernity and its Discontents*, New York: New York University Press.
Blain, J. (2000) Speaking Shamanistically: seidr, academia, and rationality, *DISKUS*. Available online at: http://www.unimarburg.de/religionswissenschaft/journal/diskus/#6.
Blain, J. (2001) Shamans, stones, authenticity and appropriation: contestations of invention and meaning, in R.J. Wallis and K. Lymer (eds.) *A Permeability of Boundaries: New Approaches to the Archaeology of Art, Religion and Folklore:* 47–55. BAR International Series 936. Oxford: British Archaeological Reports.
Blain, J. (2002) *Nine Worlds of Seid-Magic*. London: Routledge.
Blain, J. and R.J. Wallis (2000) The 'ergi' seidman: contestations of gender, shamanism and sexuality in northern religion past and present. *Journal of Contemporary Religion* 15 (3): 395–411.
Blain, J. and R.J. Wallis (2002) A living landscape? Pagans and archaeological discourse. *3rd Stone: Archaeology, Folklore and Myth – The Magazine for the New Antiquarian:* in press.
Blain, J. and R.J. Wallis (2001) Ritual reflections, practitioner meanings: 'performance' disputed. Paper given at BSA Study Group of Religion conference, April 2001.
Blain, J. and R.J. Wallis, Sacred Sites Contested Rites/Rights project, available online at http://www.sacredsites.org.uk
Borovsky, Z. (1999) Never in public: Women and performance in Old Norse Literature, *Journal of American Folklore* 112: 6–39.
Bowman, M. (2000) Contemporary Celtic Spirituality. In: A. Hale and P. Payton (eds.) *New Directions in Celtic Studies:* 69–91. Exeter: University of Exeter Press.
British Druid Order website, available online at http://www.druidorder.demon.co.uk.
Carmichael, D.L., J. Hubert, Reeves B. and Schanche, A. (1994) *Sacred Sites, Sacred Places*. London: Routledge.
Chadbourn, M. (2001) Landscapes touched by the Light. *The Times*, London. Jan 27, 2001.

Davies, P. (1997) Respect and Reburial. *The Druid's Voice: The Magazine of Contemporary Druidry* 8 (Summer):12–13.

Eliade, M. (1964) *Shamanism: Archaic Techniques of Ecstasy*, New York: Pantheon.

Flaherty, G. (1992) *Shamanism and the Eighteenth Century*, Princeton, NJ.: Princeton University Press.

Gallagher, Anne-Marie (1999) Weaving a Tangled Web? Pagan ethics and issues of history, 'race' and ethnicity in Pagan identity. *The Pomegranate*, 10: 19–29.

Geertz, C. (2000) *Available Light*. Princeton, N.J: Princeton University Press.

Greene, S. (1998) The shaman's needle: development, shamanic agency, and intermedicality in Aguarina Lands, Peru, *American Ethnologist* 25,4: 634–658.

Green, D.A. (2002) The Season of the Witch? Pagan Magic in Psycho-Social Context. Ph.D Thesis, University of the West of England.

Greenwood, S. (2000) *Magic, Witchcraft, and the Otherworld: an Anthropology*, Oxford: Berg.

Guédon, M.F. (1994) Dene ways and the ethnographer's culture, in D.E. Young and J.G. Goulet (eds.) *Being Changed by Cross-Cultural Encounters: the Anthropology of Extraordinary Experience*, Peterborough, Ontario: Broadview Press, 39–70.

Harner, M. (1990) [1980] *The Way of the Shaman*. London: Harper Collins.

Harvey, G. (1997) *Listening People, Speaking Earth: Contemporary Paganism*. London: Hurst and Co.

Harvey, G. and C. Hardman (eds.) (1995) *Paganism Today: Wiccans, Druids, the Goddess and Ancient Earth Traditions for the Twenty-First Century*: 242–251. London: Thorsons.

Hutton, R. (1996) *The Stations of the Sun: a history of the ritual year in Britain*. Oxford: Oxford University Press.

Hutton, R. (1999) *Triumph of the Moon: A History of Modern Pagan Witchcraft*. Oxford: Oxford University Press.

Jakobsen, M.D. (1999) *Shamanism: Traditional and Contemporary Approaches to the Mastery of Spirits and Healing*, New York and Oxford: Berghahn Books.

Larrington, C. trans. (1996) *The Poetic Edda*, World's Classics, Oxford: Oxford University Press.

Letcher, A. (2001) The Role of the Bard in Contemporary Pagan Movements. PhD Thesis, King Alfred's College, Winchester.

Lindquist, G. (1997) *Shamanic Performance on the Urban Scene: Neo-Shamanism in Contemporary Sweden*. Stockholm Studies in Social Anthropology 39. Stockholm, Sweden: University of Stockholm.

Maffesoli, M. (1996) *The Time of the Tribes: The Decline of Individualism in*

Mass Society. London: Sage.

Marcus, G.E. (1999) *Ethnography through Thick and Thin*. Princeton: Princeton University Press.

Matthews, J. (1991) *Taliesin: Shamanism and the Bardic Mysteries in Britain and Ireland*. London: Aquarian.

Merkur, D. (1992) *Becoming Half Hidden: Shamanism and Initiation among the Inuit*, New York and London: Garland.

Meulengracht Sørenson, P. (1983) *The Unmanly Man: concepts of sexual defamation in early Northern society*, trans. J. Turville-Petre, Odense: Odense University Press.

Romain, J. (2000) *Your God Shall Be My God*. ASCM Press.

Saunders, N.J. (1994) At the mouth of the obsidian cave: deity and place in Aztec religion. in Carmichael, D.L., J. Hubert, B. Reeves and A. Schanche, *Sacred Sites, Sacred Places*. London: Routledge.

Shirokogorov, S.M. (1935) *Psychomental Complex of the Tungus*, London: Kegan Paul, Trench, Trubner & Co.

Smiley, J. and. Kellogg, R. (eds.) (2000) *The Sagas of Icelanders*. Harmondsworth: Penguin.

Taussig, M. (1987) *Shamanism, Colonialism and the Wild Man: A Study in Terror and Healing*. Chicago: The University of Chicago Press.

Wallis, R.J. (1999) Altered States, Conflicting Cultures: Shamans, Neo-shamans and Academics. *Anthropology of Consciousness* 10 (2–3): 41–49.

Wallis, R.J. (2000) Queer shamans: autoarchaeology and neo-shamanism. *World Archaeology* 32(2): 252–262.

Wallis, R.J. Forthcoming (2003) *New Shamans: Ecstasy, Alternative Archaeology and Contemporary Paganism*. London: Routledge.

Wallis, R.J. and Blain,.J. (2002) Sites, sacredness, and stories: Interactions of archaeology and contemporary Paganism. Conference paper presented at Folklore Society Conference, *Folklore and Archaeology*, 24 March 2002.

York, Michael (2000) Defining Paganism. *The Pomegranate*, 11: 4–9.

10. Mass Media

Barry King

Traditional approaches to the relationship between the mass media and identity, whether considering an individual or collective level, have tended to assume that the effect of the mass media is to undermine the connection between the individual and her immediate context of life. Thus in the historical development of media theory, a strongly established theme is that the overall impact of the mass media leads to the fragmentation of collective consciousness, eroding or impeding the emergence of an awareness of the structural realities of class, race, gender and ethnicity and sexual orientation. Despite some internal variation, the dominant research traditions – direct influence theories and uses and gratifications both conjure an opposition between the media and the individual consumer/spectator implying that these factors are in someway independent of each other. In the theory of Mass Culture and its Marxist variants, the individual brings to her interaction with the media, a fixed identity that is then dissolved into a structurally indeterminate mass identity which causes the individual to conceive of her self as enclosed monad with private needs and desires that eventuate in an attitude of escape, loss of responsibility and self indulgence. Through the tutelage of the mass media the individual develops a mass consciousness which, in the Marxist variant, is a false consciousness based on the denial of the reality of class relationships. For cultural conservatives on the other hand, mass consciousness is a condition of decadence through which cultural standards essential to the good society are debased and corrupted by immediate self-gratification.[8]

In the uses and gratifications paradigm, by contrast, the consumers' needs have been conceptualised as autonomous and sovereign, existing independently from the 'encounter with the media'. However considerable the power of the media to structure perception, the individual is securely anchored in primary group relations, which, through the influence of opinion leaders, serve to filter out media influence (see Gitlin, 1978: 205–253 for a demonstration that Katz and Lazarsfeld's *Personal Influence* (1955) does not rule out of more direct media effects).

---

[8] These latter complementary positions almost universally condemned in professional literature as simplistic are by no means dead as the writings of Harold Bloom indicate.

Sometimes media influence on the total texture of everyday life is recognised as a problem. Thus, for example, longitudinal studies of popular heroes show a decreasing interest in local heroes whose values and beliefs derive from the community. Such *proximate* heroes are increasingly replaced by hero-types whose existence is intimately tied up with the mass media (Gash & Conway, 1997: 349–372). If it seems clear that mass media heroes are qualitatively different from "local" heroes, the fact that such heroes are voluntarily chosen is taken as a sufficient guarantee that they still arise spontaneously from popular experience (see e.g. Fiske, 1987; Jenkins, 1986). Catastrophic events such as the September 11th 2001 attack reveal this difference in a sharp form, especially when publications like People Magazine announce that they are abandoned their usual celebrity driven fare (see Gloss off Mags in New Reality, New Zealand Herald, 26/9/01, p6).

The Contingent self

The concept of identity implicit in these early formulations – as desirably fixed within a collective framework or alternately as vigorously self-sufficient like the subject of market liberalism – were not at the outset conceptually adequate to the complexity of the interaction between the individual and the media. G.H. Mead, for example, claims that the self is a construction. In Mead's view, the development of a concept of a self with a discrete identity is the outcome of a socially grounded interaction through symbols. During socialisation, via involvement in play, language use and games, the individual learns to distinguish between a social self or "me" and "I". For Mead, "me" is not what actual individuals expect of one, but rather the conventional definition of what is expected of an individual in a particular situation. This expectation is trans-individual, arising from social norms, which inform what actual individuals feel and think, functioning as a *generalised other*. 'I' by contrast, is the individual's response to the prevalent definition of "me". The individual's response to the social world is active; deciding what to respond to in prevalent attitudinal structures, but not entirely determined by them (Mead, 1934: pp. 175–178).

Any social setting contains a manifold of generalized others which the individual may selectively encounter as a matter of circumstance or choice. She may, simultaneously and serially, belong to different groups and thereby engage in a gamut of relationships with generalized others. Again not all generalized others have the same scope of relevance, some having a local and some a societal purchase, the individual may switch allegiances or balance out immediate involvements with a larger and more inclusive one than the one in which she is currently involved. In the balancing of commitments according to a personal calculus of commitment and identity, the mass media are a generalised other with an apparently universal register of relevance and penetration. The mass media, in other words, appear as the most generalised of generalised others and from this fact have a great 'referent power' (McQuail, 1994) in respect of the popular. In the light of the distinction between proximal and distal heroes raised at the end of the last section, we can observe that "mass" heroes, if filtered through local and individual perceptions, are nonetheless constructed to the script of national and even global markets. It is from inside a pre-established framework of authority and power that local or individual "readings" are obliged to work if seeking a comparable level of collective recognition.

Varieties of the contingent self

The concept of self-identity implicit in the foregoing counter-positions as an independent form that the media corrupts or obediently extends, is no longer tenable. In broad agreement with Mead's views, self-identity is seen as a kind of construction or a performance that is, consciously or unconsciously, engaged in negotiating its position, powers of agency and action in relation to others. Increasingly these others are found not in the context of everyday life but in the media representations of everyday life (Caughey, 1984). The folk notion of identity or, for that matter, traditional notions of character as virtue, which regard identity as an extension of a fixed inner personality, is regarded as treating as natural what is actually an appearance sustained by an ideological process. In the contemporary view, the self is merely contingent and limited to specific situations and conditions that have a social or discursive rather than a natural basis (see Laclau, 1990). Change the terms of discourse and the social setting and the self itself will change either deliberately or as result of processes that cannot be resisted.

Yet if there is wide agreement that self-identity is contingent, there are differing views on the degree of contingency and how fundamentally flexible or protean the self is and what this means for the nature of social life.

In the line of thought that descends from Erving Goffman, the self is a performance tactically deployed to fit in with some ongoing strip of action, all the while reserving a back region in which the performer lays aside the mask adopted to impress others (Goffman, 1969). Conceptualising identity as a kind of performance puts the self in everyday life on par with an actor in the theatre. But this analogy runs the risk of disguising the fact that in real life the action has substantial rather than merely symbolic consequences. An argument on stage does not lead to real injuries whereas in real life an antagonistic performance may. It can be asserted that symbolic actions have their consequences but these are meaningful rather than substantial. The games people plays are at once less elegant than on the stage and graver in their consequences. (On the para-theatrical and real see Wiltshire, 1990: 169–178).

Perhaps a more substantial criticism is that in Goffman's dramaturgical conception of the self, the notion of an essential self persists, hiding behind a front, manipulating verbal and visual behaviour like an homunculus behind a screen. Other theorists take a more fundamental view of the infirmities of identity.

> We must replace the starting point in a supposed thing...located within individuals, with one located...within the general communicative commotion of everyday life (Shotter quoted in Gergen, 1991: 156).

For Judith Butler, if the self is a performance, it is a performance *in depth* constrained and differentially enabled by a confluence of discursive practices, centred on sex, gender, sexual practice and desire. The individual is born with a particular anatomical endowment in which some features are defined as fundamental to his or her sexual identity; these significant features are further articulated around factors of personality and intellect that are deemed within the discursive practices of gender to arise from biological differentiation (Some individuals are anatomically "ambiguous" of course but these are exceptions that prove the rule). Within the apparent ground of gender, the individual has desires that may conflict with, if not contradict, his or her gendered identity. These desires may lead the individual to engage in acts – or conversely different acts may lead to the discovery of latent desires – which do not fit the dominant prescriptions of gender. Identity as experienced by the self and others (and even the very concept of a unitary essence called a self) do not reside in the individual but in the particular configuration of the discursive practices that surround the individual in a particular cultural setting. These practices – ways of identifying, equating and naming personal qualities – require the construction of an appearance of an essential self:

> In other words, acts, gestures and desires produce the effect of an internal core or substance, but produce this on the surface of the body, through a play of signifying absences that suggest, but never reveal, the organising principle as a cause. Such acts, gestures and enactments generally construed, are *performative* in the sense that the essence or identity that they otherwise purport to express are *fabrications*, manufactured and sustained through corporeal signs and other discursive means. (Butler, 1990: 136) (For a critique of Butler's arguments see Schatzki, Schatzki and Natter, 1996: 49–77.)

In contrast to Goffman, Butler's formulation renders the self radically dependent on the process of representation. The self cannot step back from that process because it is fundamentally a product of it, limited and extended by it, like the translation of a letter to a loved one into a foreign language that loses some of its desired nuances (see Butler, 1997: 149).

Surprisingly given their pervasiveness as providers of identity imagery, Butler has little to say about the impact of the visual media (Gender Trouble, 1989, for example, offers only passing comments on film to illustrate the arguments. Schatzki (loc. cit.) makes a parallel argument that Butler's conception of discursive practice is fundamentally tied to language. The pervasiveness of language may also explain Butler's tendency to have a totalistic conception of performance.

If recognition is given to the diversity of different kinds of visual performances and their multifarious patterns of interaction, it seems appropriate to suggest that the dialectic of gain and loss, adequacy and inadequacy that marks self-identity formation is not just an intra-personal but also a transpersonal process. If the pervasiveness of the media is taken into account, identity management is not a process internal to a specific identity position but ranges across a series of positions, some complementary and some disparate, all in circulation in a cultural field. Are the media not specifically influential in the provision of an endless stream of "possible" selves? Indeed, the mere fact of the existence of a variety of role models and the intrinsic limitations of any particular subject position might be said to intensify the search for alternate identities at a conscious level, however unsuccessful the sought after sense of integrity proves to be.[9]

Kenneth Gergen argues that the saturation of social experience by media forms has reached a point where the process of identity construction has become unstable and offers the individual no sure purpose or compass:

> ... as social saturation proceeds we become pastiches, imitative assemblages of each other. In memory we carry others patterns of being with us. If the conditions are favourable, we can place these patterns into action. Each of us becomes the other, a representative, or a replacement ... we are not one or a few, but like Walt Whitman we contain "multitudes". We appear to each other as single identities, unified, of whole cloth. However, with social saturation, each one of us comes to harbour a vast population of hidden potentials – to be blues singer, a gypsy, an aristocrat, a criminal. All the selves lie latent, and under the right conditions may spring to life. (Gergen, loc. cit: p71)

For Gergen, the development of a pastiche conception of the self which might otherwise be seen as a release from the straitjacket of 'normality' is

---

[9] Butler's critique of the Althusserian notion of interpellation whilst powerful, still remains couched at the level of the formation of an individual identity. Individuals must already be constituted as an "I" in order to be hailed. What if the "I" is not able to attain the level of "hailable" coherence? Is it more likely to be susceptible to the call?

fraught with negative consequences. In a media saturated culture, the subjective processes of self identity formation are overwhelmed by a profusion of role models, which leads to a condition he terms, *multiphrenia – the vertigo of unlimited multiplicity* (ibid: 49, 73–74, 150). Compared to the tendency within post-modern theory to celebrate the protean self, the multiphrenic self is infused with guilt over not measuring up to the demands of multiple and mutually conflicting standards and norms of behaviour. The very sense of disengagement leading to a pervasive feeling of superficiality.

The social and cultural correlates of the Pastiche Self

The approaches to self-identity formation just examined tend to give a primary causal weight to ideological or subjective factors. The development of a self-identity is, for the most part, a cognitive issue.[10] Two issues surface here – are there social structural reasons for the pastiche self and secondly, are some categories of individuals more dependent on media provided scripts of identity than others? Anthony Giddens (1991) examines a range of social structural conditions that affect general conceptions of selfhood in late modernity – his preferred term for what others term post modernity:

- In late modernity, the conditions of existence are structurally inflected around the intersection of the local and the global. If the individual still continues to live a local life, the conditions of life – security of income, employment, safety and well-being – are increasingly subject to developments such as capital flight, downsizing and outsourcing that are beyond the individual's control. Even the natural environment becomes increasingly at risk from ecological threats that emanate from elsewhere to the point where the biosphere itself may be jeopardised.
- What Giddens terms the intrusion of distance into local activities and the ensuing transformations of time and space interface with the centrality of mediated experience, radically transforming the texture of the life world. An important element in the nurturance of identity is the capacity of institutions that envelop the individual to provide a coherent and continuous narrative of self-identity. As the institutional order retreats from the grasp of the logics of locality and self-identity, the individual lacks the resources to congeal his or her experience into a personal narrative. As a consequence, the self is confronted with a series of dilemmas or problems of integration: can experience be unified as the individual is obliged to accommodate to endemic change or is any contingent self identity subject to an inevitable process of fragmentation

---

[10] Even Gergen who critically implicates the media in the processes of identity formation inclines to speak of a unitary process affecting in all selves in a media -saturated environment.

and a loss of personal meaning? Will the individual, practically unable to control the conditions of his or her existence be overwhelmed by a pervasive sense of powerlessness or will she be able to repose trust in forces that are beyond his or her control. Will the exercise of trust, ontologically necessary at some level, lead to a complete disillusionment and an overwhelming sense of powerlessness or to irrational feelings of omnipotence? What kinds of authority structures can the individual appeal to bolster themselves against uncertainty and given that all authority structures have become just one option amongst many, what will the individual chose and in choosing be able to justify? Does dogmatism or universal doubt prevail?

- Lastly, since late-modernity is marked by the pervasive commodification of experience and increasing penetration of the globe by capitalist marketing process that are premised on selling life style products. Such products, emphatically centred on appearance and self-grooming, seem to celebrate, whilst reducing the options for, individual expression to the consumption of life-style packages, available to anyone that can afford it or can at least obtain the necessary credit (Giddens, 1991: 187–201).

In these general life circumstances, the mass media, already empirically pervasive, become a major and powerful resource for the promulgation of life style options and the notion that how one lives is a matter of choice governed by commodity relationships. Even more substantial perhaps is the narrative modelling effect of the media, as filtered through forms and genres such as soap-operas, action films, reality Television and celebrity gossip, which feed the 'narrative deficits' that viewers encounter in the context of their own lives (ibid.).

As a depiction of a new social psychology that fits the experience of individuals in late modernity, Giddens' arguments are persuasive. Yet at the same time it is necessary to caution against an interpretation of his arguments that lends credence to the idea that identity today is solely influenced by the interface between the individual and the global media. Obviously not all individuals live under the conditions of late modernity. But more important, even for those that do, the binary contrast between the individual and the global is both too abstract and too individualised. An important mediating factor between the local and the global is national culture or what Anderson termed an 'imagined community'. Imagined communities work to establish a sense of a deep, horizontal comradeship, regardless of the actual extent of exploitation and inequality within the society in question (Anderson, 1991: 5–7). Historically, the axis around which an imagined community has been constructed in Britain is social class. So that other aspects of the individual such as gender, ethnicity and nationality have only served to exclude or limit the capacity of "others" to fully participate in the deep, horizontal comradeship of a class order. For those admitted to the community of the nation, the psychological and economic impact of class structuration was moderated by the honour of belonging or respectability. – a status normally reserved for those who were white, male and heterosexual (Skeggs, 1997). Contemporary developments in late modern societies, such as the USA or Britain, have shown a steady de-coupling of the relationship between class inequality, which as a structural process is evermore pronounced and the process of collective action and ideologies. For example Eder (1993) argues class today is a structural reality that lacks a cultural texture that will translate class existence into collective action. This state of affairs is very much a contemporary phenomenon and may not last.

I would argue that socio-economic class provides the fundamental causal dynamic in the relationship between social structure and identity formation. Identity as subjectively experienced is conditioned by the social valuation placed on personal attributes such as skin colour, ethnicity and gender. But the degree of consequentiality of the valuation of an attribute is determined by the individual's objective class position. This is not to claim that these other dimensions are unimportant but rather that the degree to which they are important and consequential is dependent ultimately on class position in the socio-economic sense. This claim would need considerable qualification if applied outside the orbit of late modern societies however. Yet even apparently independent status determinants such as lightness or darkness of skin colour have an historical root in class relationships in American slavery and British colonialism. (See for example. James, 1964.)

The relationship between class and other dimensions of inequality is that class processes extend or moderate the effect of the latter. Thus in relation to gender the sorting of individuals into male and female is a predominantly binary process. But in order to account systematically for the differences in life chance differences between *men and men* and *women and women* it becomes necessary to address the dynamics of class as a structuring process. Conversely status attributes such as skin colour or personal culture (habitus) only assume the power to influence life chances if coupled with class relationships of power and domination. The full weight of class structuration processes falls on individuals whose personal characteristics fall outside of the roster of preferred attributes (For a general discussion see Giddens, 1981; Bourdieu, 1987). At the same time, status group conflicts can become the discursive conduit through which class struggles are misrepresented and diverted. Thus for example black workers may unite with white workers to fight against the capitalist class. But there is also the chance that black workers see the conflict as a racial issue and attack racist white workers instead of capitalists, thereby promoting intra-class struggle at the expense of interclass struggle.

189

If the subjective impact of class inequality rests on the degree to which other factors – being black or white, male or female, young or old – ameliorate or aggravate its impact, respectability is a discipline of self-fashioning that can at least subjectively stay the full brunt of class determination (Giddens, op. cit. p. 82). Regardless of one's objective socio-economic position, he or she can maintain this belief about his or herself. If they cannot guarantee a place amongst the well-heeled and comfortable one can get the look and who knows? – the look may lead to the place after all. Being respectable is the historically proven strategy of those who would be, or precariously maintain a claim to be, middle class – not so rough as to be outside of fashionable, and not so rich as not to have to care about falling behind the latest fashion (Skeggs, op. cit. pp. 2–13).

Modularity, media and Identity

As a proposition about the nature of reality, modularity has the following features:
- The principle that all totalities are nothing more than an aggregation of components. These components can be combined in various ways because they are conceived to be functional equivalents permitting substitution, addition and recombination.
- Given the principle of functional equivalence – all cultural practices are equally valid – new configurations are sought and desired.
- Since no specific combination is deemed to be integral to cultural organizations, any given order of content has no more than a present validity since new configurations are not only desired but are certain to emerge.
- The dominating goal of any given configuration is short-term coherence. (see Kroes (1996) on the Americanisation process).

Described in this way modularity might seem to be merely a restatement of the well-rehearsed features of post-modernism – quotationalism, flattening of space-time, loss of historical sense etc. However, as a formation, modularity lacks the notion of semiotic play and 'drift' which for many is the over-riding feature of post-modernity. For even though in theory, the modular worldview should lead to the endorsement of change and plasticity, it paradoxically transpires into a search for, if not the perfect, then the *situationally best* rendition. What follows from this is a procedural version of the sublime, which intimately celebrates and valorizes the essential rendition or performance.

Contrary to the notion of the sublime as a state of experience that inspires astonishment and awe, a procedural sublime implies a process, and acting upon a substance or event in order to produce superlative effects. Invariably this effect is conceptualized as affirming the integrity of the individual as the fundamental unity of reality. Individuals are sovereign subjects that stand apart from the world and impose their (his or, not until recent times, her) will upon it or at least are served by those who undertake to produce a particular effect. Finally, the procedural sublime is increasingly commodified which is to say that the application of technology is increasingly oriented towards producing spectacles as part of the tourist and entertainment industry, driven by a logic of excess, bigger, better, more inclusive of the sensory range (Nye, 1999: 283, 291).[11]

The audio-visualisation of a modular self began with the hyper-real encoding of commercials that came into prominence in the production of commercial in the 1980's and then spread to the cinema. It is useful therefore to focus on the Television commercial as a précis of effects that are in circulation in media culture. Modular commercials flaunt their constructedness through the deployment of coding strategies that signal a distance from the everyday ecology of perception, as reproduced within the conventions of "classical" cinema. Strategies such as hypersignification of detail, reflexive camerawork, elliptical narrative forms and intertextuality seem to imply that the viewer is too savvy to mistake the represented for the real (Goldman & Papson, 1994: 11, 23–53, esp. 36). The purpose seems not to directly persuade – the actual product is only mentioned fleetingly or is presented in a frankly exaggerated way that foregrounds the fictionality or hype. What is suggested to the viewer is that he or she can make use of the product or service as a means for self-expression. However, in accomplishing the latter the text becomes the uniquely privileged site of an experience that cannot be encountered outside of the process of signification itself. In this sense, the spectator is doubly positioned outside the text as an onlooker. We are external to the look of the camera which, with swish pans and jump-cuts and other effects, never pretends to be anything but a technological manipulation; a camera eye whose formal permutations are a meta-pattern that interdict an immersion in content and because what is shown abides nowhere else but in the utopian power of the cinema and elector-optical apparatus to visualise improbable conjunctions and scenes. Modular texts cannot be said to suture the viewer into the text so much as create a distance that hopefully nurtures a mimetic desire – *the desire to be like*. The profound implication of the photographic and electronic optical imagery in this practice gives it the specific dynamic of *defensive physiognomics*. The realm of appearances is asserted to be a valid indicator of personal worth – if one

---

[11] As Nye points out the process of domesticating the technological sublime has merographically drawn on the metaphors of feminisation. Generally speaking the discourse of modularity seems driven by gender equality. But representing gender differences as easily transcended is a ruse that effects a reduction to mere function.

looks right then one *is* right. This claim is parasitic on the power of photography to *sequester* the referent temporally and spatially. Photography as a medium has the tense of ***Now/Then*** which in globally circulated images is intertwined with the spatial condition of being ***Here/There***. Not only does this offer the opportunity to the living to represent themselves outside of any present context; by re-articulating the relationship between the present and the past, it also allows those outside of any sphere of cultural activity to fashion themselves as insiders on the basis of remote observation. Because images are pre-tested in the realm of publicity by association with celebrities, or simply by the fact of being out in the public realm, they have the status of collective representations that are authentically global rather than purely local in the span of visibility. Not the least because the photo-effect of presence in absence is articulated in terms of professionally realized ego ideals, which even insiders must imitate. The conquest of space and time – of being here and everywhere regardless of temporal or geographical barriers – bestows on the image offered the character of a rescue, or, at least, a respite from the viewer's life world.

Nor should it be supposed that the modular self is simply a mediated phenomenon. Increasingly employers are demanding that employees manifest certain qualities in appearance and behaviour. The 'new' experiential market is deeply implicated in process of theatrical representation. Whether one considers the design of products for niche markets, the process of advertising, the staging of promotional events, the actors who appear in commercials or the sales personnel who strive to build a durable and repetitious commodity relationship (*Lifetime Value*) with customers, the production and distribution of commodities is a performance saturated process. The recognition of the importance of the image has led some to identify the movie studio as the paradigm of enterprise. Even where the product is not directly cultural, the theatrical metaphor still applies: what do Human Relations do but cast the actors to play the roles, the producers – the investors and shareholders – provide the finance, the directors transform treatments into operational scripts and performances, the scriptwriters attend to total quality management and process, the technical staff build the sets, provide the props and costumes and the stage crew work behind the scenes to make the performance happen (Pine & Gilmore, 1999).

The existential correlates of modular identity

In the modular text, the viewer/spectator is addressed as one who is ready to play the codes of appearance to her advantage. In a world in which the importance of place and locality no longer prevails over the flow of global information and power, the viewer can find in modular imagery a small place, which is simultaneously local and global.

But there is a cognitive price for this defensive sequestration of a self-identity: the overall scheme of performance, if seemingly based on popular cultural practices, is mimetically defined by experts. The realm of the popular here answers modernity's dream of rendering everyday existence as an art form.

In the broadest terms, the modular texts deploy a visual rhetoric that represents the media, particularly the computer graphic media, as a realm of freedom, effortless contact and effortless technique. The actual commodity being pitched is positioned as a pretext or a means towards an effect/affect the consumer (virtually defined) is seeking. Perhaps most decisively what is projected here is a prosthetic utopia, which offers the possibility that the self as formed by biological and socially intertwined processes (race, ethnicity, gender, sexual orientation, nationality and so forth) can be out-contextualized – transported to other contexts without loss of the capacity to function as a viable unit (Lury, 1998: 3). The subjects of prosthetic utopia must be highly flexible and open to the immanent possibility of re-deployment in any new context.

Reduced to the register of the personal and therapeutic, these modular texts announce that the service or commodity will confer mastery of body and appearance. As Celia Lury has argued, prosthetic technologies encourage experimental individualism – the view of the self as an experimental identity or object that does not say I am what I am, but I am what I can become (ibid: 19). But the theme of self-transformation or "make-over" is not without its own version of physiognomic responsibility – if the "look" is optional then how you look is how you chose to look, a freely expressed revelation of your desired identity. People who do not choose to be what they could be are, rightly, condemned to the consequences of their ill-fitting appearances.

If physiognomic responsibility is accepted then a number of attitudinal conditions are set in train. The individual must have the capacity to live in the moment; gratification must be immediate and functionally specific because there is no tomorrow in the world of fashion or desire. One is gratified or not; up to the minute or not. Second, the individual must see conformity as freedom, honoring the Orwellian equation of opposites. Rather than being seen as the loss of authenticity, painstaking conformity to another's scripts is converted into, and represented as, a superlative rendition.

193

Doing it my way, even if it is far from unusual. This means more than behavioural conformity to the dictates of the programme. It means showing that one is not just committed to but also psychologically attached or in love with a specific task or practice. The requirement is that one manifests a level of enthusiasm, willingness and sincerity that will overshadow what any other individual might offer. Unless this is achieved, one cannot be an individual *and* a conformist. Moreover, since performances can be faked, the capacity to fake must become a kind of sincerity (Goffman, 1972).[12] Third, the primary existential dynamic is completism. The modular self is permanently open to the potential for any detail to be significant and must therefore master all the nuances and details. In search of the endless renewal of markets and the desire-to-desire, modular scenarios encourage the individual to know all there is to know rather than to know what is meaningful (Eco, 1992).

Lastly, modular scenarios encourage magic individualism – the individual is depicted as automatically freed from collective determinations. Logically, the very concept of the individual presupposes the negation of cultural and social influences – race, class, ethnicity, and gender (Balibar, 1992). This logical negation is matched in modular scenarios, thanks to the commodity, by a stream of self sufficient transformations: either the individual is not what he or she seems, becomes something else, or is translated to a different realm of being. The definition of advertising as a magic system is not new, but Williams' definition reflected the state of the "art" at the time in product pitches that promised to fulfill fixed identities – beer drinking leads to more manliness etc. (Williams, 1997). What is being normatized now is closer to magic realism or, to use Castells' term, "real virtuality" – a system in which people's symbolic and material existence is entirely immersed and captured in a virtual setting. The setting does not communicate an experience; it *is* the experience.

Class Respectability for the Fourth World

Modular identifications like popular cultural projections in general, have both a utopian and reifying aspect (Jameson, 1979: 189–199). In its utopian prospect, it constitutes a denial of the necessity of given identities, as implied by the concept of performativity. Yet, when opportunistically deployed such a concept is not without internal contradictions – for one thing not all performances are equally valid or for that matter equally valued by peers, let alone larger constituencies. If some performances can be said to be better than others then questions of essentialism creep back in. More mundanely, not all those who would "pass" have access to the same level of resources or

---

[12] Usually the commodity is shown as the little helper that controls the anxiety that otherwise would vitiate the appearance of a natural emotional investment in the role.

conversely, the same capacity to deflect scrutiny. Nor is it entirely clear that performances are independent of standpoint experiences – of being a particular kind of socially defined being.

The Utopian aspect of modular audio-visual texts is that they propose that differences of culture and background can be overcome – indeed, in such texts one can literally morph inside another's skin. This claim is all the more advanced by the codes of visualization which depend on appearances and events as the primary means of manifesting the mind. Here the photo-effect of presence-in-absence can be turned to pragmatic advantage. If one can assume the look and the demeanor, one can have an edge – mastery of the codes of real virtuality.

But at the same time modular processes feed on the notion of a life-style as an exemplary performance undertaken by individuals who are not just stereotypes but idealizations of stereotypes (see Baudrillard, 1988, his notion of 'ecstasy' is relevant here). For example, gender identity is declared an act but an act so accomplished that it approaches the paradoxical state of willed essentialism. Pamela Anderson Lee or Arnold Schwarzenegger (and their real time and game world clones) may be exaggerations to the point of parody, but they alone can rise to the level of such a definitive, qualitative exemplification.

Modular identity processes are deeply implicated in the notion of the perfect, complete rendition or performance. In this sense, it is discourse that is founded on hyper-tokenism – the formation of symbolic representations that, emerging from popular experience, are subjected to a level of realization that renders them as the reified essence of their collective referent. Hyper-tokenism is all the more efficacious because corporate capital has seized control of the process of collective representation. Into the widely accepted notion that we are all pretending, it insinuates the notion that pretences can be more or less complete, more or less willed. Of course, we cannot all be beautiful, clever or skilled, but are there not aspects of ourselves that could achieve a kind of studied perfection with a sufficient application of effort and monetary outlay?

In the realm of leisure and romance, the submission of the individual to demands of modularity does bestow a measure of individual autonomy, an agency in circumscription. However, there is a more repressive aspect when modular expectations enter the realm of work. The driving force behind the aesthetics of modularity is a transformation in the geometry of class, the shift from a national to a global process of class formation. As a process of cognitive mapping, modularity is a response to the social order of the network society. One of the features of such a society is a structural split between a core labor force of information-based employees and managers and a larger disposable labor force. At the core, there is affluence, relative security of employment and a cosmopolitan culture based on networking with peers in a global cultural environment. The disposable labor force, shuttled in and out of employment as market conditions suggest, by contrast is poorly paid and shut out from the networks of information upon which corporate decision-making is based. This distinction between those who are programming and those who are programmed is replicated – imaginatively – in the world of leisure and entertainment.

In a network society the tendency towards polarization is endemic and subject to rapid and unpredictable shifts so that even those at the core cannot guarantee they will hold their place against technological change, corporate take-over, outsourcing and downsizing, and the willingness of similarly qualified groups located elsewhere to do the same work for less. In a situation of chronic uncertainty it is not unlikely that individuals will seek to improve their chances of surviving by adopting a façade of willingness to comply and to change – thus the new "ideal" worker becomes a modular self, one who fits into the team and is yet at the same (hopefully) unique and irreplaceable. Work, from the sides of both capital and labor, becomes an individualized process (Castells, 1996: 265).

In the light of this global development, what might be said of exemplary modular texts such as *The Matrix* and *Men in Black 2* is that they attempt to map as a condition of existence the new parameters of the network society in which power and domination depends on whether one is in a network and just as important which network one is in (ibid: 469). More exactly modular texts offer maps for those who are excluded from the cosmopolitan culture of the digital elite, and yet have not fallen out of the labor market into the Fourth world of the terminally unemployable (ibid: 279).

> It is through the promotion of 'life style' by the mass media, by advertising and by experts, through the obligation to shape a life through choices in a world of self-reflexive objects and images, that the modern self is governed. (Rose, 1990: 256–258)

Nor are the therapies of individual freedom confined to the realm of consumerism. The self who consumes is a self that works, or a self who works at consuming. More tellingly in advanced capitalist societies, good work (and the dominant form of work itself in services) is increasingly being represented as a process of self-expression. In the realm of work, the worker is enjoined to fit in and yet to be flexible – to have the ability to be focused in depth and yet open to pragmatically effective re-calibrations of the self as required (Du Gay, 1996: 182). Furthermore, in the search for the good job, it becomes important to signal these qualities in advance as a technique for self-presentation and selection. Metaphorically, those who work approximate to the condition of the ideal method actor who identifies absolutely with a part until the part changes. Those who seek work must be, so to speak, prepared as though answering a rehearsal call. And as work itself becomes flexible – as individuals circulate like so many units of energy among a variety of jobs – the requirement of fitting in to new work settings becomes a process of re-presenting the self. No wonder there is all the good advice on being presentable and the steeply increasing expenditures on personal care products. In work or leisure, it is now imperative to get with the programme.

Bibliography

Abercrombie, N. and Longhurst, B. (2000) *Audiences*, Sage.

Anderson, B. (1991) *Imagined Communities: reflections on the origin and spread of nationalisms*, Verso.

Balibar, E. (1992) *Race, Class and Nation*, Verso, London.

Baudrillard, J. (1988) *The Ecstasy of Communication*, New York, Semiotext(e).

Bourdieu, P. (1987) *What makes a Social Class? On the Theoretical and Practical existence of groups*, Berkeley Journal of Sociology.

Butler, J. (1997) *The Psychic Life of Power. Theories of Subjection*, Stanford University Press.

—— (1989) *Gender Trouble: feminism and the subversion of identity*, London, Routledge.

Castells, M. (1996) The Information Age: Economy, Society and Culture, Vol. One: *The Rise of Network Society*, Oxford, Blackwells.

Caughey, J. *Imaginary Relations*, University of Nebraska Press, 1984.

Du Gay, P. (1996) *Consumption and Identity at Work*, Sage, London.

Eco, U. (1992) *Interpretation and Overinterpretation*, Stephan Collini (ed.) Cambridge University Press, England.

Eder, K. (1993) *The New Politics of Class*, Sage.

Fiske, J. (1987) Television Culture, Routledge.

Gash, H. and Conway, P. (1997) *Images of Heroes and heroines: How Stable?* Journal of Applied Developmental Psychology.

Gergen, K (1991) *The Saturated Self*, Basic Books.

Giddens, A. (1981) *The Class Structure of the Advanced Societies*, Heinemann.

—— (1991) *Modernity and Self-Identity: Self and Society in the Late Modern Age*, Stanford, CA: Stanford University Press.

Gitlin, T. (1978) *Media Sociology: the dominant paradigm, Theory and Society*.

Goffman, E. (1972) *Encounters*, Penguin, London.

—— (1969) *The Presentation of the Self in Everyday Life*, Penguin (first published 1959).

Goldman, R. and Papson, S. (1994) *Advertising in the age of hypersignification, Theory, Culture and Society.*

James, C.L.R. (1964) *Beyond a Boundary*, The Sportsman's Book Club, Chapter 4.

Jameson, F. (1979) *Reification and Utopia in Mass Culture, Social Text*, Winter, 1.

Jenkins, H. (1988b) "*Star Trek:* Rerun, Reread, Rewritten: Fan Writing as Textual Poaching." *Critical Studies in Mass Communication* 5 (2).

Katz, E. and Lazarsfeld, P. F., eds. (1955) Personal Influence: The Part Played by People in the Flow of Mass Communications. Glencoe, IL: Free Press.

Kroes, R. (1996) *If You've Seen One You've Seen The Mall*, University of Illinois Press.

Laclau, E. (1990) *New Reflections on the Revolution of Our Time*, London & New York, Verso.

Lury, C. (1998) *Prosthetic Culture: photography, memory and identity*, London, Routledge.

McQuail, D. (1994) *Mass Communication Theory*, 3rd Edition. London: Sage Publications.

Mead, G. H., 1934, *Mind, Self and Society*, Chicago: University of Chicago Press.

New Zealand Herald, *Gloss off Mags in New Reality*, 26/9/01.

Nye, D. (1999) *American Technological Sublime*, MIT Press, Cambridge, Mass.

Pine J.B. and Gilmore, P. (1999) *The Experience Economy*, Harvard Business School Press.

Rose, N. (1990) *Governing the Soul*, Routledge, London.

Schatzki, T. and Natter, W. (1996) *The Social and Political body*, Guilford Press.

Schatzki, T. Practised Bodies: Subjects, Genders and Minds, in *The Social and Political Body*, New York, Guilford, Press.

Shotter, J. Texts of the Self (in Gergen 1991 p 156).

Skeggs, B. (1997) *Formations of Class and Gender*, Sage.

Williams, R. (1997) *The Magic System, in Problems in Materialism and Culture*, Verso, London.

Wiltshire, B. *The Concept of the Para-theatrical*, Drama Review, Winter, 1990.

11. Ethnic Communications

Victor Horboken

This chapter addresses the issue of the ethnic minority media and examines their role in the construction of a symbolic cultural place. More and more ethnic minority groups are willing to challenge the allegedly unifying power of modern information technology and mass communications. Operating in 'alien' cultural environments and co-existing with the mainstream and increasingly international media, ethnic communications are seen by the ethnic minority groups and movements as a vehicle of ethnic ideology and an instrument of resistance. While the international media tend to diffuse group identities and create a culture, which is not linked to, or characterised by any particular geographical place, the ethnic minority media may act as agents of cultural continuity, contributing to boundary formation and adding to an ethnic group's otherness and 'uniqueness'. In view of the increased movement of people and information across the globe, the ability of ethnic and transnational communications to reinforce or 'dilute' the minority identities and cultures deserve special attention and will, obviously, remain part of the agenda of cultural and media studies for quite a long time. If the ethnic minority media, as many believe, can play a key role in developing attachment to the ethnic cause and create an ethnic cultural and psychological 'safe haven', then they may be instrumental in setting the political agenda of their communities and in shaping the outlook and attitudes of the younger generations of 'ethnics'. In this respect, the ideas of 'an exile' as opposed to labour migration, and the resultant political 'consciousness of exile', an important but still under-researched phenomenon, which may turn ethnic minority media into a tool of political propaganda, are given special consideration. This chapter also attempts to show that, by evoking historical memory and provoking imagination, the ethnic minority media can promote social and political mobilisation of diasporic communities and turn the discourse of cultural continuity into a political issue of resistance and empowerment.

The preceding chapters examined different aspects of social identity and you already know that the feeling of belonging and the idea of cultural continuity have special significance for any social group. Identity is a key issue in contemporary academic discourse. Obsession with individual or collective identity seems to become characteristic of our time, which is only natural since identity imposes a set of cultural patterns upon a society and every individual; it 'offers coherence and integration in social life' and allows individuals to '…interpret their experiences and define their preferences and prejudices' (Aarebrot, 1982 in De Marchi: 52).

As the here and now fail to provide geographical and historical extensions, – those co-ordinates which presumably create cultural ideas and, thus, identities – cultural continuity and historical justification of the present are vitally important for human beings to live within the dimensions of space and time. So Americans, whose history is relatively short, try to endow every artefact of culture with historical significance, Romanians seek inspiration in their 'Latin origin', while Russians and Ukrainians are still in dispute over whose ancestors laid the foundations of the Kievan Rus Empire of the 9th–12th centuries.

As is known, identity is not just about belonging. It is also about differences and boundaries. The otherness, so valued by ethnic groups, which constantly negotiate their place and role in multicultural societies, is an outcome of a sufficiently long and 'independent' historical development in a unique geographical environment. For social groups, ethnic communities, in particular, boundaries, both physical and cultural, with their dual function of inclusion and exclusion, are important means of self-identification.

Just as individual identity is formed through membership of a group with simultaneous psychological and territorial protection of one's 'self', collective identity is built through the in-group – out-group relationships, through emphasising differences (often exaggerated or even invented) between groups, communities and cultures. One can say with certainty that it is the idea of difference and opposition that unites people within their particular groups or communities and, thus, the feelings of belonging and otherness are the most important and necessary feelings needed by any social group to survive and preserve its unique cultural profile. Concern over identity and shared culture, or even a memory of the formerly shared culture, acquire special significance for ethnic minority groups surrounded by dominant cultures of others, and for so called diasporic communities which, for different reasons, left their countries of origin and settled in foreign lands.

It is not easy to provide an exhaustive definition of a minority. For the purpose of this chapter, however, it is enough to mention Gerard Chaliand's (1989) suggestion that a linguistic or ethnic minority is defined, first of all, by its group consciousness, collective memory and collective will to survive.

> There is no minority without collective memory….Only groups
> that see themselves different…and are concerned to preserve their
> special features, however integrated they may otherwise be as
> citizens of the state, should be described as minorities (Chaliand,
> 1989: 6).

This does not mean, of course, that ethnic minority groups are fixed entities with never-changing cultural differences. Although, fearing assimilation, minority institutions usually try to set the bounds of community, the communities do interact with other groups and their culture changes as a result of this interaction (Rex, 1996: 151). The identities of such groups are rather formed 'through discursive practices' and their differences and even the continuation of their cultural practices depend, to a certain extent, on a result of '...a process of boundary formation and maintenance.' (Barker, 1999: 63) In this respect, modern mass communications and, especially, ethnic minority media, with their ability to reproduce stereotypes and create a symbolic cultural place, can make a significant contribution to reinforcement of boundaries and consolidation of ethnic identities.

The major concern of ethnic minority media, be it Aboriginal broadcasting in Australia, Jewish newspapers in New York or the Persian radio in London, is ethnic survival and community-building. We will focus on the media's ability to consolidate their communities later in this chapter. But first let us look at some issues which may help us better understand the social role of ethnic communications and why '...the relationship between the media and ethnic minorities is typically characterised by continuity, conflict and change' (Cottle, 2000: 1).

Diaspora or exile?

Following Chaliand (1982), we can provide two 'classic characteristics' of the development of the minority communities: historic minorities, which found themselves surrounded by larger nations (e.g. Basques of France and Spain, Native Americans of the US and Canada or Tatars of Russia), and minorities, which left their mother countries for political, economic or religious reasons. The latter, who live in host countries and don't have territorial claims, are known as extra- or non-territorial minorities, or diasporas.

The term 'diaspora', which was originally applied to the exodus of Jews from Palestine, is now widely used to characterise communities of people who left their ancestral homes and settled in foreign countries, but who preserve the memory of and links with the land of their fathers or forefathers. As a result, we can read nowadays about Armenian, Chinese, Irish or Ukrainian diasporas, to name but a few.

It is the trans-national, diasporic communities that are the particular concern of this chapter. Keeping in mind extra-territoriality of diasporic communities, we can update our definition of the ethnic minority in motion, making it more relevant to the present discussion.

201

Normally, diasporas exhibit several of the following features: (1) dispersal from an original homeland, often traumatically; (2) alternatively, the expansion from a homeland in search of work, in pursuit of trade or to further colonial ambitions; (3) a collective memory and myth about the homeland; (4) an idealisation of the supposed ancestral home; (5) a return movement; (6) a strong ethnic group consciousness sustained over a long time; (7) a troubled relationship with host societies; (8) a sense of solidarity with co-ethnic members in other countries; and (9) the possibility of a distinctive creative, enriching life in tolerant host countries. (Cohen, 1997: 180)

In other words, the concept of diaspora incorporates the ideas of the centre or the mother-country and the periphery, the majority and the minority, the empowerment and the relative powerlessness, the integration and secession, the accommodation and resistance, the consciousness of exile and the memory of the original place, as well as the myth of eventual return. The last feature, however, the myth of eventual return or 'a return movement', seems to undermine our attempt to construct an exhaustive definition of the phenomenon, as a community's attachment to the lost 'centre' does not necessarily imply a desire for return.

The availability (or lack) of a desire for return allows some writers to draw a line between 'more diasporic' and 'less diasporic' formations or 'quasi diasporas', which show 'only some diasporic features or moments'. (Clifford, 1994: 306) South Asian diaspora, which does not demonstrate a desire for return and is, mainly, preoccupied with recreating a culture and a symbolic 'place' in new locations, is often used as an example of 'quasi diaspora'. As pointed out earlier, it is not easy to provide a comprehensive definition of diaspora. Not all trans-national communities correspond to the above-mentioned nine-point description of the phenomenon. Some features or 'moments' may be missing and, thus, the whole discourse of diaspora is the process of accommodation and modification of our knowledge of diasporic histories and present-day experiences.

In an attempt to classify diasporic communities researchers provide five different interpretations of the phenomenon with strong emphasis on the cause of displacement. Their special concern is the nature of factors, known as push factors, which make people leave their countries of origin and try their luck abroad. The five types of diaspora suggested by Robin Cohen (1997) are 'victim', 'labour', 'imperial', 'trade', and 'cultural'. The 'victim' type includes communities which were forced to leave their homeland as a result of political, ethnic or religious conflicts. Among them were Armenians, African captives in Americas and Palestinians. 'Labour' diasporas (Italian, Chinese, Japanese, Turkish communities) emerge when the movement of people is caused by unsatisfactory economic conditions in their home countries, while the case of 'trade' diasporas does not necessarily mean an escape from home, but is the result of both an individual and a collective (state-sponsored) effort. Chinese trade communities in many countries of South East Asia illustrate this form. Europeans, who found themselves outside their countries of origin after the collapse of colonialism, like the British in Africa or Russians in the former Soviet republics of the USSR, represent the 'imperial' or 'colonial' type of diaspora. The 'cultural' or 'hybrid' type of diaspora is best illustrated by the Caribbean peoples abroad. The peoples of the Caribbean are the descendants of the European colonists (imperial diasporas), the Indian migrant workers (labour diaspora) and the African slaves from West Africa (victim diaspora).

For the purpose of this chapter, however, which examines the role of ethnic communications in the process of maintenance or reconstruction of ethnic minority identities, it is enough to introduce the distinction between economic and forced migration or 'an exile'. By drawing a line between the two categories, one can argue that economic diasporas, which may include labour, trade or imperial ones, are the products of voluntary migration, while the notion of 'an exile' or a diaspora formed by forced migration implies that the 'centre' (the homeland) has fallen under foreign rule or has become the arena of the home political and military conflicts. In other words, the difference between economic migration and an exile reflects the nature of the push factors, economic or political, in a particular 'centre'. Interestingly, the members of the Ukrainian ethnic community in Great Britain, which, in this writer's view, is a classic, although neglected, example of a militant political emigration, seldom use the word 'diaspora'. They call themselves 'Ukraintsi v ekzili', which means 'Ukrainians in exile'.

According to some commentators, there is a close relationship between the state of exile and the consciousness of exile. It is this consciousness of exile and a thoroughly cultivated desire for return that make some ethnic communities 'more diasporic' than others and influence their attitude to accommodation and secession. Political considerations lie behind the activities and the very existence of exile communities. The struggle for political goals is the ideological cement that keeps them together. In other words, it is not the availability of a culturally and politically strong 'centre', but the lack of such 'centre' and a desire to create or recreate it that consolidates the 'peripheral' communities and reinforces their identity. This is important for understanding of the role of the ethnic minority media and their contribution to the construction of social identity. The consciousness of exile determines political and cultural orientation of diasporic communities, while the content of their media may depend on whether they take a secessionist or so called pluralistic position. By pluralistic minority we mean a diasporic formation willing to preserve its identity within a wider context of multicultural society, with simultaneous respect for, and co-operation with other ethnically different groups.

Ethnicity and the challenge of globalisation

The reason for giving special attention to transnational communities and their media is obvious. We live in a time which reveals a seemingly paradoxical combination of trends toward cultural unification and globalisation on the one hand, and the upsurge of nationalism and regionalism on the other. It is also the time of the large-scale movements of people across the globe and the increasing political and social activity of ethnic minority groups.

According to UN figures, the world has witnessed a rapid increase in migration. The number of people living outside their countries of origin has grown from 85 millions in 1975 to almost 120 millions in 1990. Russians alone, who found themselves outside their homeland (Russian Federation) after the collapse of the Soviet Union, make up 25 million people (Koslowski, 2000: 1). In the last ten years, more than 20 million people have become forced migrants as a result of wars, ethnic and religious conflicts in their countries (Dhussu, 2000: 207). The ongoing global migration, which is both the product and the contributor to the process of globalisation, has become a key issue in international politics. It brought about noticeable changes in the receiving countries, both in demographic, political and cultural terms.

In some cases migrants may outnumber the indigenous, local population, like in the United Arab Emirates, where foreign workers make up 90 percent of the population, and cause changes in the editorial policy of media organisations targeting the region (ibid). The sheer scope of international migration makes one believe that, with increasing globalisation, the influence of trans-national communities and their contribution to the international political, cultural and economic processes will become ever more significant. Migrant communities have already become important political and economic actors. They '…challenge assumptions of territoriality, influence the foreign policy-making of host and home states, and develop alternative diasporic identities'. (Koslowski, 2000: 16) Interesting in this respect is Avtar Brah's (1996) attempt to define 'diaspora' and, particularly, her concept of *diaspora space*, 'which seriously problematises the subject position of the "native". (Brah, 1996: 181) In a diaspora space which, according to Brah, is the site where 'the native is as much a diasporian as the diasporian is the native' (ibid: 209), the issue of minority identities become irrelevant and new cultural, political or religious formations continually challenge the dominant cultures.

The primary concern of trans-national migrant communities is the preservation of their ethnic cultures and languages. Often this concern becomes a political issue and takes the shape of cultural resistance. The reason why ethnic communities, which find themselves on the fringes of mainstream cultures of host societies, are so sensitive to any speculations about their cultural and religious practices, their languages, traditions, values and other cultural objects is that every cultural object (traditions, rituals, values, etc.) reinforces a particular life-style and mentality, ensures stability of a particular social structure and guarantees survival and continuation of the whole of the community. In other words, ethnic communities themselves can be regarded as cultural objects which provide meaning to themselves and other communities (Billington, 1991: 87), and the role of a carefully preserved ethnic culture is to separate insiders from outsiders and to consolidate the group. Indeed, one's 'own' community provides psychological and cultural 'safe haven', a system of co-ordinates and meaning.

Culture reflects social order to reproduce and maintain, through its ideas, myths, rituals and the whole system of ideology, this very social order (See for example Levi-Strauss, 1963; Barthes, 1952; Althusser, 1984). The protection of a society's cultural heritage and values is of paramount importance for the maintenance of that society. Discussion of theories of culture exceeds the limits of this chapter, but what is worth remembering is that assimilation and gradual loss of otherness is not just the loss of cultural memory or change in cultural practices. In fact, it is the loss of a particular vision of reality. Raymond Williams claimed that all '... human experience is an interpretation of the non-human reality' (Williams, 1961: 20) and interpretations may differ. Fiske argues that human perception is an attempt to match the external stimuli with internal pattern of thought. This matching is controlled by our culture and '... people of different cultures will perceive reality differently' (Fiske, 1990: 26).

Language and construction of difference

Writings on minority and diasporic existence usually emphasise the common bonds of myth, habit and language (Sreberny, 2000: 179), the triune cultural force which unites people within their ethnic communities. Language is also believed to be the most important aspect of ethnicity, an instrument which shapes our vision of reality and, consequently, contributes to the construction of difference. If we accept Karl Marx's view that '... language is as old as consciousness, language is practical consciousness' (Marx, 1961: 85), then it becomes clear that the very existence of a group's distinct ethnic consciousness is problematic without this basic element.

But how can the language shape our vision of reality? The answer was suggested by Edward Sapir, one of the most influential of the American 'descriptive' linguists. According to Sapir, a language operates 'by means of some kind of inherent structuring principle' (Hawkes, 1987: 29), which overrides the objective observations and affects the habits of perception and response of the speakers of this particular language. Thus, the language determines the cultural setting and the whole way of life of a community, since the objective reality is perceived and encoded according to the structure of the language used by this community.

> The fact of the matter is that the 'real world' is to a large extent built upon the language habits of the group...The worlds in which different societies live are different worlds ...We see and hear and otherwise experience very largely as we do because the language habits of our community predispose certain choices of interpretation. (Sapir, ibid: 31)

Although Sapir's views (also known as Sapir-Whorf hypothesis) are criticised sometimes as too straightforward, they still have their effect on some of today's social scientists. It has been argued that language expresses distinct patterns of thought and that patterns language and discourse '...do not *represent* objects or reality but *constitute* them, bring them into being, so that social reality and social relations are discursively constituted in and through language rather than represented by language.' (Barker, 1999: 23)

For trans-national, diasporic communities, the authentic language of their forsaken home is important both as a creator of a specific cultural environment and, simply, as a means of communication which makes possible the very existence of non-territorial, not geographically bound, ethnic groups. It is the language that sustains culture and creates experience. It is the language that gives the feeling of sameness and belonging.

Even if the language of an ethnic group is not in active use anymore, it may still preserve its value as a symbol, as a rallying point of identity. The Irish (in the Republic of Ireland), for example, still show attachment for a language '...whose communicative revival is neither feasible nor generally desired.' (Edwards, 1996: 227). Ukrainian communities in Canada have always regarded the retention of the native language as their most important task. They managed to win a place for Ukrainian in the public school system, started Ukrainian private schools, introduced Ukrainian Studies to many Canadian universities, including the Universities of Saskatchewan, Alberta and Manitoba. At the same time, only 50 percent of the Ukrainian Canadians recognise Ukrainian as their mother tongue and only 20 percent speak it with any regularity (Gerus & Rea, 1985: 20). But if the language is still spoken by the 'ethnics' and used by their community media, it becomes a powerful boost to ethnic consciousness and national identity. The use of native languages adds to the uniqueness of ethnic media representations and reinforces their ability to produce and reproduce a symbolic ethnic environment.

Language, media and national identity

The idea of the media's exclusive role in the production and reproduction of national identities is often linked to Benedict Anderson's writings on the arrival of print and the emergence of 'imagined communities'. For Anderson (1983), the invention of the printing presses, also known as the 'Gutenberg Revolution', had far-reaching social, economic and cultural implications. It was a turning point in the history of human civilisation, which linked together communications and communities.

The invention of the printing presses was the first step towards print capitalism and mass production of books. And mass production, as is known, requires mass consumption or mass markets. The first publishers motivated by economic interest wanted to sell as many books as possible, but the 'divine' languages of knowledge (Greek and Latin) used by the Church and aristocracy could not satisfy them. The market they served was too narrow to meet the requirements of mass production.

Most people could not speak or read Greek and Latin. Most people spoke vernacular languages and, thus, vernaculars were ideal for the expansion of print capitalism. Book-printing turned the formerly humble vernaculars into print languages, assembled related vernaculars, those dialects of medieval Europe, 'polished' and standardised them for the needs of fledgling national markets.

Some of the dialects died out, while others (more successful ones) were elevated to the status of official, national languages. It is these national languages that helped millions of people learn about the existence of other millions of their 'compatriots', speaking the same languages and living on the same territories. Print capitalism contributed to the spread of literacy, to unprecedented dissemination and exchange of ideas. It created a single communication space, the forerunner of the sphere of public debate. Print capitalism and national language worked hand in hand, '...generating imagined communities, building in effect particular solidarities' (Anderson, 1983: 133).

For Anderson, the nation and nationalism are the products of non-biological forces. Nationalism was invented by print-language and the whole idea of 'nation-ness' was inseparable from political consciousness. Although Anderson focused on the newspaper as generator of national sentiments, one can assume that the impact of modern electronic communications, with their pervasiveness and seemingly unlimited power to create a particular version of reality, can be even more dramatic. True, many writers are cautious about the

207

effects of media representations on the process of identity formation. They believe that those effects 'must be studied not assumed' (Bernstein, 2002 in Newbold et al: 60) and that, generally, the interaction between media representations and identity is very complex.

At the same time, there is no denial that representations, actually, make sense of reality, of the physical and social space we inhabit. Cottle claims:

> It is in and through representations, for example, that members of the media audiences are variously invited to construct a sense of who 'we' are in relation to who 'we' are not, whether as 'us' and 'them', 'insider' and 'outsider', 'coloniser' and 'colonised', 'citizen' and 'foreigner', 'normal' and 'deviant', 'friend' and 'foe', 'the west' and 'the rest'... At the same time, the media can also serve to affirm social and cultural diversity and, moreover, provide crucial spaces in and through which imposed identity or the interests of others can be resisted, challenged and changed. (Cottle, 2000: 2)

The media of ethnic communities can play a key role in rediscovering and maintaining the language and culture of the indigenous people, as in the case of broadcasting for the Mapuche Indians of Chile. The minority media can contribute to the sense of community and can act as agents of empowerment, like the Spanish-language television and, generally, Latino media in the greater New York region. Transnational, community oriented media can sustain diaspora formations and consciousness. The identity of British Asians, which is continually reinvented through the use of 'ethnic' video and television programmes, is a good proof of this.

The case of Greenlandic nationalism as a product of the local media activity (Stenbaek, 1992) provides a relatively recent example in support of Anderson's conclusion that nationalism was invented by print-language, and nation-ness is inseparable from political consciousness. The print media and, later, the radio played an exclusive role in the development of national identity and the emergence of local nationalism in the indigenous Innuit societies of Greenland. The Greenlandic-language newspapers and radio acted as a gathering force, which united the scattered population. It was the print media and local radio that became a forum for debate, made Innuits accept one dialect, the western Greenland-Nuuk dialect and raised it to the level of the 'national' language. This, perhaps, more than anything else, unified the country, developed political consciousness and gave birth to the local nationalism and independence movement.

The leaders of ethnic communities seem to understand the importance of the language as 'the distinctive characteristic which marks the community from other groups' and at the same time, 'strengthens the unity and bridges the difference within the community'. (Van den Bulck & Van Poecke, 1996:

220). The linguistic issue is always high on the ethnic community agenda. Special attention is also given to funding and the development of the ethnic minority media, which are supposed to ensure loyalty to the community and cultural continuity.

Although electronic communications are believed to be ideal for the creation and recreation of ethnic cultural environments, one should remember that many diasporic communities are not rich enough to invest in broadcasting and new media and have to confine themselves to the community press. Actually, the ethnic minority press remains the main and, in many cases, the only means of ethnic mass communication. In other words, it is the newspapers in minority languages that, along with other cultural practices, formulate, through their representations, the ideas of identity, community and cultural affiliation.

Media and attachment to 'place'

Territoriality is an important aspect of ethnic identity and extra-territorial, trans-national communities always emphasise their memory of and attachment to a particular place. This attachment, which is a widespread human sentiment, is believed to be a memory of particular, often highly idealised, home-based social relationships. It is this memory that reveals itself as an attachment to place (Mewett, 1982 in Cohen: 240). Having found themselves in a new society, which requires new skills and new patterns of behaviour, migrants seek refuge in their communities. Such diasporic communities provide them with cultural, psychological and, often, economic security. Although immigrants usually want to adapt to a new environment and new sets of cultural and social relations, their vulnerability, both cultural and economic, makes them maintain loyalty to their old traditions and even take pains to restore them in the form of assertive ethnic cultures.

Previously, these diasporic peoples had identities of place or geographic identities, but in the role of migrants they have had to adapt themselves to the mainstream culture of the majority. The minority experience is that of accommodation and resistance, empowerment and relative powerlessness. The dominant ideology of the majority will not always permit the idea of multiple identities. Often, the minority can have equal civil and political rights with the majority on the level of individuals, but not as a community (See F. St Leger in Alcock, 1979: 72).

The idea of cultural practice as a form of resistance and refuge in a secure ethnic 'place' is especially important for minority cultures which see their environments as hostile and threatening. Resistance is always associated with strict observance of rituals and conservation of traditional life-styles. The creation in new countries of residence of mini-Ukrainian, mini-Italian or mini-Chinese environments, with all their ethnic rites, ceremonies and their own media, is, actually, an attempt to recreate the 'place' and to preserve the memory of the abandoned home. It is also an attempt to create solidarity and regain self-esteem.

The above-mentioned self-esteem is, obviously, an important factor, since the minority status prevents the 'ethnics' from full participation in the host countries' social and cultural life. According to Fitzgerald, at the foundation of identity lies '…the issue of self-esteem (self-affirmation) providing feelings of pride in the group' (Fitzgerald in Scannel and Schlesinger, 1992: 126). It is the minority media in the minority language, with their ability to generate imagined communities, that provide ample opportunities for such self-affirmation. While the mainstream and increasingly international media tend to alter 'the informational characteristics of place' (Meyrowitz, 1985: 117) and diffuse group identities, the close-knit ethnic community and its ethnic media are seen be the community members as a symbolic 'place', a cultural and psychological safe haven. This symbolic place is the keeper of national consciousness and promoter of communality.

The national consciousness and self-esteem are fed by tradition and ethnic symbols. They need deep-rooted memories and a noble goal. So it is only natural that the ethnic minority media give much room to the two things, which, according to Renan, constitute the nation:

> One is the possession in common of a rich legacy of memories; the other is present-day consent, the desire to live together, the will to perpetuate the value of the heritage that one has received in an individual form. (1990: 19)

Transnational communities see their media as a powerful means of narrating the nation and developing the national and political consciousness. For them, to narrate the nation means to recreate tradition and reconstruct a history. Indeed, the past works for the future. Myths of common ancestry and some shared historical past provide legitimacy for the present and hope for the future. Even tragic periods of national history can be exploited in an attempt to consolidate communities in crisis. Thus, according to Gans (1996), young Armenians in the US try to revive the memory of the Turkish massacre of Armenians (which took place more than 80 years ago, in 1915–16) '…at a time when acculturation and assimilation are beginning to make inroads into the American community in America'. (Gans, 1996 in Hutchinson & Smith: 149)

Gans goes even further and claims that the memory of the Holocaust may serve as a symbol of group destruction at a time when intermarriages are on the rise, the interest and participation in Jewish religious life is in decline, and American anti-Semitism is no longer a threat to the American Jewish community. In other words, the Holocaust may serve as a rallying symbol at a time when there are '...real fears about the disappearance of American Jewry altogether'. (ibid:148–9)

The reconstitution of national memory and cultural myths by the media is a highly selective process. The past is 'improved' and interpreted in line with today's requirements, as appeals to the past have to interpret and justify something in the present. Following Eric Hobsbawm (1983), the strategy for reconstruction of social memory can be presented as a double process. Firstly, to legitimate the present, continuity is established with the historical past, which must be lengthy and stretch back into the time immemorial. Hobsbawm points out that many political structures and ideological movements were so unprecedented '...that even historic continuity had to be invented, for example, by creating an ancient past beyond effective historical continuity, either by semi-fiction...or by forgery' (Hobsbawm, 1983: 7). Secondly, continuity is established not just with the past, real or invented, but with a suitable historical past. In both cases old models are used in new conditions and for new purposes, and the media, especially those recreating the 'place' or preserving the memory of the 'place', are inevitably involved in this process.

In his book *The Long Revolution* Raymond Williams argues that the survival of cultural objects of a certain period depends not on that period itself, but on new historical periods which make the final selection and compose a tradition (Williams, 1961: 50). For Williams, the traditional culture is not something absolute, but a lengthy process of interpretation and selection, and this selection and interpretation within a particular society is usually affected by special interests. Therefore, a diasporic group's loyalty to its traditional life-style and symbolic acts is a component part of the group's ethnic ideology and media propaganda.

As generally accepted norms and shared values, common aspirations and historical past create a particular ethnic environment and unite the 'ethnics' in their attempt to withstand assimilation, traditions and other manifestations of 'humanitarian legacy' are of paramount importance for ethnic groups' self-preservation, and the ethnic phenomenon can not be properly studied and understood without careful attention to the 'invention of tradition' Hobsbawm, 1983: 14).

The desire for another place, sentimental 'memories' and shared 'heritage' are believed to be the best antidotes for assimilation and estrangement of the ethnic community members. The idea of connection with some 'centre', real or mythical, disseminated by the ethnic media, appeared so valuable and effective in the strategy of ethnic survival that some ethnic communities, which did not identify in this way before, decided to reclaim their diasporic origin (Clifford, 1994: 310).

211

So the ethnic minority media contribute to the creation (invention) of tradition (historical memory), serve as a bridge between the past and the future, lend their audiences moral and psychological support, and promote political mobilisation of their communities. Often, the minority media, especially in the majority language, act as defenders of their community's interests. They try to win a 'worthy' place in the host society's cultural and political life. Ethnic minority groups and their media understand that cultural pluralism is an important condition of their own ethnic survival. The Ukrainian organisations in Canada, for example, pioneered the idea of multiculturalism, and the formal recognition of Canada as a multicultural nation (1971) was in part due to the effort of the Ukrainian Canadian Committee. The activities of the close-knit Ukrainian communities in Canada and their media, their persistence and their drive for multiculturalism '... served as a model for other ethnic minorities, including the native people'. (Gerus & Rea, 1985: 19). Therefore, the ethnic minority media, especially in the majority language, which operate in multicultural societies, can be regarded as a means of promoting both cultural and political empowerment of their communities.

Ethnic symbolism and cultural change

The geographic identity of migrants, estranged from their home environment and physical 'places', has always been influenced by new conditions of life and by the 'alien' cultures of their new countries of residence. But with the advent of modern mass communications, and especially television, the process of modification and assimilation of ethnic minority cultures has greatly accelerated. Modern electronic media eliminate the isolation of ethnic communities and deliver the unifying messages of the increasingly interconnected world to every particular 'place'. The mainstream culture and electronic media, which are usually majority-controlled, can change the meaning of social situations and reshape identities. According to Meyrowitz:

> As a result of electronically mediated interactions, the definition of situations and of behaviours is no longer determined by physical location ... The evolution of media has begun to cloud the differences between stranger and friend and to weaken the distinction between people who are 'here' and people who are 'somewhere else'. (1985: 117, 122)

By their concerted effort, the ethnic minority cultures and the mainstream (majority) culture of the host country can create a special type of the second-generation ethnic communities often referred to as hyphenated Canadians, Americans, Britons, etc. Dual cultural surrounding (being a part of a diasporic community, but consuming the products of the mainstream culture and media) causes a significant cultural change called, sometimes, cultural mutation, which produces the second-generation identities of 'combined places'. In terms of their life-style, language and even cultural memory, they form entities which are different both, from the non-hyphenated Americans, Canadians or Britons, and from the people in the countries of their origin. The diasporic identities of 'combined places' may preserve the emotional attachment, '...while the actual cultural content has dramatically changed'. (Fitzgerald, 1992: 114). This is because '...the children of immigrants...can not return to a 'former culture' that they never had. Any second or third-generation culture is truly a 'cultural mutation'...(ibid: 116).

Children of immigrants, raised in a foreign-language environment, educated on foreign ideas and influenced by the mainstream culture and the media of the host countries, may have little cultural or psychological attachment to their ethnic communities. Such evolution of identity and ethnic consciousness seems to be a normal aspect of diasporic existence, for even the elder migrants, who still remember their homeland and feel strong attachment to it, gradually become more multicultural and develop a certain 'plurality of vision'.

The fact that the second and third generation 'ethnics' are less susceptible to ideological pressure of their ethnic community media is a serious challenge to the media's attempt to reinforce diasporic identities and consolidate communities. In view of cultural mutation, the messages of patriotism, collective distinctiveness and sentimental allegiance to the culture of the first-generation migrants may have a limited effect. Any further attempts to change the attitudes of the second-generation 'ethnics' born and educated in the host country may become counterproductive. The symbolism of 'fathers' may fail to inspire the younger generation, while the effort of the ethnic minority media to pass on this symbolism may result in the loss of interest in the ethnic community life.

To remain afloat and adapt themselves to the changing cultural environment, the ethnic minority media have to make compromises and modernise their content; market considerations and universalist agenda come to the fore. Ethnic newspapers, for example, introduce pages in the majority languages, take a more flexible approach to ethnic ideology, to the ideas of otherness and ethnic loyalty, gender and sexuality. Even the secessionist diasporic media, whose main objective is to preserve the status quo and reinforce the boundaries at all costs, have to take into account the aspect of newness. This 'continuity vs. newness' challenge affects the whole process of construction and consumption (reception) of the diasporic media representations. It affects both the media and the ethnic minority audiences. By modernising media representations and propagating universal values, the ethnic minority media may involve their audiences in the circle of cultural ideas and life-style of the host country. As a result, the minority media may perform a dual function (Riggins, 1992: 4). On the one hand, they help to preserve the culture and express ethnicity of a particular immigrant community, even if it is just a memory of culture and a symbolic ethnicity, and, on the other, they can promote the assimilation of this community making it vulnerable to the outside influences.

Conclusion

Although the minority experience can be interpreted as the practice of resistance and the ethnic communications provide a sort of oppositional ideology, the resources of such communications and their oppositional power are rather limited. The ethnic minority media are usually informal and non-commercial organisations wholly dependent on community leadership. Ethnic minority periodicals have small audiences and fail to attract an adequate advertising support.

The lack of funding, personnel and equipment problems prevent the ethnic minority media from full participation in the host country's cultural life, from properly responding to xenophobic and racist stereotypes disseminated, sometimes, by the mainstream media. In other words, the ethnic minority media, which in many cases are fully dependent on financial support of their community leadership, are extremely vulnerable to both outside and inside influences. This reduces the ethnic media's critical potential and their ability to convey the truth about their communities and a wider cultural and political environment.

The minority journalists may have their own ideas of objectivity and professional standards, yet solidarity with, and loyalty to their ethnic communities may take priority. As a result, they exercise 'considerable self-censorship' and 'tend to be understandably biased' (ibid: 278). As the scope of events covered by these ethnic communications is actually limited to their community life and the information conveyed by ethnic media has a restrictive character, the younger audiences, as it was mentioned earlier, may start losing interest in their cultural and ideological heritage. This may be especially noticeable in the highly politicised and close-knit exile groups with their constant political excitement and never-ending war of words between different factions and other political organisations.

The ethnic communications cannot compete with the increasingly globalised media and cannot challenge mainstream cultural and ideological values. Yet, the arrival of private, market-oriented transnational information networks offers them a gleam of hope. Globalisation in the sphere of mass communications is not necessarily a one-way process with inevitable superiority and dominance of the Western media products. Access to satellite technology allows the media of the developing countries, and especially private, profit-seeking companies, to reach lucrative markets of diasporic communities. Examples of such 'cultural imperialism in reverse' are Univisa broadcasting to Latino audiences in the US, Turkey's TRT transmitting its programmes to Turkish diasporic communities in Europe and TRT AVRASYA TV broadcasting to Turkish-speakers in the former Soviet Central Asia (Thussu, 2000: 208).

Transnational communications operating from the territories of the mother countries can consolidate the ethnic enclaves and add to their otherness. Modern transport and the media have a potential to create a 'border effect': they reduce distances and establish closer contacts between diasporic groups and their mother countries. The diaspora acquires a characteristic of a borderland, where the previously dispersed ethnics '... increasingly find themselves in border relations with the old country'. (Clifford, 1994: 304). Consequently, the 'centre' has an opportunity to influence the development of the 'peripheral' ethnic groups in the countries of their residence. Consequently, the 'centre' and its media can contribute to the emergence of 'transnationalism', which, according to a number of writers, unites diasporic communities on the basis of cultural, political and economic activities, in more than one country (Van Hear, 1998: 4).

Ethnicity is a dynamic process influenced by different cultural, social, political and economic factors. Ethnic minority communications have an important role to play in the struggle for cultural survival. Although recent years have seen a growing interest in the issue of ethnic communications and their role in the cultural and political life of transnational communities, many aspects of the diasporic media environment and the relationship between the media and ethnic consciousness, especially the consciousness of exile, remain relatively unknown and still await their researchers. This paper attempts to make a contribution to this broader debate.

Bibliography

Aarebrot, F.H. (1982) On the Structural Basis of Regional Mobilisation in Europe. In De Marchi, B. & Boileau, A. M., *Boundaries and Minorities in Western Europe*, Franco Angeli, Milano, 33–93.

Althusser, L. (1984) *Essays on Ideology*, Verso.

Anderson, B. (1983) *Imagined Communities Reflections on the Origin and Spread of Nationalism*, Verso, London, 1983.

Barker, C. (1999) *Television, Globalisation and Cultural Identities*, Open University Press, Buckingham.

Barthes, R. (1952) *Mythologies*, Paladin.

Bernstein, A. (2002) Representation, Identity and the Media. In Newbold, C. et al, *The Media Book*, Arnold, London.

Billington, R., et al (1991) *Culture and Society*, MacMillan, London.

Brah, A. (1996) *Cartographies of Diaspora*, Routledge, London.

Chaliand, G. (1989) *Minority Peoples in the Age of Nation States*, Pluto Press, London.

Clifford, J. (1997) *Diasporas*. In Cultural Anthropology, 9(3), 1994, 302–338.

Cohe, R., *Global Diasporas*, ULC Press, London.

Colle, R. (1992) A Radio for the Mapuches of Chile: From Popular Education to Political Awareness. In Riggins, S. *Ethnic Minority Media*, Sage, London, 127–148.

Cottle, S. (2000) *Ethnic Minorities and the Media: Changing Cultural Boundaries*, Open University Press, Buckingham.

Downing, J. (1992) Spanish-Language Media in the Greater New York Region During the 1980s. In Riggins, S. *Ethnic Minority Media*, Sage, London, 256–275.

Edwards, J. (1996) Symbolic Ethnicity and Language. In Hutchinson, J. and Smith, A. (1992) *Ethnicity*, Oxford University Press, Oxford.

Fiske, J. (1990) *Introduction to Communication Studies*, Routledge, London.

Fitzgerald, T. (1992) Media, Ethnicity and Identity. In Scannel, P. and Schlesinger, P. *Culture and Power*, Sage, London, 112–130.

Gans, H. J. (1996) Symbolic Ethnicity. In Hutchinson, J. and Smith, A. *Ethnicity*, Oxford University Press, Oxford, 146–155.

Gerus, O. and Rea, J. (1985) *The Ukrainians in Canada*, Canadian Historical Association, Ottawa.

Gillespie, M. (1995) *Television, Ethnicity and Cultural Change*, Routledge, London.

Gillespie, M. (2000) Transnational Communications and Diaspora Communities. In Cottle, S. *Ethnic Minorities and the Media*, Open University Press, Buckingham, 165–178.

Hawkes, T. (1987) *Structuralism and Semiotics*, Methuen, London.

Hobsbawm, E. (1983) *The Invention of Tradition*, Cambridge University Press, Cambridge.

Koslowski, R. (2000) *Migrants and Citizens. Demographic Change in the European State System*, Cornell University Press, Ithaca & London.

Levis Strauss, C. (1963) *Structural Anthropology*, New York, Basic Books Inc.

Marx, K. (1961) *Selected Writings in Sociology and Social Philosophy*, Penguin Books, London.

Mewett, P. (1982) Exiles, Nicknames, Social Identities and the Production of Local Consciousness in a Lewis Crofting Community. In Cohen, P.

Belonging, Identity and Social Organisation in British Rural Cultures, Manchester University Press, Manchester, 222–246.

Meyrowitz, J. (1985) *No Sense of Place. The Impact of Electronic Media on Social Behaviour*, Oxford University Press, Oxford.

Priest, S. (1996) *Doing Media Research*, Sage, London.

Renan, E. (1990) What is a Nation? In Bhabha, H. *Nation and Narration*, Routledge, London.

Rex, J. (1996) *Ethnic Minorities in the Modern Nation State*, MacMillan Press, London.

Riggins, S. (1992) *Ethnic Minority Media*, Sage, London.

St Leger, F.Y. (1979) 'The Mass Media and Minority Cultures' in Alcock, A. *The Future of Cultural Minorities*, Macmillan: London, 1979.

Sreberny, A. (2000) *Media and Diasporic Consciousness: An Exploration Among Iranians in London. In Cottle, S. 179–196: Ethnic Minorities and the Media*, Open University Press, Buckingham.

Stenbaek, M. A. (1992) *'Mass Media in Greenland: The Politics of Survival'* in Riggins, S. 44–62: *Ethnic Minority Media*, Sage, London.

Thussu, D.K. (2000) *International Communication. Continuity and Change*, Arnold, London.

Van den Bulck, H. and Van Poecke, L. (1996) *National Language, Identity Formation and Broadcasting.* In European Journal of Communication, Vol. 1 (120): 217–223.

Van Hear, N. (1998) *New Diasporas*, UCL Press, London.

Williams, R. (1961) *The Long Revolution*, Columbia University Press, New York.

217

12. Music

Dave Waddington

> ...from Bebop to Hip Hop, black music has been shaped by the
> material conditions of black life (Lusane, 1993: 42)

In 1992, the 'gangsta' rapper, Ice T, offended mainstream white America
with the song 'Cop Killer', a fantasy of violent retribution for police brutality.
Though, strictly speaking, a *heavy metal* rather than rap record, the lyrics of
the song were seen as typifying rap's dangerous, incendiary potential. Replete
with its almost obligatory references to 'bitches', 'hoes' (whores), 'niggas',
gang feuds, 'slinging dope' and 'icing cops', the sometimes violent,
misogynistic, anti-Semitic and invariably profane themes of hip hop have
induced widespread condemnation from all quarters of American society
(Lusane, 1993; Rose, 1994).

While the extent of establishment outrage towards hip hop is admittedly
unprecedented, African American music has traditionally attracted more than
its fair share of controversy. Similarities have been drawn, for example,
between the attitudes of present-day hip hoppers and the surly, 'anti-
assimilationist' stance adopted by the bebop jazz players of the early 1940s
(Rose, 1994), while rap music itself echoes the rebellious sentiments of the
'soul anthems' that ruffled conservative white sensibilities during the Black
Power era of the 1960s (Neal, 1999).

This chapter reaches far beyond the incomprehension and indignation often
accompanying such genres to explore the way that bebop, rhythm and blues,
vocal pop, soul and hip hop have each played a fundamental role in helping
African Americans to psychologically survive and/or create oppositional
identities during times of injustice and oppression. The following analysis
borrows extensively from general commentaries on post-war black American
popular music by Gilroy (1989) and Neal (1999), and from the more
specialised analyses by Kofsky (1970, 1998) on jazz, Haralambos (1974) and
Ward (1998) on rhythm and blues and soul, and Rose (1994) on hip hop. Its
overriding aim is to outline the cultural, political and psychological
significance of each of these musical genres by paying close attention to the
particular socio-political contexts – prior to, during and since the civil rights
era of the 1950s and 1960s – in which they emerged and developed.

In drawing on these existing works, the chapter will emphasise how
'psychological resistance' to racial subjugation is often expressed via musical

and social devices which are *obliquely*, rather than directly, oppositional to mainstream culture (Ward, 1998: 4). As Rose explains:

> Under social conditions in which sustained frontal attacks on powerful groups are strategically unwise or successfully contained, oppressed people use language, dance and music to mock those in power, express rage, and produce fantasies of subversion. These cultural forms are especially rich and pleasurable where oppositional transcripts or the 'unofficial truths' are developed, refined, and rehearsed. (Rose, 1994: 99)

Particular emphasis is placed on Ward's point that black cultures are never entirely monolithic or autonomous. Thus the chapter will endeavour to explain how the separate musical genres of the past sixty years have sometimes co-existed and been mutually influential. It will also make the point that cultures are constantly evolving in relation to changing circumstances:

> World views change as worlds change, or rather as they appear to change. Consequently the dominant means of cultural adaptation to, and representation of, the black experience have changed with every perceived oscillation of black fortunes. (Ward, 1998: 58)

Subsequent sections of the chapter will deal in turn with the underlying social psychological significance of the rhythm and blues era of the early 1950s, the pop vocal period of the mid-1950s to early 1960s, the soul years of the 1960s and early 1970s, and finally, the hip hop era of the 1980s and beyond. We begin this chronological analysis, however, by looking at the social and musical characteristics of the 'bebop revolution', instigated in wartime New York City by such legendary jazz players as the alto saxophonist, Charlie Parker, the trumpeter, Dizzy Gillespie, and the pianist, Thelonious Monk.

The Bebop Revolution of the 1940s

Jazz music is generally acknowledged as the first major African American art form (Neal, 1999: 19). Its initial development coincided with the mass exodus of southern rural blacks between 1910 and 1920 to major northern cities like Chicago, Detroit and New York. Migrant New Orleans instrumentalists in particular introduced their wildly exuberant, highly polyrhythmic and 'vaguely African' music to the adoring nightclub and dancehall audiences of the north, laying the foundations of the 1920s Jazz Age (Peretti, 1997: 54). However, by the early 1930s, jazz had ceased to function as a marker and conduit of racial pride, having been musically transmogrified into the showy dance and pop craze known as 'swing':

> Despite its obvious debt to black expressive culture and the significance of black musicians in its production, swing...was

largely the domain of mainstream culture. It had a large white audience base and a discriminating 'racial-tocracy' that often afforded less talented white musicians access to the better paying venues and the more profitable recording contracts. Some of the more popular swing recordings of the period lacked any indication of significant African-American influence. (Neal, 1999: 19)

Most jazz writers generally agree that the Bebop 'revolution' of the 1940s constituted an attempt by black musicians to replace the 'saccharine overtones' of the swing era …in favour of a purer conception of jazz: an art music with the emotional pungency of a battle cry' (Gioia, 1998: 208–9). DeVeaux (1997) insists that this urgent, explosive, blues-based innovation was commercially, rather than politically, inspired. According to DeVeaux, bebop emerged organically from after-hours jam sessions involving black swing musicians, who quickly recognised the new music's potential to provide a separate market niche from that of white 'competitors'. However, such analysis underplays the role of political factors in bebop's evolution.

By the early 1940s, it was apparent that 'New Deal' legislation of the previous decade had not succeeded in eradicating glaring racial inequalities in housing, education, employment and social security (Panish, 1997: 4–5). America's involvement in a second World War was another important factor. The hundreds of thousands of African Americans enlisting in the armed services or munitions industries took understandable pride in their contributions to the fight against fascism, but this only heightened their sense of resentment at the social inequalities continuing to exist on the home front (Jones, 1963: 178). America's largest urban ghetto, the sprawling Harlem borough of New York, was a particular focus of black disaffection. Finding itself 'ravaged by economic neglect, structural erosion, and the spawning grounds of an angry and frustrated community' (Neal, 1999: 19), Harlem was affected by major rioting in 1943. It also became the epicentre of the bebop revolution.

By viewing things in this context, it becomes possible to interpret the bebop revolution as an expression of cultural self-worth in the face of social injustice. This strategy comprised an attempt by bebop players, firstly to re-take possession of 'their own' music from whites and, thereafter, to invert white evaluations of jazz music as 'pop' or 'entertainment' and re-cast it as a serious art form:

The deliberate complexity of the new style was designed to discourage a casual audience, and even exclude undesirable players from taking part in jam sessions, while the renewed emphasis on improvisation and blues progressions restored those elements of Afro-American jazz that had largely been ignored by white bands. Members of early bop groups emphasised their difference from mainstream players by cultivating a self-conscious appearance; both Gillespie and Monk wore berets and goatees to promote their image as bohemian intellectuals rather than musicians who merely supplied dance music (as in the Swing Era). Bop set itself up as a style worthy of respect and analytical attention. (Cooke, 1998: 123).

It is not difficult to speculate why the bebop innovators were, almost invariably, younger, black musicians schooled in the last throes of the Swing Era (Kofsky, 1998). Here was a small artistic elite whose particular talents had gained them a unique access to white commercial markets and offered the tantalising prospect of integration and betterment. However, as Stowe (1994: 156) points out, 'swing's utopian promise was betrayed' by a wartime experience which saw enlisted black musicians enduring uncommonly high levels of segregation and degradation.

The notion that bebop represented a strident critique of American society is rejected by DeVeaux, who maintains:

> The bebop musicians' relationship to politics was oblique at best, and certainly very different from that of their counterparts on the street corners. If bop was a revolution, it was hardly a revolution aimed directly at the black masses, who insisted on a music that satisfied their taste for bluesy dance and entertainment. Rhythm and blues, not bebop, became the soundtrack for the urban black experience of the late 1940s and 1950s. (DeVeaux, 1997: 26)

Rose's earlier point regarding the need for black musicians to resort to coded, rather than outspoken, critiques of the political system is clearly relevant here. As Kofsky points out, due to the obvious physical danger involved, '...[the bebop] manifesto had to be proclaimed primarily in musical terms and its social correlates left tacit...A Negro musician just couldn't come out and say, "Hey! The situation stinks" (Kofsky, 1970: 57–8). Nevertheless, DeVeaux's point does have some validity. The repositioning of the bebop musicians as avante-garde artist-intellectuals split them off, culturally and psychologically, from America's black working class. As we shall see in the following section, it also laid the foundation for the reappropriation of jazz by white West Coast musicians emerging in the Cool Era of the late 1940s and early 1950s.

'Dancing to Keep from Crying': Rhythm and Blues Music

Despite the first stirrings of localised unrest in northern ghettos like Harlem, the immediate post-war years formed an era in which African Americans still found themselves subjected to *de facto* – and, in the southern states at least, *legally endorsed* – exclusion from most aspects of American society and politics (Ward, 1998: 2). In this context, the majority of American blacks turned for psychic refuge, just as they had done in the 1940s, to the 'essentially danceable', highly energised 'race' music, otherwise known as rhythm and blues (Bane, 1982: 92).

As Haralambos points out, the entire blues/rhythm and blues genre was founded on a collective sense of fatalism and the need for people to accommodate to a bad situation:

> The world of blues is a 'mean old world', a 'world full of trouble'. Against a background of black nights and midnight hours, time travels slowly, 'minutes seem like hours and hours seem like days'. Life is hard and unrewarding. The blues singer rarely has 'a cent to pay the rent'. His relationships with women are usually unsuccessful. He either sits alone, unloved and 'blue and lonesome', or worries about his women with her 'back door friend'. His footsteps are dogged with bad luck and trouble. Few comforting fantasies exist in this world of harsh reality. The sun might be shining but 'it's raining in my heart'. (Haralambos, 1974: 80)

The public venting of these anxieties, combined with the empathy and mutual support arising from audience participation, induces collective feelings of release and well-being. Thus the main function of the urban blues music of the 1940s and early 1950s was one of *catharsis* rather than political opposition.

According to Haralambos, the withering demand for blues recordings post-1955 reflected a massive change of heart by African Americans. Starting from this time, black people began launching a concerted and initially successful mass protest against the Jim Crow system of racial subordination. Where once previously feelings of powerlessness and disaffection were internalised and eventually relieved via the blues, now such feelings were directed towards the system itself, rendering the blues tradition defunct (Haralambos, 1974: 150). The transplantation of rhythm and blues by 'soul' must therefore be read against the backdrop of the civil rights era, the evolution of which is also central to our understanding of the eventual emergence of hip hop.

The Civil Rights Era

One of the most momentous developments in the history of the American Civil Rights movement occurred in May 1954 with the Supreme Court ruling in *Brown v Topeka Board of Education* that school segregation between blacks and whites was fundamentally unjust. Further progress by the movement was initially stymied due to foot-dragging by local state governments, and confusion and indecision regarding the timetabling of reform. However, the movement gained fresh impetus in 1956 when the twelve-month Montgomery bus boycott resulted in the abolition of segregated seating on local public transport. Also that year, a black student, Athene Lucy, won her three-year campaign to be accepted by the previously segregated University of Alabama (Ward, 1998). However, this far from ended the struggle for racial equality. White opposition remained resolute. For example, in 1957 a violent confrontation took place in Little Rock, Arkansas, when Central High School admitted its first black students. Generally speaking, between 1955 and 1959, there were 530 instances of racial violence allegedly perpetrated by the renascent Ku Klux Klan (Ward, 1998).

In the early 1960s, a sustained campaign of passive resistance, epitomised by hundreds of high-profile 'freedom' marches, was eventually rewarded by the introduction of the Civil Rights Act 1964, a statute designed to eliminate racial discrimination in employment, housing, voting and civil justice. Nevertheless, the early 1960s were framed by unremitting white resistance, including racially motivated bombings and murders by white supremacists.

Ward makes the sobering point that, notwithstanding the 'Herculean efforts' of the Civil Rights movement and the legislative and political achievements it secured, concrete, everyday manifestations of black advancement were few and far between. This point is exemplified by the fact that, ten years on from the Brown ruling, a mere two per cent of southern black children were attending integrated schools (Ward, 1998). As the 1960s wore on, previous successes began to seem like '...markers on the road to a half-finished racial revolution' (Ward, 1998: 339). Meanwhile, American involvement in Vietnam fuelled black cynicism regarding the nation's commitment to racial equality:

> It was bad enough that blacks were disproportionately victims of the draft and tragically over-represented in the body bags. It was worse still that they were still being denied full access to the freedoms at home for which they were ostensibly fighting and dying abroad. (Ward, 1998: 339–40)

The significance of such inaction was soon felt: Black Power and Black Nationalism emerged as key organisational and inspirational forces, and between 1964 and 1968, there were over 500 riots in major US cities (Waddington, 1992). Black people's faith in the promise of justice and equality was further undermined by the assassinations of Martin Luther King and Robert F. Kennedy. The election in 1969 of the conservative Richard Nixon as president was a prelude to the violent suppression of the Black Panthers, a militant and occasionally violent organisation committed to black nationalism.

By the early 1970s, a familiar pessimism had descended upon the nation's black communities:

Government aid did help many African Americans gain college educations and secure firmly middle-class careers (especially as administrators of local social programs), but the ghetto would remain, a product of lingering poverty and discrimination' (Peretti, 1997: 153).

This situation continued to prevail for the remainder of the century.

All Sweetness and Harmony: The Black Pop of the 1950s

The evolution of soul music has paralleled that of the movement for civil rights. Between 1954 and 1963, amidst growing optimism that racial equality was within reach, rhythm and blues artists like T-Bone Walker and Elmore James were outstripped in popularity by solo performers like Brook Benton, or groups like the Platters, who purveyed a sweeter black vocal music which made obvious concessions to white musical and lyrical preferences.

This new black music was in sharp contrast to rhythm and blues. For one thing, the latter had employed huge measures of misogyny and boasted unashamedly of sexual conquest and marital infidelity. This had helped to reify a 'powerful, resolutely masculine, compensatory male identity' which simultaneously undermined the power and dignity of black women (Ward, 1998: 74). Women rhythm and blues singers had responded with correspondingly unflattering depictions of male sexual and economic inadequacies (ibid: 79). Such themes were consciously eschewed by the post-1954 vocal groups, reflecting mutual perceptions of a '…better future and a sense of empowerment and self-respect they had previously sought in sexual warfare and internecine competition' (ibid: 152). Moreover, far from being solely preoccupied with surviving the immediate future, the new music 'imagined a future bursting with exciting possibilities' (ibid: 88).

Stylistically, rhythm and blues music had been characterised by a 'dirty-toned' vocal expressiveness:

> The vocal groups, however, embraced a rather more 'European' conception of close harmony, even as they, like the gospel groups before them, radically subverted it to suit their own needs, and recast it to preserve the primacy of the testifying individual voice in a group context. Without seeking to make the link between musical forms and the societies which produce them too mechanistic, the increased deployment and popularity of 'sweet', 'Euro-American' harmonies after the Second World War does appear to have been related to emergence of a new urbane black audience which was heavily exposed to and influenced by nominally 'white' musical forms, imbued with deep integrationist aspirations and, at least from the mid 1950s, armed with a

guarded faith in the potential of the nascent civil rights movement
to realize those dreams. (Ward, 1998: 68–9)

The gradual transition towards a blacker, more *Africanised* brand of vocal
music is closely linked to ongoing developments in jazz. As mentioned earlier,
the late 1940s and early 1950s had witnessed the emergence of a new
generation of white 'cool jazz' successors to the earlier bebop revolutionaries.
The so-called Cool School eschewed any tendencies towards 'hot' or 'dirty'
instrumentalism in favour of a more elegant and restrained, classically
influenced style. This European-inflected style of jazz became primarily
associated with white, middle-class practitioners, its emphasis shifting from
America's east to west coast and from the jazz club to the college campus.
According to Kofsky, the onset of cool jazz represented a culturally
imperialistic strategy, a conscious attempt to 'bleach out' the idiom's African-
American roots; to 'divest jazz from its historical black moorings', and
thereby '...assert the primacy of white, or Western, values over black, or
African, ones' (Kofsky, 1970: 32–33).

Cool jazz was supplanted in the mid-1950s by the hard-bop era, which
paralleled the early crusade for civil rights. Fundamentally deriving from
bebop, this new style was self-consciously 'funkier' or more 'soulful' than
cool. Groups led by such hard bop luminaries as Art Blakey, Horace Silver and
Charles Mingus employed rasping, rhythm and blues-style saxophones and
other blues and gospel musical foundations both to reclaim and reassert their
art, as well as to reconnect it to its black, working-class audience:

> In the 1950s, these men had rescued jazz from some of the more
> esoteric extremes of be-bop and West Coast cool by revisiting
> their gospel and blues roots. The word ['funk'] and the music
> reeked of earthiness, blood, sweat and semen, and proudly
> proclaimed its connection to the essential forces of human, but
> more particularly black, existence. (Ward, 1998: 350)

Like their bebop ancestors of the 1940s, the hard bop players of the mid- to
late 1950s clearly occupied a more advanced stage of cultural resistance than
their counterparts in other popular musical genres. While hard bop clearly
borrowed from earlier forms of black vernacular music, it also predated and
influenced the next major form of black vocal music to arise in the civil rights
era, the 'funkier' soul sounds of the mid- to late 1960s.

Back to the Roots: The Soul Years of the 1960s

As we saw in the previous section, this was an era in which initial black
optimism gradually disintegrated in the face of white resistance and eventual
repression. Correspondingly, the 'integrationist' style of black music
represented by the 'sweet' vocal singers of the 1950s was abandoned in favour

of a tougher, avowedly *blacker*, musical form, incorporating gospel sensibilities. Ward refers, in particular, to such elements as 'the style's tumbling gospel triplets, its call and response instrumental and vocal patterns, the regular rustle of sanctified tambourines, and the energizing slap of get-happy handclaps'. Such features were set against a 'solid rock' of instrumental repetition which nonetheless permitted 'a breathtaking expressive freedom' for individuals and groups (Ward, 1998: 184). Initially, this 'Africanisation' of black popular music was more evident on the Memphis-based Stax record roster than on the Detroit-based Motown record label, which had longer to relinquish the assimilationist aspirations that had driven 1950s pop (Guralnick, 2002; Werner, 2000). By the end of the 1960s, though, the styles became highly syncretic (Neal, 1999).

Soul's incorporation of gospel was a logical development. As Gilroy explains, gospel was the 'least outward of black musical forms' which had 'always addressed itself to the oppressor, through a complex of dense codes and rich biblical symbolism' (Gilroy, 1989: 172). Haralambos also observes that gospel is full of anticipation of better days ahead, placing a priority on togetherness and unity, a fundamental tenet of soul (Haralambos, 1974: 131).

Importantly, this musical development occurred alongside other everyday elements of the soul style, such as the way that African Americans walked, talked, ate, dressed and generally led their lives. It was in this way that black Americans '…sought an antidote to white assumptions of cultural superiority by self-consciously valorizing their own culture and celebrating peculiarly African-American experiences and practices as the critical repositories of identity and worth' (Ward, 1998). As Ward and Haralambos each emphasise, this process of re-definition and re-evaluation was psychologically empowering, laying claim to worthy and highly distinctive black cultural forms previously 'ignored, denigrated or consumed as exotic novelties' by the white mainstream (ibid: 211).

As black progress was stymied and optimism progressively waned amidst the white opposition of the late 1960s and early 1970s, internecine conflict between the sexes gradually reappeared and was reified in a Black Nationalism ideology which nullified female ambition and autonomy (ibid). Generally speaking, the soul movement became progressively less assertive. Initially, its stylistic trappings became more muted, oblique and satirical in emphasis and the '…iconography of soul shifted away from the pseudo-military macho imagery of clenched fists in black leather towards the dress and cultural emblems of ancient Africa' (Gilroy, 1989: 178). Soon afterwards, this dominant imagery was supplanted by escapist and utopian notions of magical outer space realities and 'weird parallel universes', epitomised by the techno-funk of George Clinton. As Gilroy explains:

The futuristic emphasis in these images served to underline the impossibility of strategic political calculation. The means by which black America was to get from where it was to its reconstituted future was as inconceivable as time travel itself. The political repertoire which stretched between mass non-violent direct action to open militarization appeared to have been exhausted. (Gilroy, 1989: 180)

Soul's displacement by the more unashamedly dance floor-oriented funk and, eventually, by disco represented a regression to the type of musical accommodation inherent in the blues: as in the early 1950s, black Americans were 'dancing to keep from crying' (Ward, 1998: 354).

Black Voices from the Margins: Rap Music

The onset of the mid-1970s, and the coming of age of what the renowned music critic and journalist, Nelson George, has called the 'post soul' generation, heralded the next significant black musical innovation in the form of rap. According to George, this was an era in which a vast cohort of black American youth, too young to have felt the disillusionment of the early 1970s, perceived a confusing and hurtful paradox: that despite their supposedly newly-won equal status with whites, black youth was considerably worse affected by the most crippling economic conditions witnessed since the 1930s Great Depression. In George's words, rap (and the hip hop culture it forms part of) is '...the spawn of many things. But, most profoundly, it is a product of schizophrenic, post-civil rights movement America' (George, 1998: xiv).

A helpful definition of rap and its place in hip hop culture is provided by Rose who explains:

Rap music is a black cultural expression that prioritizes black voices from the margins of urban America. Rap music is a form of rhymed storytelling accompanied by highly rhythmic, electronically based music. It began in the mid-1970s in the South Bronx in New York City as part of hip hop, an African-American and Afro-Caribbean youth culture composed of graffiti, breakdancing and rap music. (Rose, 1994: 2).

Hip hop emerged from within a late-twentieth-century economic crisis marked by the 'growing immiseration' of young, working-class African Americans. The 'talented tenth' comprising the African-American middle class, managed to rise above the ghetto, only to leave the remainder impoverished, leaderless and demoralised (Lusane, 1993; Lipitz, 1994). Young African Americans fared especially badly in this period. Having gradually quadrupled since the mid-1970s, black youth unemployment had

227

reached over 40% by 1986 (Lusane, 1993). Such crisis paved the way for the emergence of an illicit crack cocaine economy among some sections of innercity youth (Kelley, 1996: 123; Neal, 1999: 133). According to Lipitz, successive moral panics since the 1970s, focusing on drug use and related gang violence, served to criminalise large tracts of urban youth and justify the abandonment of affirmative action programmes and other forms of political assistance for the poor.

Hip hop developed in those cities suffering the worst effects of 'Reagonomics': initially, in the South Bronx borough of New York, and thereafter, in places like Houston, Los Angeles and Oakland. Rose links the origination of hip hop in the South Bronx to a 1970s urban renewal programme which enforced the relocation of poor ethnic minorities into the region whose erstwhile communities had literally been destroyed.

Lipitz pertinently explains that people '...resisting domination can only fight in the arenas open to them; they often find themselves forced to create images of themselves that interrupt, invert or at least answer the ways in which they are defined by those in power' (Lipitz, 1994: 20). It was those black youths who found themselves passed over and 'dissed' by white and black politicians alike for whom rap, graffiti and breakdancing provided a political outlet and a way of contesting the negative identity imposed on them by mainstream America. Eventually, as we shall see, the opprobrium heaped on ethnic minority youth was answered and returned in the form of sophisticated and highly politicised rap poetry, promulgated via a billion-dollar record industry. From the outset, however, rap music has emphasised the significance of local reputation as a bulwark of social esteem.

The primary social unit in hip hop culture is the local crew or posse. Such units form part of the larger 'home' or 'hood' (neighbourhood) and great importance is attached to the practice of 'turning the 'hood out' or 'representing' thus extolling the virtues of the home turf and acknowledging its support (Forman, 2000: 73). This process helps satisfy the need among black youths 'to have their territories acknowledged, recognized and celebrated':

> Identity in hip hop is deeply rooted in the specific, the local experience, and one's attachment to and status in a local group or alternative family. These crews are new kinds of families forged with intercultural bonds that, like the social formation of gangs, provide insulation and support in a complex and unyielding environment and may serve as the basis for new social movements. (Rose, 1994: 34)

The earliest generation of hip hoppers showed great inventiveness by making the most of the limited resources available to them. Consistent with their overall objective of 'symbolically appropriating urban space', rap DJs attached their customised turntables and speakers to street light electricity sources, creating open-air 'theatres' for their trials by music and competitive breakdancing displays (Rose, 1994; Toop, 1984). The spray-painting by graffiti artists, not only of local buildings and walls, but also the sides of urban passenger trains, fulfilled another primary objective – that of proclaiming their identities across a much wider public sphere (Rose, 1994).

Other authors have joined Rose and Toop in emphasising that hip hop represents an outgrowth of earlier African American and African Caribbean diasporic traditions:

> Rap music is rooted in the Black oral tradition of tonal semantics, narrativizing, signification/signifying, the dozens/playin' the dozens, Africanized syntax, and other communicative practices...
> The rapper is a postmodern African griot, the verbally gifted storyteller and cultural historian. (Smitherman, 1997, 4–5, quoted in Richardson and Lewis, 2000: 253)

Similarly, Thompson (1996) maintains that hip hop's breakdancing is the product of migratory processes converging on the Bronx. Immigrants settled from such diverse areas as Barbados, Jamaica, Cuba and Puerto Rica, in addition to the southern states of the USA. Each of these brought continuing traditions of African dance, most notably those originating from the African Kongo which had entered the Americas via the slave trade. Significantly, the Kongo dance incorporates a 'dropping out' or 'performance break'. Griffin confirms that breakdancing follows the tradition of competitive neo-African dances like the 'juba' and 'kalinda' (Griffin, 1987: 37–38).

Since the innovative and pioneering days of the late 1970s, rap music and the characteristic dress codes of hip hop have been rampantly commercialised. Paradoxically, with the passing years, hip hop has become increasingly loud, assertive and more politicised. Kelley (1996) asserts that in-group references to 'niggas' are loaded with political symbolism: a reminder that the bearers of that title are the 'authentic' representatives of black culture, unlike their middle-class black contemporaries who seem to have disowned their ethnic roots. Even the loudness with which rap recordings are issued on the streets is suffused with political significance:

> Frequently employing high-decibel car stereos and boom boxes, they 'pump up the volume' not only for their own listening pleasure but also as part of an indirect, ad hoc war of position to take back public space. The 'noise' constitutes a form of cultural resistance that should not be ignored (Kelley, 1996: 134).

Since the 1970s, the lyrical content of rap music has become more explicitly politicised. Two dominant genres have emerged, offering contrasting representations of the contemporary urban black youth experience and suggesting alternative 'solutions' to the problems it entails. So-called message rap rekindles the early 1970s Black Power 'Afrocentric' emphasis on black nationalism, sometimes extending to a Pan-African emphasis on global black unity (Decker, 1994). The sub-genre is most closely associated with American east coast hip hop groups such as Public Enemy, whose leading spokesperson, Chuck D, famously referred to rap music as 'black folks' CNN' (Lusane, 1993).

Message rap's west-coast counterpart, 'gangsta rap', developed, as its name suggests, amidst the gang culture and street conflict of the post-industrial metropolises of California: South Central, Compton, North Long Beach and East Oakland. Gangsta rappers are invariably scornful of the east coast accent on black nationalism:

> Publicly echoed in Dr. Dre's ever-popular "Dre Day" we hear a complete disregard for "medallions, dreadlocks, and black fists," obvious markers of the more political aspirations of those interested in Black nationalism' (Boyd, 1997: 39).

While conscious of the everyday consequences of class oppression, the primary emphasis in gangsta rap is on the 'lessons of lived experience', involving gang life and gun retribution, police brutality and misogynistic references to women (Kelley, 1996). Thus, as Forman points out, 'The two subgenres are addressing generally common phenomena in their focus on black struggles for empowerment, yet they are deploying spatial discourses and programmes of action that do not fit easily together' (Forman, 2000: 76).

Following the precedent set by the 1960s Black Power movement, message rap has been quick to characterise black women operating outside the strict confines of the patriarchal family structure as 'ungrateful wives or gold-digging lovers' (Decker, 1994: 107). Such sentiments are equally discernible in gangsta rap. For example, NWA's 'One Less Bitch' focuses on the anger of a black pimp convinced that one of his prostitutes is deceitfully holding back a portion of her takings. Dr. Dre's accounts of a retributive lynching are followed by the repeated chant of: 'One less, one less, one less bitch you gotta worry about' (Kelley, 1996: 144).

As Rose (1994) explains, the primary thematic focus of female (or 'sista') rappers is that of sexual politics. Many female rappers ironize the attitudes of their male contemporaries by recounting tales of how they 'got one over' on men by duping them into spending lots of money on dates or buying them expensive presents. In the main, however, women rappers are concerned with rejecting charges that they systematically exploit their menfolk. Equally, as Rose points out, women rappers are aware that 'sexism against black women is being used to attack black men, rather than reconstruct power relations between black men and women,' and tend to dissociate themselves from white metropolitan feminism (Rose, 1994: 178).

Despite, or – as many would argue – *because of* rap's lyrical content, the genre has been instrumental in promoting a resurgence of ethnic pride, rooted in the recovery of neighbourhood prestige and unity and in the deconstruction of the negative identities conferred on black youth by the American middle classes. The immense commercialisation of hip hop culture has meant that riches and racial integrity can happily co-exist (Lusane, 1993: 44). As Holmes Smith maintains, the black urban ghetto has become the unlikely focus of a latter-day gold-rush:

> Like many conscientious prospectors, rappers work hard to maintain the boundaries around their bunkers beyond the barricades of mainstream America's public spaces, since such far-flung positions are essential to both the idiom's market potential and what remains of its oppositional politics. (Smith, 1997: 347)

Conclusion

In the latter half of the twentieth century, successive black musical genres emerged which enabled socially beleaguered African Americans to cope with and/or resist conditions of injustice and oppression. In some cases, this involved the creation or maintenance of oppositional identities which hinted at or, in some cases, stridently proclaimed, the need for social change.

The earliest of these, the bebop revolution of the 1940s, sent out an oblique but daring demand for artistic and racial respect. Certainly, Kofsky seems well justified in maintaining that '...bebop was more than just a set of musical procedures: it was also a musical vehicle for expressing black dissatisfaction with the status quo' (Kofsky, 1998: 110). However, bebop's esoteric symbolism was far too complicated and impenetrable to strike an appropriate chord among the black working classes, for whom rhythm and blues provided a more accessible and intelligible antidote to social and political exclusion.

In the mid–1950s, the first, faltering steps of the black struggle for civil rights were accompanied by a growing preference among African Americans for a 'sweeter', more Europeanised, brand of popular music. This reflected black faith in a more integrated and egalitarian America of the not-too-distant future. However, as white resistance to black civil rights became increasingly resolute, black popular culture took on a funkier, more nationalistic character:

> The evolution of soul music closely parallels the stages in the black movement for civil rights and self-determination. The scattered soul records from 1954 to 1960 correspond to the black struggle during those years which was intermittent and sporadic and never reached the proportions of a mass movement. The convergence of styles towards soul music from 1960 to 1964

231

> corresponds to the protest movements of the early '60s when the
> civil rights struggle became a mass movement. The establishment
> of soul music as the dominant style of black musical expression in
> the mid-'60s correlates with the rise and development of the Black
> Power Movement. (Haralambos, 1974: 154)

The eventual shattering of black optimism in the 1970s heralded the
reintroduction of accommodatory musical forms, such as funk and disco.
Nevertheless, the 'post soul' era, stretching from the mid-1970s to the present
day, has witnessed the revitalisation of black oppositional culture in the form
of hip hop, a musical genre which resuscitated community and ethnic pride,
subverted dominant racist stereotypes and recommended practical, if highly
controversial, solutions to those experiencing the crippling effects of
disadvantage and discrimination.

Unlike the black pop and soul eras of the 1950s and 1960s, hip hop culture
does not subscribe to a single monolithic or utopian vision of a better and/or
more integrated society. Moreover, it represents an unwelcome return to the
misogynistic ideology of the early 1950s, into which unsavoury stereotypes of
Jews and homosexuals have also been incorporated. For such reasons, many
academics have presented highly condemnatory assessments of rap's
contemporary cultural significance.

According to Cashmore, for example, the genre has done little more
than reproduce the threatening racist stereotypes first constructed by white,
western overlords to justify slavery and exploitation. The only difference is
that black people are now actively contributing towards their own
subjugation (Cashmore, 1987: 171). Lipitz further maintains that the outright
sexism and homophobia embodied in rap is an obstacle to community
advancement:

> Binary oppositions like those dividing men from women or
> heterosexuals from gays and lesbians turn 'different from' into
> 'better than'. They betray the instincts of intersectionality and
> conjuncture that inform the most constructive creations of youth
> culture. Most important, they leave people longing for real or
> imagined domination over others as a kind of psychic reparation
> for their own pain. But they offer no way to change society so that
> mutuality, reciprocity and justice can replace exploitation and
> hierarchy. They make it impossible to build the kind of organized
> political struggle necessary to redeem youth culture's
> emancipatory promises. (Lipitz, 1994: 24–5)

Such conclusions may be too harsh and unequivocal. Whilst it is fair to say that
some of rap music's grossest sentiments have been 'abjectly dehumanising'
(Lusane, 1993: 54), hip hop culture can justifiably lay claim to having rescued
black unity and self-worth from political annihilation.

Bibliography

Boyd, T. (1997) *Am I Black Enough for You? Popular Culture From the 'Hood and Beyond*. Bloomington: Indiana University Press.

Cashmore, E. (1987) *The Black Culture Industry*. London: Routledge.

Cooke, M. (1998) *Jazz*. London: Thames and Hudson.

Decker, J.L. (1994) 'The state of rap: time and place in hip hop nationalism', in Ross, A. and Rose, T. (eds.) *Microphone Fiends: Youth Music and Youth Culture*. London: Routledge.

Deveaux, S. (1997) *Bebop: A Social and Musical History*. Berkeley: University of California Press.

Forman, M. (2000) ' "Represent": race, place and space in rap music', *Popular Music*, 19(1), 65–90.

Gilroy, P. (1989) *'There Ain't No Black in the Union Jack': The Cultural Politics of Race and Nation*. London: Hutchinson.

Gioia, T. (1998) *History of Jazz*. Oxford: Oxford University Press.

Griffin, C.D. (1987) *Afro American Music*. London: Dryad Press.

Guralnick, P. (2002) *Sweet Soul Music: Rhythm and Blues and the Southern Dream of Freedom*. Edinburgh: Mojo Books.

Haralambos, M. (1974) *Right On: From Blues to Soul in Black America*. London: Drake.

Holmes Smith, C. (1997) 'Method in the madness: exploring the boundaries of identity in hip hop performativity', *Social Identities*, 3(3), 345–74.

Jones, L. (1963) *Blues People: The Negro Experience in White America and the Music that Developed From It*. New York: Apollo Editions.

Kelley, R.D.G. (1996) 'Kickin' reality, kickin' ballistics: gangsta rap and postindustrial Los Angeles', in W.E. Perkins (ed.) *Droppin' Science: Critical Essays on Rap Music and Hip Hop Culture*. Philadelphia: Temple University Press.

Kofsky, F. (1970) *Black Nationalism and the Revolution in Music*. London: Pathfinder.

Kofsky, F. (1998) *John Coltrane and the Jazz Revolution of the 1960s*. London: Pathfinder.

Lipitz, G. (1994) 'We know what time it is: race, class and youth culture in the nineties', in A. Ross and T. Rose (eds.) *Microphone Fiends: Youth Music and Youth Culture* London: Routledge.

Lusane, C. (1993) 'Rap, race and politics', *Race and Class*, 35(1), 41–56.

Neal, M.A. (1999) *What the Music Said: Black Popular Music and Black Popular Culture*. London: Routledge.

Panish, J. (1997). *The Color of Jazz: Race and Representation in Postwar American Culture*. Jackson, Mississippi: University of Mississippi Press.

Peretti, B.W. (1997). *Jazz in American Culture*. Chicago, Illinois: Ivan R, Dee.
Richardson, E. and Lewis, S. (2000) " 'Flippin' the Script"/"Blowin' up the Spot" 'Puttin' hip-hop online in (African) America and South Africa', in Hawisher, G.E. and Self, C.L. (eds.) *Global Literacies and the World-wide Web*. London: Routledge.
Rose, T. (1994) *Black Noise: Rap Music and Black Culture in Contemporary America*. London: Wesleyan University Press.
Smitherman, G. (1997) 'The chain remain the same: communicative practices in the hip-hop nation', *Journal of Black Studies*, 28(1), 3–25.
Toop, D. (1984) *The Rap Attack: African Jive to New York Hip Hop*. London: Pluto Press.
Waddington, D.P. (1992) *Contemporary Issues in Public Disorder: A Comparative and Historical Approach*. London: Routledge.
Ward, B. (1998) *Just My Soul Responding: Rhythm and Blues, Black Consciousness and Race Relations*. London: UCL Press.
Watkins, S.C. (2001) 'A nation of millions: hip hop culture and the legacy of Black Nationalism', *The Communication Review*, 4, 373–98.
Werner, C. (2000) *A Change is Gonna Come: Music, Race and the Soul of America*. Edinburgh: Payback Press.

13. Cyber Identity

Anthony Rosie

In this chapter I explore aspects of 'cyberworlds' and their implications for the study of identity. The study of cyber life and culture has gained impetus since its inception in the 1960s and 1970s. In this chapter I suggest the potential for ongoing research derives from two features: (i) an eclectic European philosophical background that is open to other traditions of thought, (ii) an emphasis on the interdisciplinary. This interdisciplinary focus has enabled anthropologists, architects, information specialists, novelists, software engineers, theorists, web designers, and many others, to explore cyber worlds in ways that illustrate their complexity (See Bendikt, 1991; Bell and Kennedy, 2000; Bell, 2001). In this chapter the emphasis is on cyberspace and identity rather than theories of information and information usage in a direct sense (see Webster, 1995). Information theories and their social and cultural realisation are of course extremely important for the study of identity because they address issues of economic, cultural, spatial, social and temporal experience. All such are sites for the emergence of identity. A concluding section to the chapter provides a brief commentary on recommended readings, including some on information theories.

We enter cyberspace if we hold a three-way telephone conversation, or enter a newsgroup email discussion group. If we play a computer game or enter a virtual reality setting designed by an architect for a building yet to be built we enter cyberspace. One example out of many that could be cited is the rebuilding of Potsdammer Platz in Berlin. This is an area that was severely bombed in World War II and is only now under reconstruction. The funding for the rebuild is part German, part EU based and also incorporates contributions from a number of global companies interested in German markets. Throughout the construction phase (1998–2001) visitors could 'walk the building' through a virtual reality tour. But cyberspace also involves human-machine interaction through, for example, prosthetics. The replacement hip links machine and body but so does plastic surgery whether used for cosmetic purposes or for organ replacement. Films such as *Blade Runner* and *The Matrix* show humans in contest with replicants (cyborgs) who have an apparent human body but a machine technology. All these phenomena have implications for how we construe identity. Can identity be viewed as stable? Have new forms of fluidity emerged? What is the role of post-modern thought? Can existing institutions and forms of thought, particularly those inscribed in academic disciplines, say anything useful about forms of identity? These are some of the questions a philosophical analysis can help us with. However, while cyber experience may be technologically mediated and therefore different from life in the past, there is no reason to believe that the world of the cyber is completely new. Cyber worlds often involve fantasy, whether text-based 'dungeons and dragons' or arcade games. The forerunner to this is the world of myth and magic. In the ancient Greek myths the gods were able to come down to earth, eat, sleep, talk, have sex. While their movements from heaven to earth and their ability to turn into different shapes may have defied the laws of physics, their actual movements and interactions were ones we instantly recognise. There is a shared understanding. Consequently, while cyberspace will be presented as a distinctive electronic experience it has important predecessors.

A related point is the issue of technological determinism. Put as a question, is there not a risk that seeing human activity so fully in terms of technology, means seeing human identity as solely determined by technology? Surely there are aspects of our lives that are important for the construction of our identity that lie outside the technological? These are important questions. A sceptic such as Webster (1995) accepts the importance of technology but remains unconvinced by some of the post-modern claims. Webster's points are important but to accept the impact of cyber experience for the construction of identity does not require a wholesale acceptance of post-modernism (see Webster, 1995: 163–193). In this chapter some of these claims are reviewed and a phenomenological view is also given. It is important, however, to emphasise the central importance of technology and the shape of future change. While futurists provide little analysis, others are far more sanguine and provide undoubted evidence of the rapid impact of technology and its contribution to identity construction (See Martin, 1978; Toffler, 1980; Naughton, 1999; Negroponte, 1995).

Cyberspace

Our starting point comes from a well-known depiction of cyberspace – William Gibson's *Neuromancer* (1984). In this brief extract we meet Case, an ex-USA cyberspace worker in the 'Matrix' who has double-crossed his employers. His reward is to have his body reorganised with sacks sown into his organs and cavity walls. The sacks contain a deadly poison and he has gone to Chiba (Japan) to try to find an antidote:

> A year here and he still dreamed of cyberspace, hope fading nightly. All the speed he took, all the turns he'd taken and the corners he'd cut in Night City, and still he'd see the matrix in his sleep, bright lattices of logic unfolding across the colorless

void...The Sprawl (USA) was a long strange way home over the Pacific now, and he was no console man, no cyberspace cowboy. Just another hustler, trying to make it through. But the dreams came on in the Japanese night like livewire voodoo, and he'd cry for it, cry in his sleep, and wake alone in the dark, curled in his capsule in some coffin hotel, his hands clawed into the bedslab, temperfoam bunched between his fingers, trying to reach the console that wasn't there. (pp. 9–10)

Cyberspace is a very real place where people work, dream and play. A more prosaic but encompassing definition is that of Michael Benedikt):

Cyberspace is a globally networked, computer-sustained, computer-accessed, and computer-generated, multi-dimensional, artificial, or 'virtual' reality. In this reality, to which every computer is a window, seen or heard objects are neither physical nor, necessarily, representations of physical objects but are, rather, in form, character and action, made up of data, of pure information. This information derives in part from the operations of the natural, physical world, but for the most part it derives from the immense traffic of information that constitutes human enterprise in science, art, business, and culture. (1991: 122–123)

A third definition comes from Howard Rheingold's work:

Cyberspace, originally a term from William Gibson's science fiction novel *Neuromancer*, is the name some people use for the conceptual space where words, human relationships, data, wealth, and power are manifested by people using CMC technology. (Rheingold, 1995: 5)

Taken together these definitions point to a different or, apparently, new world. Of course this world lies alongside our everyday experience and we may already be part of cyberspace. Our exploration starts with some consideration of philosophy and modernity and the extracts above will inform this discussion.

The Cartesian Subject

Benedikt (1991: 3–4) discusses the philosopher Karl Popper's depiction of three worlds. World 1 refers to the objective world we experience; this material is composed of material objects with all their motion and energy. World 2 refers to the subjective world of intentions, calculations and subjectification. World 3 is a world of objective, public structures which arise but often achieve effects that were never anticipated. Such effects were not planned for. Many of these world 3 structures are purely informational. The three worlds are linked of course and Popper's depiction is close to that of

Habermas's distinction between objective, subjective and critical knowledge (Habermas, 1971; Pusey, 1983). Cyberspace is an example of World 3 where we have a set of public structures, including solely private communication, but where the outputs are not necessarily planned. In virtual reality we may move in ways which are unpredictable, often going beyond the rules of the programme.[13]

Popper's work retains notions of subjectivity and objectivity but goes beyond the simple subject-object separation found in Cartesian thought. The well known Cartesian separation has implications for how we conceptualise humans and machines. It raises the question as to whether our identity is purely subjective and therefore a private mental process. Not surprisingly, many of the machines or cyborgs in films such as *Blade Runner* are programmed to be machines without human feelings.

Many commentators have pointed out weaknesses in Cartesian thought. (Bell, 2001: 113–127; Hall, 1996; Hamilton, 1992). The emphasis on the knowing subject leaves identity as unitary and as an essential essence. There is insufficient emphasis on external structures that exist independently of us, although created through human thought. Essentialism is one outworking of Plato's idea of the 'forms' that reveal the essential part of a quality or object.[14] In such a model identity can be seen as relatively fixed. For instance, our social identity may not be the same as our political identity but both become discrete and compartmentalised. There is little possibility for change here and our identities become fixed and stabilised. A problem with this approach is that it does not do justice to changes in the external world and the way they might impact on us. It also leaves us always viewing new developments such as technology through pre-existing lenses. It does not enable us to make connections, for instance, between cyber worlds and the worlds of myth and magic referred to above.

There is a danger that the definitions of cyberspace given by Benedikt and Rheingold simply embody this approach. That is far from the case as Benedikt's own chapter on phenomenological experience shows. However, we need to consider identity and cyberspace as more mobile than is given in the Cartesian and Enlightenment viewpoints.

It is not that the introduction of cyber worlds has shattered the Cartesian approach to identity; the approach has been under attack for a long time.

---

[13] Many of the older text-based dungeon and dragon programmes are of this sort. See LambdaMOO at http://sourceforge.net/projects/lambdamoo/ A more recent virtual world where people can operate in a virtual environment is Sim City available at http://simcity.ea.com/us/guide/
[14] Plato's idea of the forms is that there is an underlying essence which is unchanging. Real objects are versions or departures from the ideal form. Plato's work and some helpful commentaries can be found at http://classics.mit.edu/ A particularly interesting virtual reality project on classical thought can be found at http://perseus.csad.ox.ac.uk/

Bell (2001) has attacked a dualistic approach using Hall's work (see Hall, 2000 in Du Gay, Evans and Redman (eds.)). To avoid the implicit problems with the term 'identity' Hall uses 'identification' (in his 1996 paper he places identity 'sous rature'). This term from Derrida's work (see Derrida, 1981) has a particular meaning, that of a concept that is out of date and of little use but at present we have nothing with which to replace it. Identity is one such term. For Hall (and many others) the term 'identity' does not capture the fluidity and shifts that characterise modern life. The term 'identification' refers to such a multiplicity of meaning and the shifting terrain of identifiers. We can identify with different groups and hold a more mobile series of relationships, particularly in different online environments. Identification may well characterise how we approach cyber worlds. Sherry Turkle (1996) refers to her use of a dungeons and dragon environment where exactly this fluidity was possible. She also describes how many student users have several windows open at one time on their computer, moving between windows and identities as they choose.

Post-modern approaches

Hall's work shows how an essentialist approach to identity is unable to capture the fluidity and mobility of people's lives. This raises the question of the potential of a post-modern approach. The work of the theorist Jean Baudrillard is often invoked in discussions of cyber worlds. Baudrillard shows how much of our daily experience is made up of simulation. As Bell puts it, 'Baudrillard suggests that in post-modernity signs have become disconnected from reality; instead of representation we have simulation' (Bell, 2001: 76). This captures the way Gibson presents cyber-space in the extract above. The post-modern world of the cyber is a world of simulation.

This is too simplistic a definition for our purposes and we can return to the definitions of Benedikt and Rheingold here. For both commentators, cyberspace is conceptual. It is based on information that uses the laws of physics we all recognise although such laws can be defied. But what is presented is a simulation because it is constructed. The possible oversimplification arises because we need to be much clearer about the relationships between constructed worlds and material worlds as Popper indicated.

A way of exploring such relationships is through different but overlapping philosophical approaches. The work of Michael Heim is wide ranging but does permit a phenomenological analysis of cyberspace. His publications link East and West and show how many of the questions that currently occupy students, academics, software engineers are prefigured in the work of major philosophers such as Plato, Leibniz and Heidegger (Heim, 1993, 1995 and

1998).[15] Sherry Turkle (1996 and 1999) provides an analysis of identity and technology with insights from psychoanalysis, sociology and philosophy that are particularly open to debates in post-modern thought.

The work of Sherry Turkle and Michael Heim

Turkle's key study *Life on the Screen* posits a constant interplay between two different forms of knowing and hence between subject and object. The study draws on an extensive series of interviews with children and adults using computers. The samples are collected from the US, Russia and the UK. She also draws on her own training and experience in philosophy, psychoanalytic thought and practice as well as computer programming to ask what it is that people do when they use a computer. Conceptually she distinguishes between modernity and post-modernity as ways of knowing in the world. This division is supported by two other distinctions: a contrast between 'hard' and 'soft' programming and a further contrast between propositional and bricoleur approaches.

There are similarities between Turkle's conceptualisations and those of Michael Heim. The latter argues that idealist approaches derived from Plato, Leibniz and Heidegger rest on a series of distinctions over relations between humans and technology. Heim and Turkle provide different positions while sharing some common ground. Both are deeply engaged in debates over the human-technology interface. However, where Turkle is a user and commentator on computers and simulations as knowledge forms, Heim goes further and engage more directly with the construction of 3-D worlds and theories of simulation. For both commentators the cyberworld of Gibson's matrix is a reality.

Modernity and Post-modernity as Forms of Space

There is a substantial literature on these fields. As a background to debates over cyberspace a number of texts engage directly with Habermas's development of the notion of public space as a way of conceptualising a cyberworld (Herman, 1995; Jordan, 1999; Nye and Donahue, 2000). While they write from different theoretical and political perspectives these writers on public space all agree on the importance of the net as such a public arena. What Jordan (1999) and Kanarch and Nye (1999) argue is that the net forms a shifting arena which can lead to new forms of political discussion that bypass political traditions such as parliament. Parliament is traditionally the source of debates over the public good. Citizens, or 'netizens', become a

---

[15] A selection of Heim's recent papers can be found at http://www.mheim.com/html/articles.htm

potential political force linked by the net and other forms of technology in ways which defy ready definition. But all such groups call for access to a public space. While Habermas might applaud this, a number of commentators have pointed out that his formulation of public space is male dominated and European (Benhabib, 1992; Brook and Boal, 1995). However, links between public and private space can be seen to shift and to relate to global communication features (see Brook & Boal (eds.) 1995; Jordan). This is an important focus for the net and cyberpolitics.

Heim and Turkle address two features of modernity that relate to the Cartesian subject-object distinction: (i) the linear representation of knowledge and its power, (ii) the dominance of particular forms of writing and representation. The contrast to this modernist position is what we will term the post-modern contrast. Texts are linear in the sense that certain arguments are presented in a particular order and some points are requisite if other points are to follow logically. Thus, a premise is introduced and certain arguments follow from it. Conclusions that do not follow logically are ruled out of order. This is the approach taken in the traditional academic essay, a ready expression of propositional thought with a long history. Plato's dialectical reasoning is more fluid than is often found in propositional thinking but the origins of the propositional lie in medieval appropriation of classical thought. Turkle (1996: 50) gives an example of how she was forced to follow this pattern of rigid expression in an academic environment, going against the grain of her natural thinking and writing processes. The principles underpinning academic argument are found in many arenas including the business memo, the political manifesto. Some texts become particularly powerful and, as Lyotard has shown (see Lyotard, 1984), particular disciplines provide a way of 'speaking the subject'. Thus Psychology as a discipline provides a base for knowledge of human behaviour as shown in the work of educational psychologists and educational welfare officers. Here the person may become an object of inquiry, e.g. the deviant. A subject-object distinction underpins this conception of the world.

Heim and Turkle both show how cybercommunication challenges this form of dominance. Heim shows how hypertext, a creation of software engineers, allows the writer/reader to make what links they choose and to relate one text to another (Heim, 1993: 12–20). We are familiar with the web page with links to other pages but the hypertext approach goes beyond this and enables the reader/writer to construct a new text from a multitude of other texts. The bot programme is a particular example.[16] In hypertext

---

[16] One example is the work of social scientists at Huddersfield University who are developing 'key thinker bot programmes where students interrogate virtual thinkers such as Mead and Foucault. The resulting text is a student/tutor construction. The start point for such programmes is the 'Julia' character developed by Michael Mauldin seeking to pass the Turing test whereby a

constructions the reader is a creator weaving ever new intertextual patterns. The use of hypertexts link do not always led to the production of a conformist singe text. They can be used to disrupt and provide alternatives (Shields, 2000). The hypertext product can produce effects that go beyond the intentions of many conventional literary texts.

'Hard' and 'Soft' Programming

Turkle (1996: 50–72) refers to 'hard' programming as a top down model of rule-following moving from abstract points to specific details. Each section of the programme is self-contained and is then linked to other sections in a complex but readily followed architecture. This model of programming dominated University computer studies departments in the 1980s. The approach follows the linear model of knowledge outlined above and is based on assumptions about machine logic. In this model there is a distinction between human and machine. The human is the subject and the machine is the object.

'Soft' programming, on the other hand, enables the programmer to move freely and to construct according to their own thought patterns. At its strongest in post-modern thought (Pearson, 1997) the programmer becomes a variable in her own programme, thereby eliding the subject-object distinction. It is this soft programming approach which we find in many virtual reality programmes and simulations. In such simulations the user is able to move freely (rather than simply respond to stimuli) and create objects and ways of acting. Turkle explores how people come to view machines differently in online or virtual environments compared with their real life experiences. In the 1970s and 1980s machines were treated as objects and as separate from human beings. The major change was the ability to invest machines with a psychological life. It was at this point (late 1980s and early 1990s) that the 'Julia' programme and other similar ones were created. 'Julia' was a 'woman' who interacted with visitors online, responding in a pre-determined way to their questions and suggestions. The early version was inevitably rather limited but an increasing sophistication in response meant that 'Julia' could hold reasonably involved interactions with questioners. Of course the environment only permitted short questions and answers but the project showed how a machine could be taken to have an identity.

The general movement has been towards an accommodation with machines whereby they are invested with a psychological reality offering a distinctive and different world. This in itself does not challenge the subject-object distinction but if 'Julia' is treated as 'a person' lines of fissure in the

---

successful artificial intelligence programme would convince a user that it was a genuine human interaction 70% of the time. See Turkle (1996: 88–111) for an account of this programme.

distinction are beginning to appear.[17] Turkle's cross-cultural comparisons show how there seems to be a pattern whereby those countries with greatest computer exposure reach this point of accommodation first. There is clearly a danger in following a simple linear curve that valorises progression. Turkle's account does not fully address issues of the ways in which markets operate and the impact of economic globalisation although there are indications of the complexities and contradictions inherent in a cyber technological world. (Turkle, 1996: 233–254).

Bricolage and the Propositional

The anthropologist Claude Levi-Strauss developed the concept of bricolage to show how different peoples around the world assemble items and concepts together to use them in different ways from that associated with the logic of modernity (as exemplified by propositional thought). As Turkle notes (1996: 55–56) Levi-Strauss failed to apply the same approach to western modernist thought, yet, bricolage can be found in the practice of modern science and in many other aspects of our daily lives. The cyberworld is very much a construction of different elements that are put together by users. The simulation is a shell that enables users to construct their own worlds.

Taken together, 'soft' programming and bricolage describe some of the features of post-modernity and identity. The argument is not over whether we live in a modern or a post-modern world; there are surely elements of both in our daily experience. We should also remember that a discussion of the influence of post-modernity is something of a luxury when many countries lack adequate water supplies and food. The post-modern world of cyberspace provides different ways of existing: there is space for forgotten or marginalised groups, a movement away from traditional political governance (Brook and Boal, 1995; Robins and Webster, 1999). Modes of communication change; contact may be by text message and a different logic to written expression appears. The post-modern position is based on playfulness, a desire to challenge, and the ability to re-organise elements of existence. What does this tell us about identity?

Turkle (1996) provides a discussion of identity drawing on Gergen's notion of 'saturation of self' (Gergen, K, 1991). This refers to how we might 'colonise each other's brains' because we absorb the rhythm and reasons people give in online interactions. Other people become part of us through

---

[17] A number of chat programmes such as AOL, ICQ and MSN enable people to talk to each other through text and image whether individually or in chat rooms. Of course a number of persona may be built up and again notions of taken for granted subject-object distinctions can become less clear.

electronic mediation. This is certainly a quality we can identify in *Neuromancer* where Case absorbs other people into his consciousness. For Gergen, according to Turkle, the loss of some identities may be a matter of anguish but this can be compensated for by the taking on of new identities. Turkle gives several examples of people taking on different online identities when faced by uncongenial work conditions. However, this in itself is insufficient. A person may find work dissatisfying and alienating but we do not have to invoke either an electronic or a post-modern position to explain this. A series of compartmentalised identities can provide forms of protection. However, electronic mediation does permit new configurations. A person may be a non-computer user, but the role of electronic mediation is still a factor in their lives. ATM machines, cinematic graphics, timing mechanisms, and many others ensure the presence of the electronic and the rapid transmission of information about us to others. As a personal computer user who is male and middle aged I have noticed how I receive messages through my home email account which indicate that my purchase of second hand books on literature, philosophy and politics has triggered a wide range of email offers I can do without. The powers of surveillance merely increase in cyberspace (Bogard, 1996; Jordan, 1999; Lyon, 1994).

Granted that, whether intentionally or not, people draw on a wide range of identifications in cyberspace, there are some potential difficulties. A multiplicity of identities can lead to immobility and confusion rather than coherence. Responses to this challenge can include a search for conformity. At its most extreme this might include fundamentalism. At the other extreme there can be a loss of moral purpose as we slide through a multiplicity of identities. In this context we can consider some forms of exploitation through the web; one such area is referred to below. We make choices using what is at hand through bricolage. Some choices reinforce stability and coherence while others offer playful possibilities of change and experimentation. It is in this sense that people may use online opportunities. Many commentators have claimed (and there is little reason to dispute the claim) that male online users sometimes take on female identities. Turkle provides some examples through her interview data (1996: 212–226). Clearly this can raise moral concerns but when considered through a notion of gender as construction the freedom for interplay becomes much clearer. Notions of gender change are hardly new as Shakespeare's plays show. But cyberspace allows not only for more variety but for greater openness of discussion. Rheingold's study of online communities bears this out (also see Uncapher, W. (1999) in M. Smith and P. Kollock). Such an emphasis on mobility can be accommodated in a wide variety of philosophical approaches.

A Phenomenological Approach

Heim is interested in questions of ontology in order to give an account of how objects exist in cyberspace. Objects in the world are approximations of an underlying ideal form. The allegory of Plato's cave is perhaps the best-known example.[18] Heim (1993: 88–94) argues that the world of ideal forms is an ontological account of cyberspace. Cyberspace is a world of ideal forms which can be compared and distanced from 'real life'. For Plato desire starts with Eros as a physical drive, usually expressed in terms of sexual activity. But the search for mental satisfaction and the world of forms derives from and extends this physical drive. Eros moves from the physical to the mental. However, as Heim shows, this is not in itself sufficient. There needs to be a powerful logic to support such a drive. The limits of Aristotelian logic are the limits of propositional logic, which cannot easily cover a large number of new situations. Leibniz's development of modal logic was a progressive response.

Heim shows how Leibniz developed a mathematical logic whereby complex arguments were derivable from primitive elements. Leibniz's logic is incorporated into the development of electronic circuitry. In principle, this model gives us a frictionless world, an idealisation – a form of cyberspace (Heim, 1993: 58–60, Dreyfus, 1985). The limits of Euclidian space are overcome and propositional logic is replaced by a phenomenological experience whereby objects are perceived in themselves. However, rules are created that permit the creation of more than three dimensions in the world. For Benedikt this phenomenological experience is what characterises cyberspace.

At first sight it might seem strange to associate Heim's work with phenomenology. The term is not used in his texts. However, his use of Heidegger's writings, and his use of Dreyfus, who has written extensively on Heidegger in ways that are interesting for a consideration of cyberspace and identity (Dreyfus, 1995), can help the development of a phenomenological analysis. Briefly, Heidegger is interested in what it is that makes a phenomenon appear and what it is that makes something an entity. He argues that we cannot search for purely mental processes because our understandings operate in the material world and we would otherwise end up with a private language as the sole means of expression of our mental states (Mulhall, 1990). Heidegger wants to explore 'covered-upness', where things

---

[18] In Book 6 of *Republic* – see Waterfield, R. (1993) Republic, Oxford: Oxford University Press. We are told of a cave where people are forced to watch shadows dancing in firelight. The shadows are simulations produced by others and the view is false. One prisoner escapes form the cave and moves up the path to the outside world where he comes to learn that what held him in thrall were false images. Now he can see reality as it is.

and events are waiting to be discovered. The phenomenologist brings them out into the open. Heidegger believes that this is what we do when we explore the background of every day practices. This applies to cyberspace and identity.

The experience of community building in cyberspace is that people will reveal different aspects of themselves, and often not only try on new identities but will be less inhibited than in face-to-face situations (Rheingold, 1995; Smith and Kollock, 1999; Wilbur, 1997; Bell and Kennedy, 2000: 45–56). This is very much a self-directed and self-revelatory process. Of course it is full of contradictions as well as the possibility of inauthentic conversation and deceit (Donath, 1999). But as beings in the world these are features we deal with everyday in bringing together Popper's three Worlds. Cyberspace does not lose its materiality but the notions of community building and self-revelation reveal a phenomenological reality.

This might be taken to suggest that cyberspace is an idealised world where all our dreams come true. This is far from so, as Gibson's *Neuromancer* and *Count Zero* make clear. Telecommunications, email, video conferencing, mobile phones change notions of community (Wellman and Gullia, 1999).

In technological terms the early advances were those of shareware software[19] for creating virtual worlds. But cyberspace is not a place of innocence or constantly satisfied illusions. The work of computer hackers, a desire to punish some for violating rules, the threats posed by various forms of extremism all characterise cyberspace. Perhaps the most discussed examples involve either impersonation to deceive or the making of sexual demands. Stone (in Benedikt, 1991 and Bell and Kennedy, 2000) describes how a male academic 'impersonated' a disabled woman and the resulting anger that broke out when 'he' was unmasked.

A similar situation surrounds 'Mr Bungle' (Turkle, 1996: 251–254, Dibbell, 1999). Mr Bungle appeared in LambdaMOO and walked into the living room where a group of characters were talking. The description is well known. He was '…at the time a fat oleaginous, Bisquick-faced clown dressed in cumstained harlequin garb and girdled with a mistletoe-and-hemlock belt whose buckle bore the quaint inscription KISS ME UNDER THIS, BITCH!' (Dibbell, 1999: 13). The crudity and violence of the resulting action and the renewed appearance of Mr Bungle over several days are well known. In terms of our account so far he provides an interesting mix of metaphors, a clown bent on humiliation using the symbols of a classical character. The

---

[19] Shareware software consisted of programmes developed by enthusiasts which were available free of charge in a minimal form. To obtain a fully working copy of the programme the user had to pay a small fee. This led to a community of users sharing highly effective programmes. However, as the user base expanded so did the availability of commercial programmes thereby undermining the shareware approach.

wider discussion of this episode showed that many LambdaMOO users were engaged in virtual sexual encounters using text to simulate a range of fantasies. In phenomenological terms sexual experience and experimentation are revealed in a different setting. They are viewed and reflected on as acts in themselves and as ones that are repeatable through re-readings of text. The possibility of experiencing, then re-analysing what is held as text means that the phenomenological search for hidden everyday practices is made possible. There is therefore an accommodation between phenomenological and post-modern approaches to identity seen here in these murky accounts.

Heidegger's phenomenology may provide a way of exploring cyberspace. However, Heidegger was suspicious of technology, (Heim, 1993: 55–64) believing that machines were capable of distorting human beings' relationships with each other. Heidegger presents the machine as enemy and as an entity that offers an apparent logic inferior to the human capacity to think creatively. He worried that human beings would become in thrall to such domination and that critical thinking would be replaced by simplistic levels of information retrieval. As librarians become information specialists and fully digitised libraries are created we can reflect on Heidegger's point. Perhaps the crucial argument is, as Heim and Turkle both suggest, to move away from seeing the machine as enemy to seeing the machine as one component amongst many that humans use for specific purposes.

Cyberspace and power

Questions of power are involved both in the management of identity and in the management of cyberspace. Jordan (1999) distinguishes between different approaches to power (1999: 1–20). Drawing on these approaches, and extending them where appropriate, we can explore some of the ways in which power and identity are linked.

Cyberspace is a context that exists alongside others so it makes little sense to talk of theories of power that are specific to cyberspace. However, there are features of cyberspace that make for distinctive power relations. Jordan distinguishes between individual and a number of social approaches. In the individual approach we can talk about domination by individuals. The Mr Bungle episode can be seen in this light. In chat rooms people may take on different ages, and genders. The anger felt when 'Julie' was revealed to be a man, particularly a man who had enjoyed online encounters, was felt to operate at an individual as well as at a social level. There was a collective response and power became a form of distributed knowledge. The perpetrators were defined through forms of collective knowledge. The fact that 'onlookers' were certainly themselves using different gender online meant that the collective knowledge was far from simple. However, this is very similar to ways in which knowledge is distributed in other settings where apparently partial and incomplete knowledge is used in different ways.

Power relations involve knowledge and the saying 'knowledge is power' has important resonance. In cyber society there are collectives. They may be highly specialist ones as with some newsgroups or dedicated groups within chat programmes, or they may be loose collectives such as those found in the WELL (see Rheingold, 1995). Cyberspace provides a means of knowledge distribution. This ranges from email contact which can be world-wide, use of videoconferencing, chat rooms and simulations. Much of the knowledge distributed in this way is used in non-cyber settings, e.g. board rooms, hospitals and universities. It is important to emphasise that cyber societies exist alongside 'real life' settings within Popper's World 3 configuration.

Power can be embodied in objects. Durkheim's study of totemism is one classic example. Football supporters investing fan regalia with significance is another. There are many fanzine sites on the net performing a similar function. However, the fanzines are global and the networking operates differently. It is not that football is place specific. Matches can be watched around the world at the time they happen just as with a rock concert. The investment of totemic objects with power does, however, differ in cyberspace. In some cases there is only textual representation, e.g. the text in a chat room has to convey a range of physical and emotional responses, e.g. intensity of debate over a shared hobby, or discussion of symptoms of depression. Through text, representations and images are made and used in cyberspace. One of the points about the 'Julie' episode was that the collective had put together mental images of how she looked. So through bricolage, images from one context are moved into other contexts.

Visual representations on the web are common, ranging from pop ups to specially designed images and major pieces of art work where site owners have considered carefully how images might be 'read' in an electronic environment. Marshall Mcluhan, writing in the 1960s, raised the issue of visual literacy and its importance. In those days he was discussing terrestrial broadcasting and passive receipt of images in terms of individual power. The situation is very different today with digitisation, the web and bulletin boards. The images themselves can of course be used in different ways as shown in the earlier discussion of hypertext. The interplay between text and image contributes to the fluidity of identity in cyberspace and requires a more sophisticated notion of power.

Foucault's work provides a distinctive approach to power. Power is no longer simply imposed. It traverses different sites and involves a series of relations. Power is involved in tactics with individuals revealing and producing power effects. Jordan (1999: 15) quotes Foucault as follows:

> There are two meanings of the word *subject*: subject to someone else by control and dependence, and tied to his own identity by a conscious or self-knowledge. Both meanings suggest a form of power which subjugates and makes subject to.

This helps us reconceptualise power in cyberspace, and indeed in other settings. Earlier sections of this chapter have emphasised that identity is not tied down and nothing Foucault says here affects that. Foucault emphasises the position of being under the control of someone else and being tied to our identity through our self-knowledge. It is exactly this aspect to which cyberspace can provide an alternative. This is not limited to the gender taking and deceit roles mentioned earlier. Some of this work has exerted a fascination beyond its value for analysis. Of greater import is what students and others actually do in cyberspace in learning and in other aspects of their lives. Some students find it much easier to discuss topics in online discussion than in face-to-face settings (Mason, 1998; Palloff and Pratt, 2001; Salmon, 2000; Hawisher and Selfe, 2000). While there is a need for more research into the effectiveness of online environments, there is evidence from these texts that for many people an online environment provides opportunities to manage personal identity in ways that differ from those used in other settings. We can therefore consider a range of meanings of the term 'subject' here. Relations of subjugation and control may change in many ways.

This is particularly true of a range of political movements.[20] A Foucauldian approach suggests that cyberspace is an arena in which power relations are played out, reconfigured and new identities are created. For Foucault, the history of discipline and punishment involved links between institutions, professionals, social structures and a range of bricolage. The questions he asked included why at one historical point people in western Europe punished in a certain way through physical control over the body while at another historical point they used surveillance and training techniques over the body instead. In cyberspace the same dynamic is present. The body as object can be 'used' as we have seen but the interrelations between cyberbodies produces a different dynamic. Electronic transfer through email provides different modes of exercise and also different strategies for reply and for response. Cyberspace extends the Foucauldian dynamic on power.

Conclusion

This chapter has adopted a theoretical approach to the study of cyberspace and identity. Drawing on social theory in all its forms gives some purchase on

---

[20] A current example is that of anti-globalisation protests which are co-ordinated on a world-wide basis. However, new social movements of many sorts reflect new ways of organisation that are not necessarily hierarchical. See Crossley (2002).

conceptualising the net. Both the proponents and the detractors of the web and electronic usage tend to shy away from the conceptual issues involved. For this reason this chapter engaged with some philosophical issues. It is inevitable that technological change will continue and some of the material discussed in this chapter will be supplanted. However, by suggesting there is a continuity between myth and magic and our current world of cyberspace it should be clear that modes of analysis appropriate to the analysis of myth have an application to the analysis of our contemporary world. Interdisciplinary research and analysis is likely to continue to provide interesting perspectives on cyber identity.

Bibliography

Bagliolo, M. (ed.) *The Science Studies Reader*, New York: Routledge.

Baudrillard, J. (1988) *America*, London: Verso Press.

Baudrillard, J. (1990) *Revenge of the Crystal*, London: Pluto Press.

Bell, D. (2001) *An Introduction to Cybercultures*, London: Routledge.

Bell, D. and Kennedy. B. (eds.) (2000) *The Cybercultures Reader*, London: Routledge.

Benedikt, M. (ed.) (1991) *Cyberspaces: First Steps*, Massachusetts: MIT Press.

Benhabib, S. (1992), *Situating the Self.* Cambridge: Polity Press.

Billig, M. (1994) 'Sod Baudrillard' in H. Simons and M. Billig (eds.) *After Post-modernism: Reconstructing Ideology Critique*, London: Sage.

Bogard, W. (1996) *The Simulation of Surveillance: Hypercontrol in Telematic Societies*, Cambridge: Cambridge University Press.

Brook, J. and Boal, I. (eds.) *Resisting the Virtual Life*, San Francisco: City Lights Press.

Butler, J. (1990) *Gender Trouble: Feminism and the Subversion of Identity*, London: Routledge.

Crossley, N. (2002) *Making Sense of Social Movements*, Buckingham: Open.

Derrida, J. (1981) *Positions*, Chicago: University of Chicago Press.

Dibbell, J. (1999) *My Tiny Life: Crime and Passion in a Virtual World*, Fourth Estate: London.

Dreyfus, H. (1985) *Mind over Machine: The Power of Human Intuition and Expertise in the Era of the Computer*, New York: Free Press.

Dreyfus, H. (1995) *Being-in-the-World*, Massachusetts: MIT Press

Du Gay, P. & Evans, J. & Redman, P (eds.) *Identity: A Reader*, London: Sage.

Foucault, M. (1983) 'The Subject and Power', in Dreyfus, H. and Rabinow, P. (2ndedn) *Beyond Structuralism and Hermeneutics*, Chicago: Chicago University Press.

Gergen, K. (1991) *The Saturated Self: Dilemmas of Identity in Contemporary Life*, New York: Doubleday Books.

Gibson, W. (1984) *Neuromancer*, (pp. 9–10), Glasgow: Harper Collins.

Giddens, A. (1991) *Modernity and Self-Identity*, Cambridge: Polity Press.

Habermas, J. (1971) *Towards a Rational Society*, London: Heinemann

Hall, S. (1996) 'Introduction: Questions of Identity; in Hall, S. and Du Gay, P. (eds.) *Questions of Cultural Identity*, London: Sage.

Hamilton, P. (1992) 'The Enlightenment and the Birth of Social Science', in Hall S., Gieben B. (eds.) *Formations of Modernity*, Open University: Polity Press.

Harcourt, W. (ed.) (1999) *Women@Internet: Creating New Cultures in Cyberspace*, London: Zed Books.

Hawisher, G. and Selfe, C. (2000) *Global Literacies and the world-wide Web*, London: Routledge.

Heim, M. (1993) *The Metaphysics of Virtual Reality*, Oxford: Oxford University Press.

Heim, M. (1995) 'The Design of Virtual Reality', in Featherstone, M. and Burrows, R. (eds.) *Cyberspace, Cyberbodies, Cyberpunk*, London: Sage.

Heim, M. (1998) *Virtual Realism*, Oxford: Oxford University Press.

Heim, M. (2nd edn) (1999) *Electric Language*, Yale: Yale University Press.

Herman, A., Swiss, T. (eds.) (1995) *The World Wide Web and Contemporary Cultural Theory*, London: Routledge.

Jordan, T. (1999) *Cyberpower: the Culture and Politics of Cyberspace and the Internet*, London: Routledge.

Lyon, D. (1994) *Electronic Eye: The Rise of the Surveillance Society*, Cambridge: Polity Press.

Lyon, D. (1999) (2nd edn) Post-modernity, Milton Keynes: Open University Press.

Lyotard, J.-F. (1984) *The Conditions of Post-modernity*, Manchester: Manchester University Press.

Martin, J. (1978) *The Wired Society*, Englewood Cliffs, New Jersey: Prentice Hall.

Mason, R. (1998) *Globalising Education: Trends and Application*, London: Routledge.

Mulhall, S. (1990) *On Being in the World: Wittgenstein and Heidegger on Seeing Aspects*, London: Routledge.

Naughton, J. (1999) *A Brief History of the Future*, London: Weidenfeld and Nicolson.

Negroponte, N. (1995) *Being Digital*, London: Hodder and Stoughton.

Nye, J.S. and Donahue, J.D. (eds.) (2000) Governance in a Globalizing World, Washington. D.C.: Brookings Institution Press.

Palloff, R. and Pratt, K. (2001) *Lessons from the Cyberspace Classroom: the realities of online teaching*, San Francisco: Jossey-Bass.
Pearson, K.A. (ed.) (1997) *Deleuze and Philosophy: the Difference Engineer*, London: Routledge.
Pusey, M. (1983) *Jurgen Habermas*, London: Routledge.
Rheingold, H. (1995) *Virtual Community*, (p. 5) London: Minerva Books.
Robins and Webster (1999) *Times of the Technoculture.* London: Routledge.
Salmon, G. (2000) *E-Moderating*, London: Kogan Page.
Shields, R. (2000) 'Hypertext Links: The Ethic of the Index and its Space-Time Effects' in A. Herman and T. Swiss (eds.) *The World Wide Web and Contemporary Cultural Theory*, London: Routledge.
Smith, M. and Kollock, P. (eds.) (1999) *Communities in Cyberspace*, London: Routledge.
Toffler, A. (1980) *The Third Wave*, London: Collins.
Turkle, S. (1996) *Life on the Screen: Identity in the Age of the Internet*, London: Weidenfeld and Nicholson.
Uncapher, W. (1999) in Smith M. and Kollock P., University Press.
Virilio, P. (1977) *Speed & Politics*, New York: Semiotexte.
Waterfield, R. (1993) Republic, Oxford: Oxford University Press.
Webster, F. (1995) *Theories of the Information Society*, London: Routledge.
Wilbur, S. (1997) 'An Archaeology of Cyberpsaces' in D. Porter (ed.) *Internet Culture*, London: Routledge.

http://classics.mit.edu/
http://perseus.csad.ox.ac.uk/
http://www.mheim.com/html/articles.htm
http://simcity.ea.com/us/guide/
http://sourceforge.net/projects/lambdamoo/

Index

253